CW00421455

THE
PRESIDENTS
OF M.C.C.

Also by Jonathan Rice

AVAILABLE FROM METHUEN

One Hundred Lord's Tests
The Fight for the Ashes 2001
1953: The Crowning Year of Sport
The Unforgettable Tests: England v Australia 2005

THE
PRESIDENTS
OF M.C.C.

Jonathan Rice

Jonathan Rice (signature)

Methuen

First published in Great Britain 2006 by
Methuen
11–12 Buckingham Gate
London SW1E 6LB

10 9 8 7 6 5 4 3 2 1

Copyright © Jonathan Rice 2006

Jonathan Rice has asserted his right under the Copyright, Designs
and Patents Act 1988 to be identified as the author of this work.

A CIP catalogue record for this book is available from the British Library.

ISBN-10: 0413 776 263

ISBN-13: 980 0413 776 266

Printed and bound in Great Britain

This book is sold subject to the condition that it shall not by way of trade
or otherwise be lent, resold, hired out, or otherwise circulated without
the publishers' prior consent in writing in any form of binding or cover
other than that in which it is published and without a similar condition
being imposed on the subsequent purchaser.

CONTENTS

FOREWORD

I was delighted to be invited to contribute the foreword to this history of the Presidents of MCC. A prolific cricket writer, Jonathan Rice has always had an eye for unusual cricketing subjects, and has mined a rich vein for this book. In *The Presidents of M.C.C.* he applies his kind humour, research skills and great descriptive talents to lay before us vignettes of the two hundred or so men who have preceded me as President of our great Club. Although they differed wildly in their cricketing skills, backgrounds and dedication to the game, it is clear that the vast majority thoroughly enjoyed their time on the 'woolsack of cricket'.

As for my own nomination, the call came one Friday morning in March 2005, the fourth to be exact, on my office phone seldom used now that I'm retired. It was Tom Graveney, President of MCC, asking if I would like to succeed him. Would I *what*!? How could anyone steeped in the summer game, as colt, schoolboy, Cambridge University and Sussex captain, not to mention fifty years both writing for the *Sunday Times* and as a subscription member of MCC, fail to be bowled over by such an offer? Or so I mumbled, barely able to believe what I was hearing; my astonishment was all the greater as only six weeks before I'd had a similar call from David Green, Chairman of my beloved Sussex, with an invitation to the Presidency at Hove. After all, I had my critics – 'talks too much', 'given to expressing sharp opinions in newspapers', 'known for putting his foot in it'. One thing is sure: I was originally involved on the MCC Committee as a rebel candidate backed by a group of malcontents.

On Sunday I called back to ask Jackie Graveney, Tom's wife (and we go back half a century), if he was pulling my leg. It was the John McEnroe moment – 'you cannot be serious.' Thankfully, he was serious.

In the fabulous Ashes summer of 2005, Tom Graveney proceeded to play an innings as President quite as immaculate as any of the 122 centuries he made as the most elegant batsman of his generation. He was a huge success with the great British public as well as with the members. Furthermore he cut the tape, without the benefit of the left-handed scissors that he needed, to reopen the Lord's Pavilion, after completion of a major refurbishment. This beautiful building, much more accessible these days, is the major reason why Lord's can justifiably claim to be the home of cricket.

Looking after this site – 'the Vatican' to some, 'the Cathedral of cricket' to others – is one of MCC's three great duties to the game. Looking after its Laws and, scarcely less important, the Spirit of the Game is another task; it is not an easy one when interpretation can threaten serious rupture within the international cricket fraternity, as we saw again at the Oval in 2006. Finally MCC, whose members provide much of the financial resource which the Club contributes to cricket, exists to provide services to both E.C.B. and I.C.C., the local and international governing bodies. These services embrace organisation of cricket tours, coaching and pure research on many topics.

As I write, my Presidential Year is almost over. To Tom Graveney I owe a great debt of gratitude for giving me one of the most memorable years of my life. My successor will be Doug Insole, whom I have persuaded to accept a position that he has declined previously for what at the time were good reasons. Doug is popularly regarded as an excellent choice and I hope he will enjoy his year as much I have done.

Robin Marlar
PRESIDENT OF MCC, 2005–06

INTRODUCTION

'The chief post cricket has to offer is that of President of M.C.C.,' wrote
Sir Pelham Warner in 1929, before he was Sir Pelham and before he
took over that chief post himself. The Earl of Clarendon (not necessarily remembered as one of the great Presidents) introduced his
successor Viscount Downe to his fellow members at the Anniversary
Dinner of 1872 by saying that Lord Downe would be 'no unworthy
occupier of the seat now vacated'. This statement could have been made
of almost all the men who over 220 years have been chosen to perch
upon what has been described as 'the Woolsack of cricket'. In its
pompous self-satisfaction, Lord Clarendon's introduction is typical of
MCC's attitudes at its social apogee in the mid to late Victorian era, and
yet it reveals an inescapable truth – the seat that is vacated every year
has been filled by very many worthy men, and those that were not
worthy at least considered themselves to be so.

I must admit that one of the daunting things about researching
and writing this book is that so many people involved with the Club
over so many years have taken themselves so very seriously. There have
not been many Presidents until recent times who have underestimated
their importance in the world of cricket (and neither can all the modern
ones be exemped from the charge) and there have been several who
seem to have listened to the flatterers who have told them how almighty

they are in their year of authority. Yet once you strip away the social splendour enjoyed by most of the men who took on this chief post, at least until the 1920s, you come to see that most of them truly had the best interests of cricket and their Club at heart, and that they would have appeared much more sympathetic to modern eyes if only they had been a little less certain of their place in society. That is not to say they were not worthy men. It is merely an indication of how far social values have changed that we look on some of the utterings of these people with amazement, amusement or horror, and sometimes with all these emotions at once. MCC is still viewed by many outsiders as exclusive, divisive and an anachronism, but to compare the Marylebone Cricket Club of the 21st century with the Club as it was even fifty years ago, in the dying years of the amateur/professional divide, is to see how far times have moved on. In St John's Wood they have perhaps moved farther than anybody could have dared believe possible.

This book is not meant to be a complete history of the Presidents and their role within MCC, although it is, as far as I know, the first book that has focused on the Presidency rather than on the Club as a whole. It is meant to be a miscellany of information about these men, and perhaps to show how their presidencies reflected the times they lived in. I have found myself rather more interested in the non-cricketers than the cricketers, and I have certainly made no attempt to retrace in detail the cricket careers of men such as Sir Pelham Warner, Peter May, Colin Cowdrey or Gubby Allen. These cricketing statistics can be found in *Wisden*.

I have, on the other hand, spent some time researching the political, military and business careers of many of the Presidents, and have been astonished by some of the connections between Presidents in the nineteenth century, and by the influence many of the great families in cricket wielded over the whole period. In the course of my research, I have come across such names as Rudyard Kipling, the Duke of Wellington, Lord Baden-Powell and Elton John, all of whom were closely involved with one President or another. I have also discovered things about Dervishes in Sudan and the boundaries of Venezuela, to take but two examples, which I had not suspected could be linked to MCC.

The whole process was started during the Presidential year of my brother, Tim, who asked me to see whether I could find a President with less cricketing skill than him. It was a hard task to be set, but I think in the end I succeeded in providing the answer (look up J. H. Scourfield, 1870, for a start, or Bernard Duke of Norfolk in 1957), and at the same time learnt a great deal about the men who have held this office. So my thanks first of all go to Tim, for setting me on the road towards the writing of this book. I have subsequently discovered that several sets of brothers have been Presidents of MCC, so my nomination in years to come would set no precedent.

I would also like to thank the members of MCC's Publishing Working Party, chaired by Dr Gerald Howat; and the Arts and Library sub-committee, chaired by Lord Fellowes, who gave the go-ahead to the project. Peter Tummons, managing director of Methuen, has also lent a sympathetic ear to my complaints and successes as the research and the writing got under way, while Adam Chadwick, Curator of MCC and Glenys Williams, Archivist, have done all that I could have wished to give me access to the Club's archive. I have also had tremendous help from Colin Maynard, Ken Daldry and Sally Goldfield at MCC. For permission to reproduce photographs, thanks go to MCC and The Roger Mann Collection.

Then there are the many individuals without whose help this book could never have been completed. Above all, my wife Jan has, as ever, put up with me locking myself away with my laptop, and emerging only at mealtimes to bore her with the antics of strange Victorian noblemen. After her, in no particular order, I should like to thank Mireille Galinou, archivist of the Eyre Estate; Tim McCann at the West Sussex County Record Office for putting me on the trail of the Dukes of Richmond; David Rayvern Allen, for his insights into the early years of MCC; David Robertson, Hon. Curator of Kent County Cricket Club, for his knowledge of Lord Harris, Lord Cornwallis and many other Kentish Presidents; Paul Smith and Stephen Baldwin, who between them know more about Lord Guernsey and Sir Edward Chandos Leigh than is strictly necessary; John Woodcock, for his memories of Harry

Altham and others; Graeme Wright, sometime editor of *Wisden*, for his encouragement; and the many past (and present) Presidents I have spoken to including Lord Bramall, Hubert Doggart, Charles Fry, the late Colin Ingleby-Mackenzie, Doug Insole, Tony Lewis, Robin Marlar, Michael Melluish, HRH Prince Philip, Sir Oliver Popplewell, Dennis Silk and J. J. Warr.

Finally, I want to thank Carl and Liz Reading, in whose home in Jakarta I wrote more than one third of this book. Carl's library of Victorian history was invaluable and their baby daughter Alice made the whole stay delightful.

CHAPTER ONE

1787–1820

THE UNKNOWN PRESIDENTS

On 28 July 1825, a few hours after the end of a match between two public schools, Harrow and Winchester, at Thomas Lord's ground in St John's Wood, the Pavilion caught fire and was burned to the ground. Both schools protested their innocence. As the Marylebone Cricket Club's earliest surviving minute book, dated 1826, rather feebly records, 'the old Pavilion was destroyed by fire on 28 July 1825, with some of the records.' For 'some', read 'all'. There are absolutely no records retained by MCC that predate the fire, and there was apparently no attempt by the Club to rebuild their archive after the fire.

The loss of priceless cricket history may not have seemed such a tragedy in 1825 – after all the Club was only 38 years old at the time, and the Committee of the time would have little idea that two centuries later their little cricket club would be one of the great institutions of British society with a history made all the more interesting for the fact that so little is known about its origins. What is more odd is that the leaders of the Club did not do anything about replacing their records by noting down, for example, the names of early Presidents, captains, players and committee men. There is general agreement of the names of the Presidents going back four years before the fire, but before then there is no record at all. Over the years, many people have tried to track down references to early Presidents, by referring to magazines such as

Bell's Life, to the society pages of other newspapers, to the local press in the St John's Wood area and to the obituaries of the prime suspects as early Presidents. No conclusive evidence at all has been found so far. As time passes, it is unlikely that it ever will.

There is not even any absolute proof that the Club came into existence in 1787, traditionally celebrated as the year when MCC was founded. The main evidence for choosing this year is that the minute book for 30 July 1836 notes that 'the Marylebone Club having been established in the year 1787, it is resolved that a Jubilee Match shall take place at Lord's Ground on the second Monday in July 1837.' The minute went on to add that 'every Member of the Club is solicited for a subscription of One Pound towards the promotion of the sport on this interesting occasion.'

It is assumed that the people who organised it must have been certain that the Club was then fifty years old. Certainly, given the very young age of some of the early Presidents and players, it is virtually certain that some of the men gathered to watch the Jubilee Match and dine at Lord's that night would have been present at the founding of MCC. The President that year was the Fourth Lord Suffield, only 23 years old at the time and the son of the Hon. William Harbord, one of the early supporters of MCC. But the actual date of foundation could have been as late as 1790. Some historians have stated that the Marylebone Club was the same club as the White Conduit Club and the Star and Garter Club and, indeed, the club of gentlemen who laid down the earliest extant laws of cricket, in 1744. This seems very unlikely, as this would predate the height of Hambledon's power, but with lack of unimpeachable evidence it can be argued that the Club is nearer three hundred than two hundred years old.

In the early years, there were two Marylebone clubs playing cricket, as well as the White Conduit Club, for whom MCC members routinely turned out to play, and vice versa, in the those early years of MCC's life. What is certain is that the name 'Marylebone Cricket Club' is first used in the late 1780s, when Thomas Lord established his first cricket ground. However, Lord's entrepreneurial spirit only serves to add to the difficulty of trying to find out the names of any of the officers of the Club before 1825, because of the fact that the ground where the fire occurred was the third ground built by Lord and used by MCC in its comparatively short life. The two moves would have made it all the more likely that early records were lost, abandoned or destroyed.

We must also take into account that Britain was often at war in the early years of the nineteenth century, and the number of games of top class cricket that were actually played dropped drastically. In the chief record of the era, Thomas Britcher's scorebook, there were an average of about eight major matches played by the Marylebone Cricket Club every year between 1790 and 1798. From 1799 to 1804, the average drops to three games a year, and in 1805, the year of Trafalgar, there were none. It is very difficult to gauge how active the Club was off the cricket field, and we do not even know when the custom of appointing a new President every year began. Although this was the custom from 1821, when Lord Strathavon was the first known President, it was also the practice during the two World Wars of the twentieth century for one man to remain President for the duration of hostilities, so there is no certainty at all that for our missing 34 years there must be 34 missing names.

So who were the likely early Presidents? We can take an educated guess as to who might have held the office of President in those early years, even if it is not possible to put a name to a year. The transfer of power from Hambledon, which had been the undisputed champion club of England for the best part of thirty years, to Marylebone was sudden and, in many ways, it was an inside job. Broadhalfpenny Down had many strong qualifications as a cricket field, but it was just too rural for the people who wished to run cricket, and who felt it was their right to do so. As society became increasingly urban from the late eighteenth century onwards, rural pastimes became town pastimes or died. Wealth was moving from the land to industry, and the recreations of the landed gentry were taken up by the new moneyed classes.

On 25 February 1774, thirteen years before the probable date of MCC's birth, some members of the Je Ne Sais Quoi Club met at the

Star and Garter hostelry in Pall Mall to prepare 'New Articles of the Game of Cricket' – a set of standard laws to allow cricket clubs geographically disparate to compete on equal terms (although almost never, in those days, on anything resembling a level playing field) rather than following a myriad of local rules that invariably favoured the home side. The self-appointed Committee who met at the Star and Garter that winter's day included several men instrumental in founding a great cricket club in London, something which would have been impossible only a couple of decades earlier. There were of course representatives of Hambledon – Rev. Charles Powlett and Mr Philip Dehany, for example – but the balance of power was already shifting. Col. The Hon. Charles Lennox, who would later become the Fourth Duke of Richmond and who was probably the most influential and energetic of the early cricket administrators, was there, as were the Duke of Dorset, the Duke of Hamilton and his brother-in-law Sir Peter Burrell, and the Monson brothers, all names that would echo down the list of MCC Presidents in years to come.

The man most commonly deemed to be the founder of the Club is GEORGE FINCH, THE NINTH EARL OF WINCHILSEA. He was the man who persuaded Thomas Lord to buy his first ground in what is now Dorset Square (on land owned by the Duke of Dorset), and who was the financial benefactor whose resources enabled the Club to get going. He must surely have been an early President, perhaps the very first, but then again, he might, like Sir Spencer Ponsonby-Fane almost a century later, have been content to be a grandee of his club without assuming any formal position. Like those of the Club he founded, the Ninth Earl's records were destroyed by fire. In Winchilsea's case, it was a conflagration of 1908 that annihilated the archive at his family home in Burley-on-the-Hill in Rutland, but the result is the same – we know far less about him than we ought to. He was an Old Etonian, unlike many of the early cricket potentates who were Harrovians or Old Westminsters, and a keen, if not particularly good, cricketer. He began life, in 1752, as a wealthy aristocrat and, as some wealthy, young and restless aristocrats were wont to do, he joined the Army. He spent four years fighting in the American Wars, raising a regiment of infantry at a personal cost of around £20,000, while other men of his age and influence were at home playing cricket, cards and backgammon. On his return, however, he wasted little time in getting back into the sporting social circles he had enjoyed as a young man fresh out of school. He was a member of a 'Committee of Noblemen and Gentlemen of Kent, Hampshire, Surrey, Sussex, Middlesex and London' who sat once again at the Star and Garter in Pall Mall and issued an updated set of Laws in 1784. As in earlier sets of Laws, there was an article covering betting on the game, which was Winchilsea's passion and one shared by many a noble supporter of the game, and indeed was their main reason for being so interested. Gambling was as much a part of cricket in the eighteenth century as it is in the twenty-first. Gambling, then as now, financed the development of the game.

However, Winchilsea's main claim to immortality as a cricketer lies in the fact that it was he who persuaded Thomas Lord, a professional cricketer originally from Thirsk by way of Norfolk, to set up a cricket ground in Marylebone, and who gave Lord the financial support he needed. Lord was a better cricketer than Winchilsea and probably a better businessman, but did not possess the capital needed to get going. Winchilsea did. If MCC had a founding President, then Winchilsea would almost certainly have been the man.

Lord Winchilsea was President of the Hambledon Cricket Club in 1787, at the very same time that he was encouraging Thomas Lord to build his first ground, a fact that encapsulates the sudden but total transfer of power from the Hampshire Downs to the capital at the end of the eighteenth century. But Winchilsea was not the only Hambledon stalwart to become heavily involved with MCC. Two of the Hambledon club's principal backers over the three decades of its superiority were also early members of MCC. The Rev. Charles Powlett and Philip Dehany, although rather older than many of the cricketers who feature on the early scorecards of MCC, were nevertheless very much involved in Marylebone cricket.

CHARLES POWLETT (pronounced, and sometimes spelt, Paulet) was the eldest son of Charles, Third Duke of Bolton, but unfortunately he was born in 1728 – some two decades before His Grace his father married his mother. There is a very strong measure of doubt as to whether the Duke was actually his father: Powlett's mother, the actress Lavinia Fenton, had been conducting a notorious affair with a Portuguese nobleman before she took up with the Duke, and her son Charles was born only six months after she eloped with the Duke. As his nephew and ward – who loathed his uncle – was to write in a letter to his fiancée 65 years later, 'His villainies are too black for me to mention, but I begin to think he cannot be a Powlett – indeed he has himself said he is not, but owes his birth to a Portuguese ambassador.' In any case, his illegitimacy barred him from inheriting his father's title and most of his money, so the only thing left for him was to go into the Church.

Even a passing study of Powlett's life will reveal that he was a most unlikely candidate for holy orders: he was thoroughly unpleasant, mean-spirited and snobbish, and had very little interest in religious matters. A bastard by name and by nature. He was a typical eighteenth squarson, squire and parson in one, interested in racing and gambling and little else. He had two younger brothers, Percy and Armand, who both went into the services – Percy into the Navy and Armand into the Army – but Charles stayed at home in Hampshire and indulged in his passion for fine clothes, fine horses and clever bets on cricket. He was twice married, but his heart wasn't in it. He admitted in a letter to his brother that

> they tell me I must marry whenever I get a living. As you know a desire of matrimony was never among my predominant foibles, and … you

will easily believe I would willingly dispense with this necessary evil, but as my friends are absolute in their opinion, I must give up mine and make myself miserable to please the world. I am not very good natured and condescending.

His first marriage lasted 35 years but produced no children and one could easily reach the conclusion that Powlett was homosexual. The Earl of Winchilsea also never married.

Powlett ended his years in Marylebone. After years of enjoying the camaraderie and sport of Hambledon cricket, he moved to London when he was almost sixty years old and lived a further twenty years in St Marylebone. There is no doubt that he was a very early member of MCC, (for example, there was a match played at Lord's in 1788 between 'Mr Paulet's Side' and 'Mr East's Side') but at a time when the Club's Presidents were probably playing members rather than committee men, he is not very likely to have been one of the missing Presidents. Only one ordained priest is known to have been President of MCC, the equally unpleasant but rather more noble (albeit still from the wrong side of the blanket) Reverend Frederick Beauclerk, who held office in 1826.

It is a coincidence that Powlett's great-nephew, Fred Powlett, emigrated to Australia in the early years of the nineteenth century and became one of the founders of the other MCC, the Melbourne Cricket Club. Young Fred also played a handful of first-class games for Victoria and, when his first cousin Frederick Temple was elevated to the Archdiocese of Canterbury, he became the first and so far only first-class cricketer to have been first cousin to an Archbishop of Canterbury.

PHILIP DEHANY, Charles Powlett's comrade in arms at Hambledon, was the son of a Bristol merchant, five or six years younger than Powlett, but educated at Westminster and Trinity College, Cambridge, where the two men would have met. Dehany was more intellectually gifted than Powlett, or else had a more pressing need to establish a career, as he went up to Cambridge at the age of eighteen, a few months before Charles came up, aged 24. Both had the same tutor, and became lifelong friends. They shared a passion for gambling and for trying to fix the races and matches they bet on, and Dehany, like Powlett, took an active part in the administration of cricket in the final decades of the eighteenth century. He was a member of MCC and may possibly have been an early President; his money, which lasted well despite his gambling urges, may well have bought him that honour had he wished it.

A third Westminster man was a prominent member of the Club in the 1790s. He was called George Louch, and was a close friend of Powlett and Dehany. He was also a good cricketer, whose name appears regularly in the early scorebooks.

The Earl of Winchilsea's right hand man in the setting up of Lord's new ground, and therefore the establishment of the Marylebone Cricket Club, was COLONEL THE HONOURABLE CHARLES LENNOX, a Scot who was heir to the Duchy of Richmond, a title he succeeded to a few years later. Lennox was a fine cricketer, twelve years younger than Winchilsea and thus only about 23 years old when MCC was founded. He too was a soldier, although rather more serious about his profession than the effete Winchilsea, and a man with an impetuous temperament. In 1789, two years after the founding of MCC, he fought a duel on Wimbledon Common with His Royal Highness the Duke of York, on the pretext of a perceived slight. Winchilsea was his second. The Duke fired wide on purpose, while Lennox apparently shot away a lock of the Duke's hair. The Duke kept himself away from Lord's for a full year after this event, such was Lennox's authority at the Club, but they were reconciled at a match between England and Hampshire in 1790. Lennox, opening for England, made a duck in each innings, while Winchilsea, opening for Hampshire, made one of his higher scores, 15. The Duke of York was merely a spectator and, although almost certainly a member of MCC, was unlikely to have been an early President.

Lennox went on to become the fourth Duke of Richmond (yet another title that began with one of Charles II's extramarital conquests), and it was his wife who gave the famous Ball on 15 June 1815 before the Battle of Waterloo. On the afternoon before the Ball, many British officers enjoyed a game of cricket organised by the Duke on the outskirts of Brussels. This was perhaps what the Duke of Wellington was referring to when he said that the battle was won on the playing fields of Eton. Richmond spent much of his life out of England, first as Lord Lieutenant of Ireland (a post also held by Charles Powlett's grandfather the Duke of Bolton) and then as Governor General of Canada, where he died in 1819 after being bitten by a rabid fox. Lennox was a fine cricketer, the scorer of the first century in Scotland, and is a very strong candidate to have been one of the early Presidents of MCC. The one thing that counts against him, though, is the fact that his grandson, then Earl of March, was President of the Club in 1842 and his correspondence at the time with his father never once mentions MCC, Lord's or cricket. One might expect that if the grandson was holding a highly visible and fashionable position in society as a sucessor to his grandfather, he might have mentioned the fact. The lack of a mention tends to make it less likely that either the Fourth or the Fifth Duke of Richmond was ever President.

The third man at the centre of the establishment of MCC was Sir Peter Burrell, who subsequently became Lord Gwydyr. Burrell was born in 1754, making him two years younger that Winchilsea, and in his early thirties when MCC was founded. He was a good batsman on his day, but spent much of his time involved in political issues rather than on the cricket field. He was elected Member of Parliament for Haslemere in Surrey in 1776, and knighted in 1781. From 1782 to 1796 he sat for Boston in Lincolnshire. He rose to the position of Deputy Grand Chamberlain and in that capacity presided over the impeachment trial of Warren Hastings, the former Governor General of India who was tried for corruption on his return to England after serving many years in India trying to improve the administration and finances of the East India Company, and trying to civilise the local population. In the end Hastings was acquitted, but only after having spent most of the money he had gained in India paying for his defence. Burrell's reward was an elevation to the peerage.

Despite his hectic parliamentary life, Burrell still found plenty of time for his cricket, and from 1790 his name regularly appears in Britcher's scorebook. He was brother-in-law to another sports-mad nobleman, the Duke of Dorset, and his sister, Elizabeth, was also a fine cricketer at a time when women rarely played. His wife Priscilla was Baroness Willoughby de Eresby in her own right, and their great-grandson was to become President of MCC in 1890. It seems very likely that Burrell was also President in the early years.

An early member of MCC was Frederick Reynolds, the playwright. In his autobiography, *The Life And Times of Frederick Reynolds*, he gives us an interesting picture of some of the personalities in the early years.

> The day I was proposed a member of the Marylebone Club, then in its highest fashion, I waited at the Portland Coffee House to hear from Tom Lord the result of the ballot with more anxiety than I experienced the month before, while expecting the decision of the audience on my new play. Being unanimously elected, I immediately assumed the sky blue dress, the uniform of the club.

Clearly the waiting list in those days was far shorter than it is today, even though the Club was in its highest fashion and the method of informing new members of their fate was rather more personal than would be possible today. To have Tom Lord, proprietor of the Club's ground, come and tell the nervous applicant he had been elected is a standard of service that few clubs today could aim for. Lord, of course, though a member of the club, was also an employee and so is not even remotely likely to have been President.

Reynolds then gives a few names of the most fashionable members of the Club in the 1790s.

> The members of the club who were most regular in their attendance were the late Duke of Richmond, the present Lord Winchilsea, Lord Darnley, Lord Cardigan (known in his active cricketing days as Hon. Robert Brudenell), Lord Frederick Beauclerk, the Honourable John and Henry Tufton, General Bligh and Richard Leigh, the Duke of Dorset, Sir Horace Mann, the Honourable Thomas Twistleton, Charles Anguish, Paulet, Louch and Dehany.

He also mentions the Marquess of Hertford and the Earl of Thanet, elder brother to the Tuftons, who were nephews of the Duke of Dorset. Most of these men are strong candidates for the role of President in those early years, with the possible exception of Charles Anguish, who died at the age of only 28. Reynolds does not, on the other hand, mention that he was ever President, so we must assume that that honour escaped him. He does however reveal the unlikely fact that the Club was 'sometimes honoured with the presence of the Duchesses of Richmond and Gordon, Lady Wallace and other ladies'. So women had invaded the halls of MCC in the 1790s! When were they first evicted?

To this list we can add the names of men such as Lord William Bentinck, the Earl of Dalkeith, the Duke of Hamilton, the Hon. William Harbord, the Earl of Sandwich, Sir John Shelley, Lord Tankerville, the Hon. Colonel Lowther and a few mere commoners: Ashton Smith, his son Thomas Assheton Smith, William Ward and Thomas Vigne.

THOMAS ASSHETON SMITH, known as plain Tom Smith to his contemporaries, was, according to George Osbaldeston, 'a very choleric man, and in consequence he had several "turns-up" to use a pugilistic term, in all of which, except one, he came off victorious.' He was a very keen huntsman, riding with the Quorn in the early years of the nineteenth century, and despite being, in Osbaldeston's opinion, 'very hard featured, not at all good-looking', he was also 'one of the most honourable men that ever existed'.

THE DUKE OF HAMILTON and his family were to play a very major role in the Presidency of MCC in years to come, and it is entirely possible that a forbear was President in the early years. Dalkeiths, Harbords and Sandwiches all feature on the roll of known Presidents and yet it is the commoners whose names keep on cropping up in any discussion of likely Presidents in the early years of the Club.

RICHARD LEIGH, a man with large estates near Wilmington in Kent, and one of the great matchmakers of eighteenth century cricket, is a strong contender. In the early years of MCC there were annual games between teams of members that might have been a 'President's XI v. The Rest', although we have no proof of the matter. In 1794, for example, 'Louch's XI' played 'R. Leigh's XI' at Lord's, but which of the two team captains, if either, was President is something that cannot be proved.

GEORGE LOUCH and Richard Leigh are, of course, clear probables for the missing Presidents' list. Other such games were Hon. Col. Lennox's XI v. Earl Winterton's XI (1795), Lord Yarmouth's XI v. Hon. H. Tufton's XI (1797) and Lord Frederick Beauclerk's XI v. F. Ladbroke's XI (1809). All or any of these men could have been President; it is very frustrating not to know. However, if Francis Seymour, Earl of Yarmouth, was ever President he would have been setting a quite different example from the high moral tone of his successors. His main claim to fame was his 'undisguised debauchery', as a contemporary put it, remarked on even in an era when what we would call debauchery, disguised or not, was a common enough noble failing.

Richard Leigh was a fairly near neighbour of Sir Horace Mann, the greatest cricketing matchmaker of the decades immediately before MCC was founded, and he was part of a long tradition of men of Kent and Kentish men who played important roles in the development of cricket and of the Marylebone Cricket Club. Sir Horace Mann managed to bankrupt himself through his extravagance in promoting cricket and in following other pleasures, which probably eliminates him from the list of potential Presidents, but all the same his place in history as a sponsor of great cricket matches is secure.

The Darnleys were another Kent family whose most famous cricketing son was Ivo Bligh, the man for whom the Ashes urn was created. He was chosen to be President in 1900, but both his great-grandfather James Bligh, the Fourth Earl, and his great great-uncle General Edward Bligh, known throughout the country as 'Skirmish' Bligh, were enthusiastic supporters of the Club at the turn of the nineteenth century. The Sixth Earl, James Bligh's grandson and Ivo Bligh's father, who had been born in Marylebone, was President in 1849. The establishment of the great MCC family dynasties, of which the Darnleys were but one, dates back to the founding of the Club.

The Duke of Dorset was probably not very involved with the earliest days of the MCC as he was at that time serving as Ambassador to France, an appointment cut short when the French Revolution put an end not only to the French monarchy but also to cricket tours from England. The Duke, like Mann and Leigh, was a Kent man and a pretty good cricketer. He owned what is now the Sevenoaks Vine ground, and gave it to the public on his death. It was when playing for the Duke's team in 1769 that James Minshull hit the first recorded century in major cricket. The Fourth Earl of Tankerville, two years older than the Duke of Dorset but still only in his forties when MCC was formed, was a Surrey man, with his seat near Walton on Thames. He was a generous supporter of Surrey cricket, and did very little else. He and Dorset were described as 'the two idlest lords in His Majesty's three kingdoms', which considering the competition they faced in that particular category is quite an achievement.

The three men who seem almost certainly to have been Presidents, if only we could put a year to their names, are Thomas Vigne, Hervey Aston and William Ward. Aston was first seen on the scorecards in 1792, and was known as the chief matchmaker for the Club in the early years. Whether 'chief matchmaker', which these days might be the equivalent of fixtures secretary in a lesser club than MCC, could ever be combined with the Presidency is not certain, but as the average age of both members and Presidents in the years between 1820 and 1850 is well under 35, we can assume that almost anybody who was a member was also a potential President, provided he had the right connections. Aston certainly did, if his matchmaking skills are anything to go by.

THOMAS VIGNE, who first appears on the scorecards in 1804, served for many years on the MCC Committee from 1825, but was never President in those years. He was born in 1771 and died, still a committee man, in 1841. His very long period of service to the Club seems to indicate that he must have been President at some point, so would surely have held that office before the fire, and that record of his Presidency has been lost. Then again, after the fire of 1825, the names of four earlier Presidents, from 1821 to 1824, were not lost, and if Vigne had been asked at the time the post-conflagration committee were remembering things past, he surely would have mentioned his Presidential year. And yet, if he had been asked, he (and many other members) could probably have listed all the Presidents from when he first started playing, so the conclusion we come to is that no one did anything about reconstituting the archive of MCC until much later, when most of the key members had died. Many researchers over the years have tried to find out more, and all have failed. The Club just did not know its own importance in those days – or perhaps it was too conscious of it, and therefore did not condescend to bother with such trivial things as history.

W ILLIAM WARD, whose XI played against Lord Frederick Beauclerk's XI in 1815, was a great cricketer. His score of 278 for MCC against Norfolk in 1820 was the first double-century ever recorded in a top match, and it remained the highest score made at Lord's for 105 years. He reportedly used a bat that weighed four pounds and lasted him fifty years: a mighty weapon indeed. He was a banker, eventually becoming a director of the Bank of England and MP for the City of London. Rather inevitably, given his career path, he ended up a very rich man, which proved of great benefit to the Club. In 1825, the year of the fire, Thomas Lord decided he would build houses on a large portion of his ground, in order to raise money for his retirement. Ward stepped in and paid £5,000 for the lease from Lord, and the houses were never built. Lord got his comfortable retirement in West Meon in Hampshire, a mere long hop from Broadhalfpenny Down, and the MCC members were saved from the developers for another half-century. In the 1870s, when William Nicholson helped the Club out of a similar pending disaster, he was rewarded almost immediately with the Presidency. As Ward was never President after 1825 it seems a fairly sure bet that he had already held the post before 1821, quite possibly in 1815 when his XI took the field at Lord's. Ward remained a loyal supporter of MCC and a regular Committee member until 1840 when the minute book records that on 12 July, Ward wrote that:

I have to request that my name may be removed from the List of members that are disposed to play in matches. I have also to request that I may no longer be considered a member of the Committee. Although I make these requests under circumstances that are most unsatisfactory to my feelings, I nevertheless beg to assure you that I have no misgiving as to the good intentions of the Committee, or want of desire to uphold it in the estimation and respect of the Club.

And so he left.

It is worth noting that there have been suspicions over the years that the fire of 1825 was more likely to be connected to Thomas Lord's attempt to develop the ground than to either high jinks after the Harrow v. Winchester game or to pure misfortune. There is no firm evidence to back up any of these theories; no one at Harrow or Winchester ever came forward, then or later, to confess. As for the Thomas Lord theory, it is nothing more than suspicion created by putting two facts together and making four, or possibly five. Lord himself was never thought of as having been involved in deliberate sabotage, but some murmurs have been heard that the people who might have been willing to buy the part of the ground that Lord was willing to sell could have organised the fire in an attempt to get cricket moved away from the ground altogether. If this theory has any validity the potential buyers underestimated the attachment to their ground that MCC members had already formed, because the Pavilion was rebuilt and cricket continues on Thomas Lord's third ground 180 years on. It seems that misfortune must remain the most likely cause of the fire.

There are well over one hundred names of MCC members that we know of from the first forty years of the Club's existence, but we have no proof of which of them may have been President, or Treasurer or Secretary for that matter, in any particular year. We do not even know whether the tradition of a one-year Presidency, which was certainly in effect from 1821, began at the formation of the Club. We certainly do not know whether anybody from those early years ever became President for a second time. This happened twice in the nineteenth century and once in the twentieth century, but on the first known occasion of this happening, in 1867 when Lord Verulam had a second year in office thirty years after his first Presidency, there is no mention of this being either a unique event or something for which there was a precedent.

So, as we move into the period when the names of the Presidents are recorded, we can only make a few firm statements about the early Presidents. The first is that the Club, although small, was extremely fashionable from its earliest years. To be President would have been an honour from the start, and it therefore seems likely that the tradition of an annual Presidency began at the beginning. Hambledon, the obvious forerunner of MCC, while not sticking to a yearly change of President throughout its years of pre-eminence, nevertheless did regularly change its President, rather than having the same man for life, as some county clubs were to do in later years. MCC probably formalised the annual arrangement from the start.

We can be pretty certain that Presidents were elected by the membership each year. This was the method followed until 1842, although the first firm evidence of this system is a minute of 1825 that states 'A President shall be chosen annually on the second Thursday in May.' It is assumed that this minute, which was written after the fire but which refers to the Annual General Meeting that took place two months before the fire, was recorded so that there would be a clear reconfirmation of the rules of the Club after they, along with everything else, had gone up in smoke. The minute does begin by saying, 'At the Anniversary Dinner on Thursday 11 May at the Pavilion, Charles Barnett Esq. President, the Rules of the Club were revised and declared to be as follows …' It is thus possible that the annual election of a President was an innovation from 1825, but as we know that there was an annual President in each of the four years before, it seems most probable that this rule was not one of the revised ones. It was merely a restatement of past practice.

We can also state with some confidence that most of the early Presidents would have been young men, still playing members. This was the case for most of the next three decades to the 1850s, and it seems logical that, in a small club, this would have been true as much before the fire as after it. And lastly we can assume that although all members were pillars of London society, well connected at the highest levels (even if they did not all involve themselves in duels with the Royal Family), there was no distinction between the titled and commoners when it came to the Presidency of MCC. It was not until the 1830s that a title became de rigueur for a President. From 1821 to 1834 there were only two lords and two honourables among the first fourteen listed Presidents. As far as it could be, the Marylebone Club was an equal opportunity organisation in its earliest years.

CHAPTER TWO

1821–1841

THE FORMATIVE YEARS

The pre-history of MCC ends in 1825, but there is a four-year period before that when we know who the Presidents were, but little else about the Club. The very first name on the list of Presidents is one that means very little today, Lord Strathavon. All the same, upon investigation he proves to be a typical specimen of the cricketing elite of his age.

CHARLES GORDON, LORD STRATHAVON, was the grandson of the Eighth Marquess of Huntly and son of the Fifth Earl of Aboyne. He was born on 30 January 1792 at one of the family seats, Orton Longue-ville in Huntingdonshire, and was therefore only 29 years old when he took over the Presidency. A keen if remarkably ungifted cricketer, who had graduated from Cambridge University in 1812 at the age of twenty, he distributed his favours around the main southern teams of the age, playing for Hampshire, Kent, Middlesex and Surrey as well as MCC. His lack of real talent may also have been part of the reason why he played for so many teams. In the 33 matches of first-class quality that he played in, he scored only 193 runs, at an average of 4.02 and with a highest score of only 19. He did not bowl and took only nine catches, so his value to the teams he represented was limited at best, and one can imagine the selection committees of those days being more than happy to pass him on to someone else. In 1819 he played in the Gentlemen versus Players match at Lord's, in those days the most important game of the season, but remarkably he was representing the Players, which is probably a unique achievement for a nobleman. As Lord Harris laconically remarked in his epic history of Kent County Cricket Club, this was 'presumably because he backed them, an arrangement that would not now be tolerated'. Actually, to back yourself to win is something that is tolerable, even today, but given Strathavon's fairly appalling career average, he either wanted the rare satisfaction of being on a winning side, or else backed the Gentlemen to lose and therefore felt honour bound not to play for them. The match finished, as was usually the case, in a win for the Players, this time by six wickets. Lord Strathavon made 5 and 6, well above average for him, but never represented the Players again.

Lord Harris also noted that a few years after this unseemly action, in 1828, Strathavon 'assisted, or at least appeared for, XVII Gentlemen v. XI Players, when he had the satisfaction of being on the winning side.' However great the moral satisfaction of being on the winning side may have been, it is doubtful whether the financial satisfaction was as great as it had been when also on the winning side nine years earlier. Strathavon's apparent lack of talent on the cricket field was all the more surprising when we learn that his father, the Earl of Aboyne, was a good cricketer who in 1791, the season before his son's birth, had played an innings of 'about 150' in a game at Aldermaston Wharf.

Lord Strathavon remained a member of MCC for about fifty years, but his direct interest in the running of the Club did not long outlast his Presidency. In 1826 he married Lady Elizabeth, daughter of the Marquess of Conyngham, but she died before any children were born. In 1844 he married for a second time, to a commoner with the semi-regal name of Marian Antoinette, and, even though he was over fifty at the time, by her he had six sons and seven daughters. In 1836 his grandfather the Marquess of Huntly died, promoting his father to this title and Strathavon himself to the title of Earl of Aboyne. At this time he ceased to be Member of Parliament for East Grinstead, a part of the country with which his family had no obvious connection but which he had nevertheless represented for twelve years. In 1853, his father died at the age of 93, so Strathavon at last became Marquess of Huntly, the tenth of that ilk.

He died where he had been born, on 18 September 1863, the year before *Wisden Cricketers' Almanack* was first published, aged 71 at his family seat in Orton Longueville.

His successor was **HENRY LLOYD**, elected President in 1822. Lloyd was a real local boy, born in Marylebone 28 years earlier, on 2 February 1794. He first played for MCC in 1815, which was probably the year of his election, and played intermittently for them over the next fifteen years. He was not as bad a cricketer as Lord Strathavon, but his career figures hardly set a high standard for future Presidents. He played one more game in his career than Strathavon, 34, and scored exactly twice as many runs – 386 at an average of 6.89. He had a top score of 37, one short of twice as many as Lord Strathavon managed in any innings, but was not a bowler (few amateurs in those days bothered to bowl). His main claim to fame is in being dismissed for 1 when playing for MCC against Hampshire, an early example of the LBW law being enforced. He gave up the game in 1828, but served on the Committee in 1827 and 1829, and quite probably in several other years before and immediately after his Presidential year.

Lloyd's successor was one of the giants, both physically and fig-uratively, of MCC's early years – **BENJAMIN AISLABIE**. Aislabie, a Londoner born and bred, was if anything a worse cricketer than either of his predecessors (career batting average 3.15, highest score 15 not out) but this statistic comes about largely because he was considerably older than both Strathavon and Lloyd, being 49 years old when he took on

the Presidency, and there are almost no scorebooks extant from the time
of his cricketing prime, such as it was. Nevertheless, Lord Harris
confirms that 'as a cricketer, he was of no account.' What is more, by
1815 or thereabouts, he had put on a huge amount of weight, and tipped
the scales at almost 20 stone. When he played he got someone not only
to act as his runner but also to field for him, and 'whilst at the wicket
creating considerable amusement' on account of his size. Aislabie was
a great huntsman, and there is a fine portrait of what looks like a tall
willowy man astride a horse in the Long Room at Lord's, but closer
inspection shows that this was painted several years before the more
full-bodied version became President.

Aislabie, an Etonian, had been elected to MCC in 1802. He was
by profession a wine merchant, but seemed to spend very little time
selling wine and rather more running the Marylebone Cricket Club.
From 1822, the year before his Presidency, he took over as Honorary Secretary and thus was, a year later, the only man on the official list to have
combined the posts of President and Secretary in the same year; it is a
record he still holds. He remained Secretary until his death, in 1842,
when, despite his huge contribution to the Club, the minute book is
sparse in its references to his demise. After seventeen years of Aislabie's
handwriting in the minute books, it is a shock to read in a different
hand the minute of 16 May 1842 which notes the 'lamentable illness of
Mr Aislabie'. On 14 June, the book notes that Roger Kynaston was
elected Hon. Sec. 'in place of B. Aislabie deceased'.

A closer study of the situation reveals that Aislabie was not much
more effective as a Secretary than as a cricketer. The financial state of
MCC when he died was not good, despite the fact that it was still a
fashionable and well-patronised sporting club. The Treasurer with
whom Aislabie had effectively run the Club for many years, Felix
Ladbroke, had died in 1840, and while there was no suspicion of foul
play on the part of either man, there is little doubt that what we would
now call the most basic of management and financial controls were
all but non-existent. Sir Spencer Ponsonby-Fane, a man who turned
down the Presidency on several occasions, recorded in the foreword to

Lord Harris's book *Lord's And the MCC* that 'I can see Mr Benjamin Aislabie, the Secretary of the Club, a big fat man over twenty stone in weight, fussing about with a big red book in which he was entering subscriptions for some desired match of which the funds of the club could not afford the expense.' That was the height of management and financial control within the Club at the time. Of course, MCC was made up of members who were for the main part very well off, and no doubt the Committee's view was that almost any crisis could be overcome by appealing to their large pockets.

The tradition of allowing the Secretary and Treasurer to remain in office indefinitely, probably begun by Aislabie through force of personality more than anything else, was not changed by the 1842 Committee, but one of their very first decisions after the death of Aislabie was to appoint two members of the Club but not of the Committee to act as auditors. Aislabie's death marked the end of the early years of the Marylebone Cricket Club.

Despite his failings as Hon. Secretary, Aislabie was a jovial man and a good companion. He was the composer of many cricket songs, several of which he could quite easily be prevailed upon to sing at the Club's Anniversary Dinner year after year, and he was also Custodian of the Club Snuff Box, a position that seems to have fallen into disuse over subsequent generations.

Aislabie handed over in 1824 to **HENRY LANE**. Like his predecessor-but-one Henry Lloyd, he was born in Marylebone, in 1793, the year before Lloyd. He was a few days short of his 31st birthday when he took on the Presidency, and still playing a few games for MCC, Kent and Hampshire. Lane was another of those early MCC Presidents elected by his fellow members for his pleasant character rather than for any distinction on the cricket field. He played club cricket in west Kent and played a handful of games for the county without any particular distinction. He also appeared at Lord's for the Gentlemen against the Players twice, in 1820 and 1827. In neither game did he achieve anything of note. Lane's life was to prove a short one. He died at the age of 40 at his home in Sussex before he could leave his imprint on fields of activity beyond the MCC.

It was the custom at this time for the President to be chosen by his fellow members and for the handover to be made at the Anniversary Dinner, held at the beginning of May. Lane handed over to **CHARLES BARNETT** at the Anniversary Dinner on Thursday 11 May 1825, and at that time several club rules were revised. The Anniversary Dinner was fixed for the second Thursday of May each year, which was also the start of the Club's playing season. The annual subscription was set at £3, a fairly large sum for the time. The rules for applying for membership were rather less onerous than they are today: 'Any Gentleman wishing to become a member shall be proposed and seconded at one meeting, and balloted for at the next.' Meetings were regular monthly affairs at worst, and sometimes held weekly, so the waiting list was never very long. However, 'Two black balls shall exclude.' On the other hand, 'not less than nine members shall constitute a ballot,' which is a very small voting base. This meant that in practice all new candidates were personally known to every influential member of the Club, and would quite probably have been encouraged to put their names forward for membership in the certain knowledge that they would be elected. At this time, there were probably no more than 150 members of the Club, but, even so, 9 is a tiny percentage of the total membership to constitute a quorum for the ballot.

At this meeting they also set the rules for electing the new President. 'A President shall be chosen annually on the second Thursday in May, together with seven members who with the President and Treasurer shall form a Committee for the general management of the Club.' A further rule noted that 'The office of Treasurer, now filled by Felix Ladbroke Esq., shall be permanent.'

Charles Barnett had been born on 31 October 1796, so was only 28 years old when he took on the Presidency. He had begun playing for MCC in 1820 and went on sporadically for eighteen seasons, but, like the majority of his predecessors, his cricketing claims to the position were flimsy. A batting average of 5.16 and a highest score of 24 not out are hardly figures to boast of, although as a bowler in important cricket he outshone all those who had gone before. He took one wicket! All the same, he played for the Gentlemen against the Players in 1823, 1824, 1825 and 1827, his appearance in 1825 being a rare but by no means unique case of the current President playing in the greatest match of the year. In 1828 he played on the same side as his predecessor Lord Strathavon for XVII Gentlemen v. XI Players, but, like Strathavon, he hardly assisted their cause, and made a pair.

Barnett, the first name on the list of Presidents in the Pavilion at Lord's, was President when the Pavilion was burned down. William H. Slatter, in his privately printed 1914 book, *Recollections of Lord's*, wrote that 'how it caught fire, no one could tell. When the excavations were dug out for the present Pavilion, a stone was found embedded twelve feet in the clay. This had all the appearance of a thunderbolt.' So it was an act of God, not of schoolboy tomfoolery.

Barnett, who served the Club as a committee man for many years after his Presidential year, died, much regretted and full of years, on the last day of 1882; he gave way to the only ordained priest ever to have been President. **THE REVEREND THE LORD FREDERICK BEAUCLERK** was 53 when he took on the Presidency, and had by that time come to the end of a very distinguished playing career. He was a younger son of the Duke of St Albans, like the Duke of Richmond descended from one of Charles II's peccadilloes. After attending Cambridge University, he took holy orders like many a younger son of the nobility, and then turned his full attention to cricket. He was a very fine cricketer but was also a bad tempered, foul-mouthed, dishonest man

who was one of the most hated figures in society. That he ever rose to
the position of President of MCC probably reflects more on the lack of
other suitable candidates than on his personal popularity. He was
renowned as one of the great single wicket players of his day, at a time
when these contests were hugely popular, but, in the words of a later
President Sir Pelham Warner, 'he sought to turn his cricketing prowess
to monetary gain,' which was totally against the ethic of the gentleman
cricketers of MCC. He was reputed to earn up to £600 a year by playing matches for high stakes. In 1805, the year of Trafalgar when there
were few cricket matches of real quality in Britain, he played eleven
innings, in eight of which he top scored for his team. He also scored
two unbeaten centuries, including his career best of 129, and this at a
time when a reasonable team score was no more than 100. His bowling, underhand of course, was slow and effective in his early career,
mainly because he imparted back spin that made it bounce sharply,
but then batsmen learnt that he did not like being hit. After that his
effectiveness as a bowler declined.

The money he earned from cricket was not merely through betting
on himself to succeed. He bought and sold matches as though
they were lots at an auction. In one well-recorded incident, he played
against a team raised by George Osbaldeston in Nottingham, and sold
the match in advance. He did not realise, however, that the Nottingham team had also bet on themselves to lose, so the match soon
descended into farce. Beauclerk never liked to lose a bet, and even
managed to break a finger in trying to stop a deliberate overthrow by
the Nottinghamshire men. In the end, the Nottingham team won
despite their best efforts.

Another story relates how Daniel Denison, a notorious criminal who
was hanged in front of 10,000 spectators at Cambridge in 1812 for
poisoning horses, on one occasion refused to travel in the same stage
coach as Lord Frederick 'on account of the latter's fluent and expressive
vocabulary', as Lord Harris puts it. Clearly Lord Frederick was no
ordinary clergyman. 'Cruel, unforgiving, cantankerous and bitter' is
how one source describes him. He was certainly the least honourable

of all Presidents of MCC – a title that he will, we hope, hold for all time. Many great cricketing names, such as William Lambert and E. H. Budd, people who otherwise led equable lives, could not stomach the man. Budd, the only man who was considered Beauclerk's equal as a cricketer, resigned from MCC in 1826, the year Beauclerk became President. When Lord Frederick died, a few days before his 77th birthday on 2 April 1850, there was no obituary notice printed in *The Times*, nor in any other publication of note. Society, and cricket, wanted to forget about its wild rebel son as quickly as possible.

Beauclerk's successor was as far away in character from the rogue clergyman as possible. **HENRY KINGSCOTE**, the first President to be born in the nineteenth century, was still a few days shy of his 25th birthday when he took office. It is interesting to note that the guest list at the Anniversary Dinner on 10 May 1827, when Kingscote was elected, does not include Beauclerk. Most of his predecessors and several of his successors were there, including Lord Strathavon, Henry Lloyd, Aislabie, Barnett, Hon. George Ponsonby, John Barnard and Sir John Bayley, together with some of the probable early Presidents, such as William Ward and Thomas Vigne. There were only 24 people at the dinner (i.e. about one fifth of the total membership), but Lord Frederick was not among them. The outgoing President has missed the annual dinner no more than a handful of times in the history of the Club, and then always with a strong excuse, such as that of the Hon. Robert Grimston in 1884: absent, dead.

Henry Kingscote was a Hampshire man, a modest right-hand batsman who had been in the XI at Harrow and made his debut at Lord's in 1823. He played for the Gentlemen against the Players several times, but in each match the games were at odds. In 1829 and 1830, twelve Gentlemen played eleven Players while in 1831 it was eleven Gentlemen against nine Players. The 1832 game was eleven-a-side, but the Players had to defend a standard size wicket 27 inches high by 8 inches across, about 60 per cent bigger than the Gentlemen's wicket of 22 inches by 6. The Players still won: by an innings and 34 runs.

Kingscote had a successful career in trade, especially with Australia, where the town of Kingscote on Kangaroo Island is named after him. His wealth enabled him to devote much of his time to the Club, serving on the Committee for over twenty years beyond his Presidential year and ending up as Treasurer from 1840, when Felix Ladbroke died, until 1848, when the post was abolished. His own Committee in 1827 comprised Beauclerk, Strathavon, Thomas Vigne, Henry Lloyd, Charles Barnett, Aislabie, William Ward and Felix Ladbroke. Of these, only Vigne, Ward and Ladbroke are not on our list of Presidents. Ladbroke, as Treasurer, would not be but surely Vigne and Ward are among the missing men.

Henry Kingscote died aged 80 on 13 July 1882. No one had a bad word to say of him. His successor as President was **ALGERNON GREVILLE**, a man who was closely connected to many of the most powerful families of Britain. He was born on 29 December 1798, and so was 29 years old when elected President. By this time he was secretary to the Duke of Wellington, having been a captain in the Grenadier Guards. Although the Duke was not known as a cricketer, we have already seen how the Duke of Richmond organised a cricket match amongst his officers on the eve of Waterloo, and there is a further rather tenuous link between the Iron Duke and MCC. In 1841 the President was the Earl of Craven, whose father the first Earl was one of the lovers of the courtesan Harriette Wilson, who published her memoirs in 1825. Miss Wilson had tried to blackmail many of her lovers into paying several hundreds of pounds to be left out of her book, but the Earl of Craven was included as was the Duke of Wellington, who had dismissed her request for money with the famous remark, 'Publish and be damned.'

Algernon Greville played in one or two important matches during his brief time as an active cricketer, first playing at Lord's in 1816 when only seventeen years old. Three years later he played for the Gentlemen against the Players (against Lord Strathavon on the Players' side), but after 1823 his name disappears from the scorecards of the important matches of the day. His brother Charles Greville was a great diarist and political commentator whose son was killed at the Battle of Omdurman in 1854. His daughter Frances Harriet married Charles, Earl of March and heir to the Duchy of Richmond, in 1843, the year after March had been President of MCC. March was the grandson of Charles Lennox, Fourth Duke of Richmond.

During Greville's Presidency, a major change in the Laws of Cricket was passed. The minute book of 19 May 1828 notes, in Aislabie's florid handwriting,

> Law 10 to be repealed and replaced by: 'The ball shall be bowled: if it be thrown or jerked, or if any part of the hand or arm be above the elbow at the time of delivery, the umpire shall call "No Ball" '

Round arm was now legal. Overarm bowling would not be long in coming.

Another significant change made during Greville's year was to the ground itself. When Thomas Lord first took on the ground there had been two ponds within the site, one being in front of what is now the Mound Stand, and the other near the western end of the Grand Stand. During 1828, these ponds were largely filled in, and a rather better drained playing area began to take shape.

In 1829 **JOHN BARNARD** was elected President. He was another Kent man, born in Chislehurst on 6 July 1794, making him almost 35 years old when he took on the Presidency. He was elected at the Anniversary Dinner, which that year was held at Grillions Hotel rather than in the new Pavilion. It would be seven years before the dinner returned to the MCC Pavilion. Barnard had been a member of MCC since 1818. He was still an active, enthusiastic and comparatively unskilled cricketer (career batting average 9.96), and the first but by no means last wicket-keeper (fifteen catches and twenty stumpings in his eighteen top class games) to have taken on the Presidency. He was the youngest of three brothers who all represented Eton at cricket. John also played for Cambridge University and Kent, as well as for MCC. In his Presidential year, he turned out for the Unmarried versus the Married. On his team were four other past and future Presidents: Henry Lloyd, Charles Barnett, William Deedes and Herbert Jenner. Jenner did not long remain in the ranks of the Unmarried – he married Barnard's first cousin Maria Norman a few years later, linking the Barnard family to the Jenners, the Hart-Dykes and the Nepeans: all famous MCC families of the nineteenth century. On the Married team were Lord Strathavon, William Ward, the Hon. Colonel Lowther and Thomas Vigne, among others. In fact, over half of Barnard's Committee that year was playing in the game, making the match the most prestigious of the year at Lord's. This was not an official MCC game, however, as Jenner for one was not yet a member of the Club.

Two small but interesting resolutions were passed early in Barnard's tenure. One involved the first recorded blackballing of potential members: at the Anniversary Dinner two men, Edward Rice and Charles Atkinson, were rejected, though their failings remain un-recorded. Rice had been proposed by Benjamin Aislabie and Atkinson by Lord Strathavon, so one might have expected their failure to become members to have caused some ripples on the Committee. If so, it is not mentioned.

The second resolution was made on 27 July 1829. 'It was ordered by the Committee that in future no charge should be made upon the Stock Purse for the Anniversary Dinner.' Clearly even at this stage the Club funds were not enough to subsidise the dinner, so in future, the ticket price would have to cover the entire cost.

Barnard handed over to the **Honourable George Ponsonby**, but his work for MCC was not yet done. In 1835 he was asked to join a committee to revise the Laws of Cricket, their work culminating in the legalisation of round arm, if not quite overarm, bowling. Ponsonby, and his brother the Hon. Frederick, another Lord's stalwart, were sons of the Earl of Bessborough, but George is the only member of that distinguished cricketing family ever to have been President of MCC – unless we include the infamous Lord Frederick Beauclerk, who was a cousin by marriage. The Bessborough family are mainly famous in cricketing terms for the efforts of the Sixth Earl, who along with his brother Sir Spencer Ponsonby-Fane and John Loraine Baldwin, founded the I Zingari club in 1845. IZ remains the leading rambling cricket club, and the portrait of the three founders hangs in the Lord's Pavilion as a permanent reminder of their contribution to cricket. Both Lord Bessborough and his brother Sir Spencer turned down the Presidency, in Sir Spencer's case several times, but the Honourable George Ponsonby was not so reticent. Born in 1783, he was 47 years old in his Presidential year and boosted the average age of Presidents of the time quite considerably. He had not been on the Committee before his election and did not serve on it after his Presidency, so his overall contribution to Club affairs was fairly slight. It seems ironic that the one member of the Bessborough clan to take on the Presidency was possibly the least involved in the Club. It is also remarkable that Ponsonby's Presidency lasted two weeks longer than any of his predecessors, because the Anniversary Dinner was postponed from 12 May to 26 May 1831 because of a clash with the General Election.

After Ponsonby came **William Deedes**. Deedes was in his mid-thirties in 1831 with his active cricket career behind him. He had been born in Sandling Park near Hythe in Kent on 17 October 1796. Remarkably, no other member of the Deedes family has ever taken on the Presidency, despite their high profile, mainly in journalism, and

their well-documented love of cricket. William is an ancestor of Bill
Deedes, the Conservative politician and journalist who was still writing in his nineties. He first played at Lord's in 1819, at the age of 24, and
also first featured in the Gentlemen v. Players match in July 1821 when
the game was held to celebrate the coronation of King George IV. The
match also featured Lord Frederick Beauclerk at the end of his playing
career and Sir John Bayley, the 1844 President, not far from the end of
his. It is worth pointing out the result of this encounter, in view of Lord
Frederick's participation. The Gentlemen made 60 all out (of which
Deedes made 4) and then 'gave up the match' when the Players had
reached 278 for six wickets in reply. How much money Lord Frederick
won on the game is not recorded.

Deedes had a reasonably good record as a batsman in the few matches
for which we still have records, which include the Gentlemen v. Players
matches of 1822, 1823 and 1825. He was also known as a fine outfielder
'at middle wicket' and a fast underhand bowler. His mother's sister,
Mary Bridges, married Edward Knight of Godmersham, no more than
fifteen miles from the Deedes family estate at Sandling Park. Knight was
the brother of Jane Austen and a keen cricketer himself. Their son,
Major Henry Knight, was elected a member of MCC in 1827.

Deedes gave way to **HENRY HOWARD**, a Sussex man about whom
comparatively little is known. He was a man who played little
cricket (he did not feature in the early Gentlemen v. Players matches),
was in his thirtieth year when he took on the Presidency, but made little
other contribution to the Club, either before or after his year in office.
He was, in fact, from a family that was rapidly becoming more distinguished. Although he himself held no title, his uncle was Bernard
Howard, Twelfth Duke of Norfolk and his father was Lord Henry
Howard-Molyneux-Howard, of Greystoke Castle in Cumberland;
Edgar Rice Burroughs stole the name when he created Tarzan. Howard
married Charlotte Long, of the family of Sir Robert Walpole, and their

daughter Elizabeth became the second wife of the Fourth Earl of Caernarvon. Their son, Hon. Mervyn Herbert, born in 1882, is the only member of his family to have played first-class cricket. Herbert played for Eton, Nottinghamshire and Somerset in the early years of the last century, but died young, aged 46, in Rome.

Howard's successor was a true original, yet a Victorian cricketer *par excellence*. HERBERT JENNER was born on 23 February 1806 in Mayfair and began his top class cricket career with Cambridge University in 1825. He had already appeared at Lord's by then, in 1822 at the age of sixteen, and captained Cambridge in the first ever University match, in 1827. The match was drawn, with only one innings for each side being possible, but Jenner made the most of his role as captain. In Cambridge's innings of 92 all out he made 47, and when Oxford batted he bowled from one end throughout their innings and kept wicket at the other end. Sir Spencer Ponsonby-Fane remembered Jenner's play, writing that he was 'an excellent wicket-keeper, although he stood five or six feet behind the wicket and walked forward to meet the ball. There were no such things as pads and finger guards in those days.' He then added two lines of doggerel:

> They didn't mind a few stingers
> And they didn't wear India-rubber fingers.

There have been better lyricists than Sir Spencer on MCC committees.

Jenner was elected to MCC on 12 May 1828, at the Anniversary Dinner presided over by Algernon Greville, just four days after having been nominated by two ex-Presidents, Benjamin Aislabie and Henry Kingscote. He became President just five years later, but did not continue his membership of MCC for many years after his Presidency. There was no record of his falling out with the Club, just a lapse in his dues. He lived in Gloucestershire, and perhaps was satisfied watching the Grace family play cricket locally rather than making the journey to St John's Wood to see lesser cricketers disport themselves. He gave up playing in big matches in 1836 when his work as a barrister took precedence, but continued to play minor matches in Kent where he lived until 1864 when he moved to Gloucestershire, the year of W.G. Grace's debut on the major cricketing stage and the year of the first publication of *Wisden*. In Gloucestershire, he carried on playing for his village, Hill, until he was in his seventies. In 1880, at the age of 74, he played his final game when he captained Hill in a match against the neighbouring village of Rockhampton. As in his university days 53 years earlier, he bowled unchanged at one end and kept wicket at the other. He was only dismissed, after scoring 11, because the only allowance he would make to his advancing years was to use a runner while batting, and the unfortunate fellow ran himself (and Jenner) out. All the same, his side won. As *Wisden* remarks in an 1898 article entitled 'The Oldest Living Cricketer', 'in this final match he used a bat made in 1829 and given to him in 1831 by Benjamin Aislabie.'

When he moved from Kent in 1864 he also added to his surname, becoming Jenner-Fust. When he died in 1904, aged 98 years five months and seven days, he was the oldest first-class cricketer; it was a record not surpassed until F. A. MacKinnon reached that age late in 1946. He remains the longest lived MCC President to date, and, along with the Earl of Coventry (1859), is one of two Presidents to live for 70 years beyond their Presidential year. Clearly, being President is good for your health. Few men have failed to reach their allotted three score years and ten, although one of the shorter-lived Presidents was to be Jenner's successor.

Herbert Jenner was the last commoner but one to hold the office of President until 1870. For the next three dozen years, it seemed that if you did not have a title you were not considered for the office of President. The first of these men was the (slightly titled) **HONOURABLE**

ANTHONY HENRY ASHLEY, younger son of the Seventh Earl of Shaftesbury, and known as Henry rather than Anthony to his intimates. Henry was born on 5 May 1807, so was 27 years and ten days old when he was elected President at the Anniversary Dinner at Grillions Hotel, which had been chosen as the venue because the Hon. Sec., Mr Aislabie, had been late in making his booking at Ellis' Hotel in St James's Street and had to make do with second best. This had happened despite a resolution of the Committee on 30 July 1833 'that the next Anniversary Dinner shall be at Ellis' Hotel.'

Henry Ashley had been elected as a member five years earlier and played a handful of matches for MCC in those first five years of his membership. However, he was never a very good cricketer: a bit of a batsman and a bit of a bowler. Like many of those who came before and after him, he was an Old Harrovian, and because of, or perhaps despite, his good connections his Presidential year was remarkably uneventful. Perhaps the only fact of interest is that he missed the 1835 Anniversary Dinner, when he should have handed over to Lord Charles Russell, through illness, which was a forerunner of things to come. Like his descendant, the cricket historian F. S. Ashley-Cooper, he was never a well man, and died aged 51 on 2 December 1858. He took the extra surname Cooper, to become Ashley-Cooper, after his year of office, and in doing so became one of three Presidents to add a second barrel to their names, the others being Herbert Jenner-Fust and Sir Frederick Hervey-Bathurst, Bt., (1857), who was just plain Frederick Hervey when he was proposed for membership in May 1830. By coincidence, Hervey's proposer and seconder were the Hon. A. H. Ashley and Mr H. Jenner.

Ashley's elder brother, Lord Ashley, who would inherit the title of Earl of Shaftesbury, was a political reformer who played a leading role in the reform of factories and public health in the second quarter of the nineteenth century. Although his father was opposed to Catholic emancipation and parliamentary reform, Lord Ashley tried, through his 'Ten Hours Bill', to limit child working hours, and later became instrumental in significantly reducing outbreaks of cholera through his leadership of the Board of Health in the 1840s and 1850s. In this, his closest ally was Lord John Russell, whose younger brother, Lord Charles Russell, took over as MCC President from Henry Ashley.

Lord Charles obviously thought very little of his Anniversary Dinner. After all that trouble to organise it at Ellis' Hotel, a Committee minute of 3 August 1835 resolved 'that in future the Anniversary Dinner shall take place at the Pavilion, the sum of £15 being allowed out of the Stock Purse, and each member paying twenty-five shillings for dinner, desert (sic), wine, tea and coffee.' In 1836, that is what happened, but only nineteen members turned up.

LORD CHARLES RUSSELL, aged 28 in his year of office, was a member of the family of the Duke of Bedford, and was born at the family seat of Woburn in Bedfordshire. His full name, Charles James Fox Russell, also showed his blood relationship to Charles James Fox, the Foreign Secretary to Lord Grenville in the short-lived 'Ministry of All Talents' of 1806. The Dukes of Bedford were also related by marriage to the Dukes of Richmond among many other noble families, and Lord Charles' half-brother was Lord John Russell, afterwards Earl Russell (1792–1878), grandfather of the mathematician, philosopher and peace activist Bertrand Russell. Lord John was a very distinguished Liberal politician, one of the drafters of the Reform Act of 1832, and towards the end of his life Prime Minister for nine months after the death of Palmerston. So Lord Charles Russell's connections through all layers of privileged society of the time were exceptional. By this time, as MCC approached its 50th birthday, the Club was becoming a true stalwart of Victorian society. As much as the Church of England was described as 'the Tory Party at prayer', one could almost describe MCC as English society – if not only the Tory Party – at play.

The main achievement of Lord Charles Russell's tenure was the revision of the Laws by a committee of no fewer than sixteen men. These included eight past Presidents and one future one, plus one more man, Col. The Hon. Lowther, who may well have held office in the early years. Their most significant revision was of Law 10, which now read: 'The ball must be bowled. If it be thrown or jerked or if the hand be above the shoulder in the delivery, the umpire must call "No Ball".' In a matter of a few years, the revolution started by John Willes and his sister Christina and her crinolines had caused bowling to progress from underhand to 'not above the elbow' to 'not above the shoulder'. True overarm bowling was on its way. There was also, incidentally, still a law covering betting on cricket: gambling was not perceived as a threat to cricket until later in the century.

Lord Charles' committee also passed one other rather modern sounding resolution on 3 August 1835, 'that in future, no person (whether Member or not) be allowed to smoke within the pales that surround the Pavilion.'

Lord Charles' successor was **EDWARD HARBORD, THE FOURTH BARON SUFFIELD**. He was a very young man at the time of his appointment, a month short of his 23rd birthday. Remarkably, he was not a cricketer of any sort, without a single appearance for MCC in any of their big matches, and yet as a man still young enough to qualify these days to be elected Young Cricketer of the Year by the Cricket Writers' Club he was elected by his fellow members to their top office. Perhaps because there were only nineteen members present at his Anniversary Dinner, several of whom had held the post already, he was elected *faut de mieux*. Yet, overall, Lord's was becoming more and more a centre where young society congregated, so much so that at this dinner a resolution was passed that a gatekeeper be appointed, to enforce the rule that 'no non-subscriber shall be admitted within the pales which surround the pavilion unless he be introduced and accompanied by a Member of the Club.' This was the origin of the famous Lord's gatekeepers, a breed that over time would acquire a legendary reputation for allowing no one past them, even if their name was bloody Sunil Gavaskar.

Harbord's Committee also approved the employment of an extra professional bowler to satisfy the needs of the members for practice. There were now to be five professionals on the staff, as well as five boys as 'scouts', to chase the balls and bring them back in the perhaps unlikely event that one of the members could hit one of the professional bowlers that far. The dominance of the professionals over the amateurs at this time was further reinforced by the Lord's Gentlemen v. Players match of 1836, which pitted eleven Players against eighteen Gentlemen, even greater odds than in the 1828 match.

Lord Harbord's focus during his Presidential year was clearly on things to come. On 25 July 1836, the following notice went up in the Pavilion and around the ground:

> Celebration of the 50th Year of The MCC
>
> The Marylebone Club having been established in the year 1787, it is resolved that a Jubilee Match shall take place at Lord's Ground on the second Monday in July 1837 for the benefit of the Players ... Every member of the Club is solicited for a subscription of One Pound towards the promotion of the sport on this interesting occasion.
>
> Lord's Ground, Monday 25 July 1836
>
> Benj. Aislabie, Secretary, MCC

That this notice describes cricket as a sport, rather than a game or a pastime, shows the importance MCC attributed to itself. To true countrymen the only sports are hunting, shooting and fishing. In their eyes, anything that does not result in the death of a hapless creature cannot be described as a sport. Cricket, with its royal patronage and its relentless march towards the very heart of society, was justifiably the first ball game to be routinely described as a sport, a title that golf and then the various codes of football would eventually earn half a century later.

Events were to overtake the Committee's plans. On 20 June 1837 Britain would wake up to the dawn of the Victorian age with an eighteen-year-old girl on the throne, as her uncle King William IV had died overnight. The national mourning and political turmoil that followed, including a general Election in July 1837, played havoc with the Marylebone Club's celebrations, but they still managed to fit in some of the festivities planned during Harbord's Presidency.

H arbord was only forty years old when he died on 22 August 1853 and his half-brother, who was also to become MCC President, in 1863, inherited the title. Harbord's successor as President took the position into his family to an even greater degree. JAMES, VISCOUNT GRIMSTON, was the eldest son of the Earl of Verulam, and was 28 years old when he made it to the top of the Club. He was elected to MCC on 25 May 1830, after being proposed just the day before, by John Barnard and Benjamin Aislabie. As far as we can see, this equals the record for the quickest election of all time, on a par with that of the 1846 President, Lord Winterton and a few others. The young Grimston wasted no time in becoming involved in Club affairs. Four days after his election he seconded the application of the Earl of Ossory, who had to wait the unconscionably long time of nine days before being confirmed as a member.

Grimston was educated, like so many other Presidents, at Harrow, but unlike his three brothers, Edward, Frederick and Robert, he did not play in the University match. Edward played for Oxford in 1836 in a match his side won by 121 runs, thanks in the main to the 87 extras that Cambridge conceded (45 byes, 33 wides and 9 no balls). Wicketkeeping was not as advanced in those days as it is now.

The connections within the social stratum that ruled MCC at that time come into focus with Grimston's Presidency. Not only was Grimston President twice (again in 1867 when he had inherited the title of Earl of Verulam), but his father (in 1840 – the only example of a father following his son to the Presidency), his younger brother Robert (1883), and his brother-in-law the Earl of Craven, (1841) all became Presidents. The only brothers to have both been President are the Grimstons, the Harbords, the Hamiltons (James, Marquess of Hamilton in 1874 and

George in 1881) and the Lytteltons (C.G. in 1886 and Alfred in 1898).
Both the Hamiltons and the Lytteltons dominated the Presidency over
the generations even more than the Grimstons and the Harbords, but
making the Presidency a family affair began in 1836. Incidentally,
the mother of the Hamilton brothers was born Lady Louisa Russell, a
relative of Charles and also of the Duke of Richmond.

Grimston is one of only three men to have held the Presidency twice,
along with the Eighth Duke of Beaufort (1853 as the Marquess of
Worcester and 1877), and HRH Prince Philip, Duke of Edinburgh
(1949 and 1974). Prince Philip is the only member of the Royal Family
to have been President, but the regal connections do not stop there. At
Queen Victoria's coronation on 28 June 1838, among her train bearers
and ladies in waiting were Lady Caroline Gordon-Lennox, sister of the
Earl of March (1842), Lady Mary Grimston, Viscount Grimston's sister
and Lady Adelaide Paget, later to marry into the Cadogan family, whose
scion, Viscount Chelsea MP, would be President in 1873. Among the
Ladies of the Bedchamber on that august day was Baroness Lyttelton,
daughter of the Second Earl Spencer, aunt of the 1861 President and
grandmother to the 1886 and 1898 Presidents. Sarah Cavendish, mother
of the 1908 President, was a Maid of Honour. The powerful families of
Britain were taking a firm grip on the Presidency of MCC just as much
as on politics and the church.

The 1838 President was the **SECOND MARQUESS OF EXETER,
BROWNLOW BROWNLOW-CECIL**, who was 43 in his Presidential
year. No great cricketer, he was nevertheless a keen sportsman, and as
well connected as anybody. His wife was Isabella Poyntz, a relation of
the Spencer family, and Burghley House, the family seat, was one of the
great houses of the era, with wonderful sporting facilities and lavish
entertaining. The Marquess' eldest son, Lord Burghley, was a better
cricketer than his father. He played for Cambridge in the Varsity match
of 1847, and made the highest score of the match, 47. A later Lord

Burghley, three or four generations down the line, won the Olympic 400 metres hurdles title in 1928 and was portrayed by Nigel Havers in the film *Chariots Of Fire*.

GEORGE STANHOPE, THE SIXTH EARL OF CHESTERFIELD, was President in 1839. The Stanhopes had also been represented at Queen Victoria's Coronation by Lady Wilhelmina, who was a train bearer. When Lady Wilhelmina grew up she became a much married lady; her first husband was Archibald, the Fourth Lord Dalmeny, and a famous cricketing name. Chesterfield, who had been a member of MCC since 1827, was far more interested in horse racing than in cricket. He became owner of the brilliant horse Priam, which he bought for 3,000 guineas (£3,150) in 1831, the year after it won the Derby, and he enjoyed many more successes with that horse. When he was retired to Bretby Park, Lord Chesterfield's stud, his fee was set initially at the outrageously high figure of 30 sovereigns, and this was raised to 40 sovereigns very quickly. In the mid-1830s he was the leading horse at stud, but Lord Chesterfield suffered from the same failing as many of the sporting gentry of his age: a serious lack of funds. In 1837 he had to sell Priam to pay off some of his debts, and Priam went to the United States for $15,000 – a huge sum at the time. Two years later, Chesterfield was President of MCC.

There is a racing connection between Chesterfield and the 1844 President, Sir John Bayley. Priam was the son of another great horse called Emilius, which ran in the Derby in 1823. The race was run at the same time that Sir John Bayley's wife was expecting her first child. Sir John, a very keen racing man, had decided that his child, if a boy, was to be given the name of the winner of the Derby. The two favourites were called Lollipop and Emilius. It was the child's good fortune that Emilius won, because, as Arthur Duke Coleridge remarked in his book, *Eton In The Forties*, 'Lollipop out of Sweetmeat would have been a very trying name for an Eton boy.'

There were changes afoot within MCC. At the 1839 dinner, Benjamin Aislabie stood down from the Committee but not from his role as Secretary, so for the first time the Secretary became an ex officio member of the Committee, like the Treasurer, rather than an elected member. This had the effect of increasing the size of the Committee by one, which was just as well as Lord Chesterfield himself barely ever attended Committee meetings, leaving his friend Lord William Beresford to act as chairman in his absence. He also failed to turn up to his final Dinner without good reason, in an act of disregard for the Club that had been previously matched only by Lord Frederick Beauclerk.

Chesterfield would have handed over, had he been there, to another Grimston. This time it was **JAMES, FIRST EARL VERULAM**, the father of the 1837 incumbent. Verulam was another whose interest in cricket was more through his sons' interest than his own, but he took on the job happily enough. He had been Member of Parliament for St Albans before being created Earl Verulam in 1815, and it was his political skills rather than his cricketing ones that MCC were looking for. There were several signs of discontent in the ranks at the way the Club was being run, and with the death of Felix Ladbroke, the Treasurer, in early May 1840, it was left to the Annual General Meeting immediately before the dinner to sort things out. They took the soft option, and Henry Kingscote, a tried and trusted worker in the MCC cause, was appointed Treasurer. The Committee had now swelled to thirteen people, an unwieldy size for a Club of fewer than four hundred members, especially when the autocratic and cantankerous Lord Frederick Beauclerk was one of its number. Yet it was the question of the role of the President that, prompted by the membership, really exercised the Committee.

In July 1840, William Ward proposed that 'it is desirable to revert to the practice that formerly existed of electing as President a Gentleman likely to preside at Table and take part personally from time to time in the matches that are played during the season.' His view was not endorsed by the Committee, although we can suspect that several members sympathised, and Ward resigned from the Committee and from the list of playing members. This was a major breach that needed swift action.

Action came in October that year, with the resolution that, in a change to Rule 9, 'the President of each year shall nominate his successor at the Anniversary Dinner.' This rule had to be ratified at the next AGM, on 24 May 1841, so it was not put into effect until 1842.

At the 1841 dinner, Lord Verulam's son-in-law, the Earl of Craven, became the last of the Presidents to be elected by the membership. WILLIAM CRAVEN, the Second Earl, had only been a member since June 1838, so his promotion to President within three years was extremely quick – probably a record. Craven was married to Lady Emily Grimston, the sister of James, Edward, Frederick and Robert Grimston. Craven's father had conducted a notorious affair with the courtesan Harriette Wilson, but the son was of a more sober cut. He was only 31 years old when elected, so could have satisfied William Ward's requirements that the President take part personally from time to time in the matches. But he didn't.

One might be tempted to write that the only really positive thing he did, as the first man to have the Presidency in his personal gift, was to hand it on to the heir to one of the great cricketing titles in MCC history, the Duke of Richmond. However, as a Committee minute of 5 May 1842 notes, 'the Earl of Craven being absent, no President was named, but it was agreed by the members present that a President should be chosen at a future meeting of the Committee.' This was the last minute that Benjamin Aislabie ever wrote.

CHAPTER THREE

1842–1859

THE YOUNG MEN

Fifty-five years after the founding of the Club, MCC was undergoing major organisational changes. The first permanent Treasurer, Ladbroke, and the first permanent Secretary, Aislabie, were dead; William Ward, the greatest batsman of his generation, had severed his connection with the running of the Club, and even the turbulent priest, Lord Frederick Beauclerk, was coming to the end of his reign of terror. In 1842, the Club turned to **CHARLES GORDON-LENNOX, EARL OF MARCH** and heir to the Duchies of Richmond, Lennox, Aubigny and Gordon. His Presidency began in a very low key, simply with a minute dated 27 June 1842, recording a general meeting of the Club which listed 'the Earl of March, President, in the chair'.

As we have seen, Richmond is a powerful name in early cricket history, and the connection continues to this day. The lovely ground at Goodwood Park in Sussex, the seat of the Dukes of Richmond and Gordon, still hosts regular cricket of a good standard every summer, and Goodwood Cricket Club, founded in 1813, is heading strongly towards its own bicentenary. The first mention of cricket and a Duke of Richmond, however, goes back right to the earliest years of cricket's recorded history. In 1727, the Second Duke, great-great-grandfather to the Earl of March, concluded an agreement with a Mr Broderick for two matches in July that year, which comprise the earliest written set of laws

by which cricket was to be played. Among its articles was the fact that
the wickets should be 'pitched in a fair and even place at twenty three
yards distance from each other'. Lord's over a century later could easily
be described as a 'fair and even place', but what happened to the twenty-
third yard?

The Earl of March, born on 27 February 1818 and thus only 24 years
old at his nomination, was about as well connected as any young man
could be. His grandmother, the Duchess who gave the famous Ball
before Quatre Bras, prided herself as being 'the first matchmaker in
England', having married her four daughters to the Dukes of Bedford,
Manchester and Richmond, and to the mere Marquess of Cornwallis,
having failed to snare William Pitt. March's mother, Lady Caroline
Paget, was the daughter of the Marquess of Anglesey (and aunt to the
1855 President, Lord Uxbridge), and his sister married the Earl of
Bessborough, bringing him into a close relationship by marriage with
Sir Spencer Ponsonby-Fane and the Hon. George Ponsonby. In 1843,
just after the end of his Presidential year, he married Harriet, daughter
of Algernon Greville, the secretary to the Duke of Wellington and
MCC President in 1828. Another uncle, Lord William Pitt-Lennox,
who wrote one of the first gossip memoirs, *Celebrities I Have Known*,
devoted many pages to the cricketing heroes of the day: Lord Winchilsea, Lord Frederick Beauclerk, Henry Tufton, General 'Skirmish' Bligh
and many others, all of whom played cricket at Goodwood, most
of whom would have known the 1842 President almost from the day
he was born.

It has to be admitted that March was not the greatest President in
the Club's history. His father, the Fifth Duke, was a land-owning Tory
of the old school, and an arch Conservative in all things political,
despite briefly accepting a position in Earl Grey's Whig government,
along with Lord John Russell among others. The Duke's interest was
in matters agricultural, notably the Corn Laws, the repeal of which he
opposed bitterly. In 1843 he established the Central Agricultural Protection Society, nicknamed the Anti-League in opposition to the
Anti-Corn Law League. The letters between the Duke and the Earl of

March at this time are entirely taken up with political issues; March was already a Conservative MP, and a close political ally of his father in the House of Lords. In all their correspondence in 1842 and 1843 there is not one mention of cricket.

March had been educated at Westminster (the Alma Mater of Powlett, Dehany and Louch of Hambledon and the first years of MCC) and Christ Church, Oxford, where he played a little cricket without proving himself to be particularly skilful. He graduated in 1839, was given a huge Coming of Age Ball by his mother and proceeded into the Army, where, like his father before him, he was briefly ADC to the Duke of Wellington, which is no doubt where he met his future wife. As a further connection with the list of MCC Presidents, one of the trustees of his marriage settlement was the Second Earl Cawdor, father of the 1908 President. March was a very conservative Tory MP for West Sussex from 1841 to 1860, when he inherited his father's title and, for the first time, the title of Duke of Gordon as well. His cricket interest did not really outlast his time at Lord's, and if he had any sporting interests thereafter they focused on racing. He had been elected to the Jockey Club in 1838, three years after he joined MCC. However, it was agricultural matters that consumed the rest of his life. He remained a leading politician, holding several important posts in Conservative governments from 1867, when he became President of the Board of Trade, to 1886, when he stepped down as Secretary for Scotland. In between he was, among other things, leader of the Conservative Party in the House of Lords. He was also President of the Smithfield Club and very proud of his achievements in improving the herd of shorthorn cattle at Gordon Castle and the flock of Southdown sheep at Goodwood. His Scottish connections led him to be Chancellor of Aberdeen University, Lord Lieutenant of Banffshire and President of the Royal Highland and Agricultural Society of Scotland. All in all, a very different life from that led by his grandfather.

One cricketing connection remained as a link to those days. When the Fourth Duke had challenged the Duke of York to the famous duel, his second had been his close friend the Earl of Winchilsea. When his grandson, George the Eleventh Earl, went bankrupt in 1865 March was appointed a trustee of his affairs. More tragically, Winchilsea's eldest son, Viscount Maidstone, was also declared bankrupt at the age of 25 in 1877. He died two years later.

M arch's choice as the next President was not someone with whom he appeared to have a close connection – a rarity within MCC in those days. HENRY GEORGE FRANCIS REYNOLDS MORETON, SECOND EARL OF DUCIE, was born on 8 May 1802, and thus was four days short of his 41st birthday when he accepted the Presidency at the Anniversary Dinner, this year held at the Clarendon Hotel. Club rules had been changed early in the year so that now the dinner would be held on the first Wednesday of May, 'when the season will commence'. This became a rule that was more honoured in the breach, as the dinner thereafter continued to be held on the first Thursday in May, as ever. Subscriptions were also raised to £3 per year, with a £1 entry fee, and at the same time two independent auditors were appointed. The first two holders of this post were Hon. Edward Grimston and Sir John Bayley.

Ducie was not a cricketer, thus hammering another nail into the coffin of William Ward's desire that Presidents would be playing members, and during his time one of the most obvious royal non-cricketers, His Royal Highness Prince Albert, was made Patron of the Club, in succession to another Royal Highness, the Queen's uncle Augustus Frederick, Duke of Sussex, who died aged 70 within a year of being made Patron. Royal patronage and social connections seemed to be taking precedence over cricket at this time. It is perhaps not surprising that, as the quality of play at Lord's was dipping, a group of cricketers came from another source to raise the standards. William Clarke and his All-England XI, based in Nottingham, were already looming on the horizon.

Ducie was another keen agriculturalist, which must have been his connection with March. While March was writing to his father asking for £630 to plant trees at Goodwood, Ducie was constructing his great arboretum at the family home at Tortworth Court in Gloucestershire. By the time he died, in 1853, over 18,000 trees had been planted.

After just one year as Hon. Auditor, SIR JOHN EDWARD GEORGE BAYLEY, BT. stepped up into the Presidency. Bayley was an unusual character. He had been born in 1793, so was already 50 when he took on the Presidency. We have already noted his unique way of naming his son (who took his eventual revenge by changing his surname by deed poll to Laurie), and a glimpse at the minute book for his Presidential year shows that he was determined to tighten up what in his view had become a rather slack place. As an example, the rule that had been passed nine years earlier about smoking in the Pavilion had clearly not been kept. On 17 June he called a General meeting of the Club, to consider, among other things 'that no smoking be allowed either within, or on the benches surrounding, the Pavilion.' The membership, however, would not agree and the resolution that was passed stated simply that 'no smoking is permitted in the Rooms of the Pavilion or under the verandah.' The benches were saved for smokers, and one assumes the corridors and hallways of the Pavilion were also havens of tobacco smoke.

Overall, Bayley's Presidency was a success. Although only fifteen members attended the Anniversary Dinner at which Bayley handed over to Thomas Chamberlayne, one of then, the long serving Hon. Col. Lowther, rose to tell the gathering that Sir John 'had filled the office of President during the last season with such advantage to the Club'. Membership was up during the year from 417 to 465, 'a fact which cannot but be highly satisfactory to those who look up to the gentlemen of the MCC as the great promoters of cricket', and the accounts showed a modest profit, in contrast to the more perilous position of the late 1830s.

Sir John still had more work to do for the Club. In 1847, he and another of his sons, Lyttelton Bayley (then aged only 20) proposed at the Annual General Meeting that

> in order to encourage good conduct on the part of professional players both of the ground or who may have been engaged in matches with the Marylebone Cricket Club, a fund be raised, to be called 'The Cricketers' Fund' (in lieu of the present reward fund which shall be abolished) for the purpose of giving donations in the case of sickness or accident, the fund to be under the sole control of the Committee of the MCC, and that the sum of £10 only be annually taken from the funds of the Club in the hope that Members will be indused [sic] to add their contributions.

The resolution was carried, and the Cricketers' Fund was set up.

This marked a small nod in the direction of the wider world of cricket by the members. Until now, the emphasis had been on the social cachet of the Club, gentlemen batsmen disporting themselves at the expense of professional bowlers, and with constant references to 'the season' rather than 'the year' of Presidential office, and with the view that people 'look up to the gentlemen of the MCC as the great promoters of cricket': God's in His heaven, I'm in my Pavilion and all's right with the world. Sir John and his son for the first time made members realise they had a social responsibility, even if by today's standards the resolution may appear very patronising with its reference to encouraging good conduct on the part of the professionals. Sir John Bayley was all in all a good man.

THOMAS CHAMBERLAYNE, who was his chosen successor, was the only untitled man to hold the office between Herbert Jenner in 1833 and J. H. Scourfield MP in 1870. These were still the high years of social privilege at Lord's however much Sir John Bayley may have hoped to turn the tide. Chamberlayne, who was forty years old in his year of office, was a Hampshire man, to such an extent that when MCC played Hampshire on 7, 8 and 9 July 1845, Chamberlayne opened the batting against the Club of which he was President. His opening partner was Sir Frederick Hervey-Bathurst, who would assume MCC's Presidency in 1857. Their apostasy reaped its due reward when MCC won the match. Chamberlayne was also very heavily involved in the formation of the Hampshire County Club, having presided over the meeting at which it was formed in 1863.

Sir John Bayley was in no doubt of Chamberlayne's qualities. When Bayley had ceased being auditor on becoming President, Chamberlayne had stepped in, and when introducing him to members at the Anniversary Dinner, Bayley noted that Chamberlayne, 'by his very munificent subscriptions … and his support of the noble game, both at Lord's and in Hampshire, has established so decided a claim to fill the distinguished office of President of the club.' Chamberlayne in his reply was more modest. As the local newspaper reports noted at the time, 'he alluded to the fact of his living in the country might prevent his attending at Lord's as often as he could wish.' Chamberlayne was right. He did not get to Lord's as often as a President should, but at least he played there once or twice, without much success.

He nominated the Fourth Earl of Winterton to take his place. EDWARD TURNOUR WINTERTON was born on 18 May 1810, one of a remarkable number of Presidents born in May, and was two weeks short of his 36th birthday when he took over from Chamberlayne. He had been proposed as a member on 19 May 1834, by William Ward and Benjamin Aislabie, and elected the following day. If Chamberlayne was not much of a cricketer (career batting average 2.65), Winterton hardly represented a major improvement (career batting average 2.68). He had played for MCC against Hampshire the previous summer, and, despite making just 1 and 4, at least finished on the winning side. His main cricketing feat, though, is to have played in a match when one team was dismissed for 0. On 13 August 1855, his home estate team, Shillinglee Park in Petworth, Sussex, played the Second Royal Surrey Militia, who suffered the ultimate indignity of nought all out. Winterton then had the task of opening the batting for Shillinglee Park. His team gained a first-innings lead, but failed to complete the victory as the match petered out into a draw.

Winterton, who was more assiduous in his attendance of Committee meetings, handed over to Lord Strathmore, a lad of 24 from Glamis Castle whose devotion to the Club was such that he failed to attend a single Committee meeting throughout his Presidency.

Thomas George Bowes-Lyon, Twelfth Earl of Strathmore and Kinghorne, was educated at Harrow, but did not get into the XI. He did, on the other hand, play half a dozen big matches for MCC, and plenty of minor ones, so perhaps his absence from Committee meetings can be explained by the fact that he was away playing cricket instead. He was described as 'a useful and steady batsman'. He died young, aged 42, on 13 September 1865, and was succeeded in the title by his younger brother. His great-niece was Elizabeth Bowes-Lyon, later to become Queen Elizabeth the Queen Mother, so this royal connection with the Presidency is not a direct one. Prince William and Prince Harry are of the same family as the 1847 President, but they are direct descendants of the 1861 President, and of course of the 1949 and 1974 President.

On 12 July 1847, a minute notes that 'a letter from the President of Victoria Cricket Club' was read to the Committee. Unfortunately, its addressee, the President of MCC, was not there at the time, but the message of goodwill it contained was the first official correspondence between England and Australia on cricketing matters. One of the founders of the Melbourne Cricket Club, and an early power in cricket in Victoria, was Frederick Powlett, great-nephew of Charles Powlett of Hambledon and St John's Wood. Fred had emigrated to Australia a decade or so earlier, but whether he was the signatory of the letter from Victoria is uncertain.

1823, Benjamin Aislabie

1825, Charles J. Barnett

1826, Lord Frederick Beauclerk.
A sketch from life by George
Shepheard in about 1790.

1833, Herbert Jenner

1835, Lord Charles Russell. 'This fell sergeant, strict in his arrest', *Vanity Fair*.

1848, Thomas Coke, Second Earl of Leicester. 'Agriculture', *Vanity Fair* by 'Spy'.

Below right: 1864, William Ward, First Earl of Dudley. 'Property', *Vanity Fair* by 'Ape'.

Below: 1861, John, Fifth Earl Spencer.

1869, Henry Fitzmaurice,
Fifth Marquess of Lansdowne

1877, Henry Somerset, Eighth
Duke of Beaufort. 'The Duke
of Sport', *Vanity Fair* by 'Spy'.

1874, James, Marquess of
Hamilton

1881, Lord George
Hamilton. 'Georgie',
Vanity Fair by 'Spy'.

1883, Hon. Robert Grimston

1886, Charles, Fifth Baron Lyttelton. 'Cricket, Railways and Agriculture', *Vanity Fair* by 'Spy'.

Below right: 1891, V. Edward Walker

Below: 1887, Hon. Edward Chandos Leigh, Centenary President.

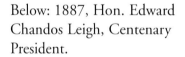

1894, Victor Child-Villiers, Seventh Earl of Jersey, just before the First World War.

1896, Sidney Herbert, Fourteenth Earl of Pembroke

1895, George Canning, Fourth Baron Harris. 'Kent', *Vanity Fair* by 'Spy'.

1893, William Legge, Sixth Earl of Dartmouth, *Vanity Fair* by 'Stuff'.

1897, Thomas Anson, Third Earl of Lichfield

1898, Hon. Alfred
Lyttelton. 'Devil' to
the Attorney-General.

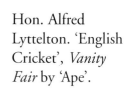

Hon. Alfred
Lyttelton. 'English
Cricket', *Vanity
Fair* by 'Ape'.

1901, Richard Curzon-Howe, Fourth Lord Howe. 'South Bucks', *Vanity Fair* by 'Spy'.

1900, Hon. Ivo Bligh. 'Ivo', *Vanity Fair* by 'Spy'.

1903, Richard Webster, Viscount Alverstone. *Vanity Fair* by Verheyden.

1904, Henry Manners, Marquess of Granby

1905,
Charles E.
Green

Below:1907,
Robert
Threshie Reid,
First Baron
Loreburn. 'Mr.
Attorney',
Vanity Fair by
'Spy'.

1906, Walter Hume
Long. 'Wiltshire'. *Vanity
Fair* by 'Spy'.

Strathmore handed on the Presidential baton to **Thomas Coke, Second Earl of Leicester**. Lord Leicester was only 25 years old when he took office, and had only been elected the previous year. His father was already almost seventy years old when Thomas was born, and he inherited the title very young. He had a half-sister who was married 28 years before Thomas was born, and he himself lived to the age of 87. His youngest son was born in 1893, 45 years after the Earl had been President of MCC and 45 years after his eldest son had been born. They were fecund old codgers, the Leicesters. By marriage, he was connected to many other cricketing families: his brother-in-law, much later in life, was C. G. Lyttelton, Fifth Baron Lyttelton, the 1886 President. The Sixth Earl of Dartmouth, the 1893 President, married his daughter Mary, and another daughter Margaret married Henry Strutt, Lord Belper, the 1882 President.

The Earl of Leicester was a keen if not particularly capable cricketer, who played for Norfolk (the family seat was not, of course, in Leicester but in Holkham, Norfolk) and I Zingari. He was also, like March and Ducie before him, a great agriculturalist whose interest lay in the land rather than in industry. By the time of his death he was Father of the House of Lords. Looking at his progeny and his skill at intermarrying his children, this title could almost be taken literally.

In 1848, the year of revolutions in Europe, Sir John Bayley proposed and the Hon. Robert Grimston seconded the motion that 'the office of Treasurer be abolished and the duties thereof be henceforth performed by the Secretary, and that the Committee in future consist of thirteen members'. This motion was carried, which allowed Henry Kingscote, the Treasurer, to step down after two decades of loyal service to the Club. It seems that Kingscote was quite happy with this arrangement and voted for the change, which concentrated the executive power of the Club in the hands of the Secretary, Roger Kynaston. The new system seemed to work, and was not altered for some time.

Thomas Leicester's next man in was **JOHN STUART BLIGH, SIXTH EARL OF DARNLEY**. Here is a cricket name to conjure with. Not only was this Lord Darnley the great-nephew of General 'Skirmish' Bligh, one of the early members of MCC, but he was also father of the Hon. Ivo Bligh, the man for whom the Ashes were created. Darnley was only just 22 years old when he became President, the youngest recorded to this time, and although he himself was no record breaker at the wicket, he was described in his obituary notice in *Wisden* as 'a great lover of cricket'. The Darnleys are yet another Kent family who played a major role in MCC's history. Their family seat is at Cobham Hall, although this Lord Darnley was born in Marylebone, like Presidents Henry Lloyd and Henry Lane before him. At Maidstone ten years later, he was the man who presided over the meeting at which the Kent County Cricket Club was formed, and he served as their President four times, in 1859, 1869, 1872 and 1882.

During the year, which was still known as the President's 'season' with all the fashionable connotations that carries, Darnley's Committee resolved on 2 July 'that as the Goodwood Races commence on 31st inst., the Gentlemen v. Players match shall take place on the 23rd instead of the 30 July'. Racing still upstaged cricket in the eyes of fashionable Victorian society. Incidentally, Darnley was not there when the resolution was passed – he arrived late to the meeting.

By this stage in the development of MCC, the qualifications for the Presidency were becoming clearer. Clearly to be, in the words of *Wisden* half a century later, 'a great lover of cricket' was important, but the connection between some Presidents and the sport seems no more than tenuous at best. Much more vital were the connections, both social and political, for a Club that was striving to achieve a position at the heart of society. They had a royal patron, Prince Albert, and a list of gentleman members that was now some five hundred strong. From among that membership each year it was important that a suitably well connected personage could take on the role of their figurehead, and make other clubs realise that MCC was the central authority of cricket, with all the right connections and therefore all the power on their side, whatever may be going on elsewhere in the country. It would be at least another 25 years before any regional cricket interests were to be represented in the person of the President.

In 1850, the man nominated to be President was **HENEAGE FINCH**, **LORD GUERNSEY**, the 25-year-old heir to the Fifth Earl of Aylesford. Guernsey made a refreshing change from several earlier Presidents in that he was both young and an active cricketer, playing many games for MCC between 1847 and 1855. In 1849 he persuaded George Parr and John Wisden to establish what they all hoped would be a 'provincial Lord's ground' at Leamington Spa. The Parr and Wisden Ground hosted many games over the next decade, although Lord's was the venue for the North against the South match in Guernsey's Presidential year, when John Wisden (playing for the North as he was by then resident in Leamington Spa, which was 'north' as far as London's cricket folk were concerned) took all ten wickets in an innings. All his victims were clean bowled, and this remains the only time this feat has been achieved in a first-class match. Guernsey also played for the North in that match, without having to contribute very much. John Wisden's sports equipment company also dates from about 1850, and it is quite probable that it flourished on the basis of regular orders from Lord Guernsey and his noble friends.

He had all the connections – Lord Winchilsea's family were also Finches, and his sister Augusta married the Earl of Dartmouth, so the 1893 President was his nephew. He himself was MP for South Warwickshire from 1849 to 1857 – his seat, Packington Hall, was near Coventry. Unlike the Leicesters, the Aylesfords were not a long-lived family, but Lord Guernsey, who became the Sixth Earl of Aylesford in 1859, had time before he died aged 46 to breed a remarkable son, Joseph, who in turn became Earl of Aylesford, if only briefly. Joseph was born in 1849 and married Edith Williams, the daughter of an MP, in 1871, just after the death of his father. The new Lord Aylesford pushed his way to the very centre of the social scene, entertaining the Prince of Wales and many of his circle at sumptuous parties at his home, and becoming one of the Prince's most boisterous intimates. Prince Edward even invited Aylesford to accompany him on an official tour of India at the end of 1875, giving him the responsibility of organising the sporting events and wild game hunts. However, Aylesford's tour was cut short early in 1876 when he had to return home to confront his wife, who had taken a lover. A divorce suit followed, and though Aylesford himself was not the guilty party, he was effectively banished from the court henceforth.

With no wife and no opportunities left to him in England, Joseph Aylesford left for the United States, and by 1883 had bought himself a 2,500 acre cattle ranch in west Texas, near the cattle town of Big Spring. As possibly the wealthiest man in the town, he was able also to buy up the hotel and the bar, and to build a meat market. His fortunes soared. It was not to last long, though. In 1885, just two years after turning up in Big Spring, he held a New Year party that went on for two weeks, at the end of which Aylesford died. His hard lifestyle had finally caught up with him. He remains, as far as is known, the only son of an MCC President to die of alcoholic poisoning in west Texas.

In 1851, Lord Guernsey handed over to **George Grey, the Seventh Earl of Stamford and Warrington**. Grey was another young President, only 24 when he took office; it is noticeable that the average age of Presidents in the 1850s was as low as it had ever been or ever would be. In the 1820s, Presidents on taking office had been on average about 34 years old; in the 1830s, they were just a little less than 32 years old; in the 1840s, the average age went up to almost 36, but in the 1850s, the average was only a month or two above 30. If it had not been for the nominations of Viscount Milton and Sir Frederick Hervey-Bathurst, both in their forties, the average age of Presidents in the 1850s would have been well below 30. In the 1860s, the average soared to 39 years

4 months, and since that decade the average has always been above 40, and usually above 50. William Ward's legacy finally died as Victorian self-esteem reached its zenith.

The Earl of Stamford died childless in 1883, despite being 'twice married to women of low social rank'. His successor as Eighth Earl was a second cousin once removed, a missionary called Rev. Harry Grey. Harry Grey had taken his missionary zeal to South Africa and had set up home, without the benefit of holy matrimony, with 'a Hottentot woman' named Martha Solomon, the daughter of an innkeeper in Wynberg, Cape Province. They had several children, but their only son was illegitimate, so when he died in 1890, the rival claims of Harry Grey's illegitimate son and the son of Harry Grey's younger brother William (who had died in 1872) were brought to court. The infamous and thrillingly scandalous Stamford Peerage Case of 1892 resulted in judgment in favour of William Grey's son, also confusingly called William, who thus became the Ninth Earl of Stamford and Warrington. Two consecutive Presidents of MCC proved to have black sheep in their family. If these facts could have been forecast in 1850 and 1851, as English society tried to rid itself of its past and the 'undisguised debauchery' of half a century earlier, perhaps neither man would have been allowed to become President.

After the ineffectual Earl of Stamford, in 1852 the Presidency passed to GEORGE HAY-DRUMMOND, VISCOUNT DUPPLIN, the 24-year-old heir to the earldom of Kinnoull. He did fit the bill as a playing President – by the narrowest of margins. He played one match in 1852, making a duck in both innings and neither bowling nor taking a catch in the field. He failed to attend either the Anniversary Dinner at which he was nominated, or the dinner a year later when he handed on the office. His attendance at Committee meetings was sparse, and all in all one wonders how he got the job. Of course, the power of blood and marriage ties was still a major factor, which also explains how comparatively new members (Dupplin had only been a member for half a dozen years) could fit in so quickly and so well as to be known by enough members – as well as the outgoing President – to be likely candidates. MCC was an extension of the house parties, wedding breakfasts and shooting parties that they all attended during the relevant season, so MCC men knew each other almost from birth, not just from the moment their membership application was accepted. This is no longer the case, but it would not be until almost the turn of the century that other factors than breeding would play an equally important part in the selection process. Dupplin was a man bred for the role, but without any other obvious qualification.

Dupplin's Committee was where MCC's authority lay. It was packed with the most committed and long-serving members, including eight past and future Presidents. Men like Lord Charles Russell, Sir John Bayley, the Earl of Verulam and his brother Robert Grimston, Sir Frederick Hervey-Bathurst, Col. Lowther and the Hon. Frederick Ponsonby were the real pillars of the Club. One of their decisions in 1852 was to suspend the Galloway pony races that used to take place around the ground after the end of each cricket season. This had been a pleasant way to amuse the members out of season, especially when so many were interested in horse racing, but the damage to the outfield was such that the Committee decided they had to end. Human athletic competitions continued at Lord's for another twenty years, but even they came to a close in 1872, because 'they did so much damage to the seats,' in the words of William Slatter.

The Committee also contained for the first time in 1852 the name of William Nicholson, who had been elected seven years earlier and now was one of only three commoners on the Committee. He was the only one of those three to make it to the Presidency, and it took him 27 years of service and the saving of the Club itself for him to be considered acceptable.

In 1848, Lord Dupplin had married Lady Emily Somerset, daughter of the Seventh Duke of Beaufort, so it was an easy decision for him to nominate as his successor the Duke's eldest son, his brother-in-law

Henry, then Tenth Marquess of Worcester. At the Anniversary Dinner on 5 May 1853 at which Worcester was nominated, neither he nor the outgoing President was present, and indeed only twelve members in total attended. The cricket may still have been a central part of Lord's, but the catering was hardly a moneymaking venture.

HENRY CHARLES FITZROY SOMERSET was born in Paris on 1 February 1824, so was 29 years old when his sister's husband handed him the MCC Presidency. He had all the usual connections: his wife Lady Georgiana Curzon was the daughter of Earl Howe and thus great aunt to the 1901 President. His mother-in-law was a Brudenell, of the family of the Marquess of Aylesbury (not to be confused with Aylesford), and the first Marquess had been a leading light in the early days of MCC. Henry Somerset, like the Earl of March and Algernon Greville before him, had worked closely with the Duke of Wellington and he was also a relation of Lord Raglan, a military leader of the Crimean War which broke out early in 1854, towards the end of his term of office.

The Seventh Duke of Beaufort, a great sportsman of his day in the hunting, shooting and fishing sense of the word, had done a great deal to build up the Badminton Hunt, as his son and grandson did after him. The Seventh Duke died on 17 November 1853, so it was during his Presidential year that the Marquess of Worcester became the Eighth Duke of Beaufort. Until then he had been a Tory Member of Parliament for East Gloucestershire for seven years while at the same time serving somewhat inactively as a captain in the Seventh Dragoon Guards. Worcester/Beaufort's sporting interests were very much what you would expect of the landed gentry: apart from the Badminton Hunt, he was a keen carriage driver (echoing the interests of another two-time President, HRH Prince Philip a century later) and a noted shot. He was an instigator of the Badminton Library of sporting books in the 1880s, including the edition on cricket, which has long been considered a classic. However, there is no strong evidence that cricket was close to his heart. His interest in homeopathy, very eccentric in his time, was much stronger.

Henry Beaufort's eccentricities were not only confined to the field of complementary medicine. It is said that, shortly after inheriting the dukedom, he presented documents which he felt proved the legitimate claim of the Beaufort line through John of Gaunt and his third wife Catherine Swynford to the throne of England. This revelation, while possibly true, would have undone four hundred years of English history and also have proven that Queen Victoria should not be on the throne. Somewhat innocently, the Duke presented these documents to Queen Victoria herself. The Queen, being a sensible and clear headed young woman, politely thanked the Duke for his efforts in preparing the documents and bringing them to her, and then promptly threw them on the fire. Thus it is that the Beauforts are not the Royal Family of Britain.

T he Duke of Beaufort was followed into the Presidency on 4 May 1854 by another nobleman born overseas, **Sir George Henry Robert Charles William Vane-Tempest, Earl Vane**, who had been born in Austria on 26 April 1821, and thus was just past his 33rd birthday when he took office. He had begun life as Viscount Seaham, but with the death of the Third Marquess of Londonderry in 1854, his father succeeded to the Marquessate and young George stepped up a rank to become Earl Vane. From 1846, when he married, he was a Member of Parliament for 26 years, and a huge landowner throughout Britain, owning Wynyard Park near Stockton-on-Tees, along with tens of thousands of acres in both Wales and Ireland. Pevsner described Wynyard Park as the 'most splendid nineteenth century mansion in the county', perhaps a comparatively uncompetitive category for plaudits, but all the same an indication of the wealth and power enjoyed by the Londonderry family at the time.

In fact, this was a great age of building mansions, palaces and estates, and architects and builders were busy men. Sir Geoffrey Wyattville, for instance, enjoyed the patronage of the Dukes of Beaufort, Bedford and

Devonshire as well as the Earls of Bridgewater, Cawdor and Chester-field: all MCC men. Londonderry House in London was designed by Benjamin Wyatt, as was Crockford's and much of the Duke of Wellington's London home, Apsley House. It is quite likely that the conversation in and around the Pavilion at Lord's at this time was as much about building a castle as it was about building an innings.

Vane's life was built around politics and estate management much more than it was around cricket. He was no cricketer, but his political credentials were formidable. His half-great-uncle was the Second Marquess, better known as Viscount Castlereagh, who was Foreign Secretary from 1812 to 1822, succeeding to the Londonderry title only the year before he died. Castlereagh's diplomacy is the probable reason that young Vane's mother and father were in Austria when he was born, but when the Foreign Secretary committed suicide in 1822, the Third Marquess, Castlereagh's younger half-brother, failed to keep up the family interest in politics, preferring less thought-provoking pastimes.

Lord Vane himself married Mary Edwards, the daughter of a Welsh MP, and they established their main home at Machynlleth, where Vane, who inherited the title Marquess of Londonderry from 1872, set himself great tasks. It was through his efforts that the railway came to Machynlleth, and he also built a hospital, some almshouses and a school. In 1874, he built a 78-foot high clock tower in the town, the Castlereagh Memorial Clock, to commemorate the coming of age of his eldest son Charles. He died in 1884, a good and worthy man, but hardly a cricketer, and certainly no strong influence on the workings of the Club where he had been President thirty years before.

The Anniversary Dinner of 1855, held on 2 May in the Pavilion, was even less successful than the previous year's. Only ten members turned up, and once again both the outgoing and incoming Presidents were absent. Nevertheless, ten members were enough to constitute a quorum for election of new members, and in the absence of their betters, the ten men there elected no fewer than 32 new members, no doubt hoping for a larger attendance at next year's dinner.

The new President was a good friend of Lord Vane and another man with Welsh connections: **HENRY WILLIAM GEORGE PAGET, EARL OF UXBRIDGE** and heir to the Marquess of Anglesey. Lady Caroline Paget, his aunt, married the Fifth Duke of Richmond, making their son Lord March, the 1842 President, his cousin. Uxbridge's sister, Constance, married George, the ill-fated Eleventh Earl of Winchilsea, in 1846, bringing the Ponsonby family within their circle. His nephew, the Sixth Marquess, married Victoria, daughter of the Eighth Duke of Rutland, who in 1904 was to be President himself. The interbreeding goes on.

The most interesting member of the Anglesey family was probably his grandfather, the First Marquess, who was Wellington's second-in-command at Waterloo (the Waterloo link comes into play yet again). A cannonball shot off his left leg during the battle and the tomb of his Left Leg, put up by someone with a strange sense of humour, still can be seen by the battlefield at Waterloo. Before the loss of his leg, Anglesey, along with ancestors of the Duke of Beaufort and the 1862 President the Earl of Sefton, were members of the 'Four Horse Club' or 'Four In Hand Club', a group of aristocrats with more money than social responsibility, who used to race their coaches in Regency times. The Beaufort family maintained their interest in carriage driving down the generations, but the Anglesey and Sefton clans switched to gentler pastimes.

The 1856 Presidency passed to a man in his forties for the first time since Thomas Chamberlayne was President eleven years earlier. **WILLIAM SPENCER WENTWORTH-FITZWILLIAM, VISCOUNT MILTON**, was a Yorkshireman and heir to the Earldom of Fitzwilliam. His Lord's pedigree was impeccable – his grandmother was Lady Charlotte Ponsonby, so he was a cousin of Sir Spencer Ponsonby-Fane and the Earl of Bessborough. His father was a politician, whose campaign to be elected for the county of York in the 1807 election was strongly supported by their family friend George Osbaldeston's mother (who of course did not have a vote). Milton's sister, Lady Anne Wentworth-

Fitzwilliam, was a Lady in Waiting at Queen Victoria's Coronation, along with the females from the Lennox, Lyttelton, Grimston, Paget and Cadogan families. There was also the Irish connection, which was very strong within MCC's higher echelons at this time. Milton's grandfather, the Fourth Earl, was Lord Lieutenant of Ireland from 1828 to 1829, as the Fourth Duke of Richmond had been, and also Milton's kinsman John Ponsonby, Fourth Earl of Bessborough. It was a position that would be taken in later years by the Sixth Marquess of Londonderry, the Fifth Earl Spencer and the Duke of Abercorn, among other key players within the MCC's hierarchy.

Viscount Milton, though no cricketer, played one innings in a top class game, for Sheffield in 1852, scoring 9. This gave him a career aggregate 9 runs higher than Viscount Dupplin, for example. He was elected a member of MCC in June 1836, having been proposed by the Hon. Capt. Spencer, and seconded by Benjamin Aislabie. The previous year his elder brother William had been elected, but died within five months of his election. Milton thus inherited his brother's title and his place at Lord's in quick succession. It was a further twenty years before he became President. A year later he inherited his father's title.

SIR FREDERICK HERVEY-BATHURST, the 1857 President, was just short of his fiftieth birthday, a few days younger than Sir John Bayley had been at his Anniversary Dinner in 1844. He was therefore the second oldest President to date, but was certainly the most skilled cricketer to take on the role since Lord Frederick Beauclerk three decades earlier. Sir Frederick, born in the Scilly Isles on 6 June 1807, was elected to MCC in 1830 and from the next season was a stalwart of their sides for thirty years. He was still playing, albeit at a lower level, in his Presidential year, and did not give up until 1861. He also played many games for Hampshire and for the Gentlemen. He was, unlike the vast majority of his amateur contemporaries, a fine bowler, even if his batting was no better than most of his Presidential forbears (career average

5.92 over 92 matches). He bowled round arm, but fast, and took eight wickets in an innings for Hampshire against MCC in 1845, a match in which he had also opened the batting with his good friend and fellow Hampshire and MCC man, Thomas Chamberlayne. He played for the Gentlemen against the Players many times, including in 1837, when, to even up the sides a bit, they did as they had done in the 1832 match and forced the Players to defend a much larger wicket than the Gentlemen. In 1837 the Gentlemen stood in front of a regulation wicket measuring 27 inches by 8 inches while the Players had to defend one twice the size: three feet high by one foot wide. Hervey-Bathurst made the most of the conditions to take five wickets, but the Players still won, by an innings and 10 runs.

The standard of amateur cricket failed to show any real improvement right through the 1840s and 1850s, and there was a real danger that clubs like MCC would degenerate purely into social clubs, where gentlemen of society watched a little cricket, gambled a little on cricket and discussed other matters of fashion and taste in the smoking rooms. There was a small nucleus of members who understood the role that the MCC needed to establish for itself: of being the unifying body of cricket like the Jockey Club was for racing, but what was going on in the north of England and in the Midlands, and the rise of professional cricket to a standard that no amateurs of the age could match, meant that MCC's chances of becoming that authority seemed slim indeed. So it was that on 1 and 2 June 1857 the first match at Lord's between the two main professional XIs, the United and the All-England, was played for the benefit of the Cricketers' Fund. All-England won by five wickets, and, for the first time, the London public were able to see the giants of the day – Wisden, Lillywhite, Lockyer, Parr, Stephenson, Willsher and all – pitted against each other rather than merely against the cream of the amateur game. In many ways, this can be seen as one of the most significant matches ever played at Lord's – for what it led to rather than for what it was in itself.

Hervey-Bathurst, as an active cricketer, a wise old head (in comparison with other Presidents of recent vintage) and an experienced MCC

Committee man, did as good a job as President as any of his predecessors, but the man he handed over to was very young, born five years after Sir Frederick had been elected to the Club.

ALAN STEWART, LORD GARLIES, was the 22-year-old heir to the Earl of Galloway, and a keen cricketer from Kirkcudbrightshire in Scotland. His mother, Harriet, was sister to the Seventh Duke of Beaufort, so the Marquess of Worcester, President in 1853, was his first cousin. His wife, whom he married after his time as President of MCC, was daughter of the Second Marquess of Salisbury, so the Third Marquess, who went on to become Prime Minister at the turn of the twentieth century, was his brother-in-law.

Garlies had been educated at Harrow, a favourite school for the sons of Scottish peers in the early nineteenth century, and was in the school XI in 1853 and 1854. He played in both years against Winchester at Lord's, and in 1853, on his first appearance at the headquarters of the Club he would preside over just five years later, he scored 17 and 23, top scorer for his side in both innings. In the second innings he was asked to open the batting, and he took three hours and forty minutes over his 23, before being ninth out. *Scores And Biographies* (Vol. 4, page 509) describes him as 'a very steady batsman indeed', which seems an understatement after that second innings during which he scored one run every ten minutes. He was also described as 'an active and energetic field, either at long-stop or at a distance from the wicket'. That report today would imply a keen but useless fielder to be kept as far as possible out of harm's way, but we are probably doing Lord Garlies an injustice at a distance of 160 years. He played a few games, occasionally even as a wicketkeeper, for MCC between 1858 and 1864, when he faded away from cricket, in London at least, and returned to his estates in his native Scotland. He became MP for Wigtownshire from 1868 until 1873 when his father died and he became the Tenth Earl of Galloway. A military man in ceremonial terms at least, he was an officer in the Royal Horse

Guards and honorary Colonel of the Royal Scots Fusiliers, as well as, in his less bellicose moments, being Her Majesty's Commissioner to the General Assembly of the Church of Scotland. He died in 1901, aged 65.

Lord Garlies handed over to the youngest President MCC has ever had, as far as records can show. **GEORGE WILLIAM, NINTH EARL OF COVENTRY**, was born on 9 May 1838, beginning his Presidential year on 4 May 1859 at the age of 20 years and 360 days. He was also the first President of MCC to have been born in the reign of Queen Victoria. He had succeeded his father to the earldom at the age of five, and was elected to the Marylebone Club in 1856, when only sixteen years old. He must still have been one of the youngest members when he took on the Presidency, the only man ever to have achieved the Presidency before he reached 21. Had he not been a peer anyway, and therefore ineligible, and had there been anything approaching a universal franchise in 1859, he would not have been old enough to vote. He lived until 13 March 1930, during the later years of the reign of Victoria's grandson George V, all but 70 years beyond the end of his Presidency, and his continuous membership of the Club, just short of 75 years, must surely be a record, at least among the Presidents. He was, almost inevitably, the Father of the House of Lords when he died, having been a peer for the astonishing period of 86 years and ten months.

Lord Coventry was a great lover of the game and an active cricketer. He played several games for Worcestershire, then for one of the lesser county sides, as well as for MCC, and was described as 'a hard hitting slashing cricketer and a slow lob bowler'. His connections with the great families of the time, through cricket, birth and marriage, were as strong as most of his predecessors – he was an active member of Lord Bessborough's I Zingari, a member of the Jockey Club from his early twenties and in 1865, when he married, he became the son-in-law of the Second Earl of Craven (1841) who was in turn son-in-law of the First Earl Verulam (1840). In cricketing terms his legacy was in siring a son,

Hon. C. J. Coventry, who played with Major Warton's touring team to South Africa in 1888/89 and retrospectively became a Test cricketer, when those early matches were accorded Test status some years later.

The question is nevertheless worth asking: why did Lord Garlies pick such a young man to be President? He himself was not much older, of course, and many of the other most active members of the Club were also men barely out of school. Yet perhaps the clue lies in the minutes of that 1859 Annual General Meeting. The second paragraph, after a long one listing over 30 members who attended the AGM and Dinner, simply states, 'The 3/ candidates mentioned in the Book of Elections pages 184, 185, 186, 187, 188, were all elected.' No one was blackballed and there was no discussion. They were all just elected. Job done. The Club was a small one, in need of members, so the number of potential Presidents was also small. Lord Garlies probably had only a handful of people to choose from, and he went for the most blue-blooded, even if he was only twenty years old.

The modern era is creeping nearer. The 1859 President sired a Test cricketer, and just over one hundred miles to the west of Lord's an eleven-year-old boy was playing cricket in his orchard with his mother, his brothers and his dog, and within five years would be starting the process of revolutionising cricket, and with it Lord's and the Marylebone Cricket Club.

CHAPTER FOUR

1860–1883

MID-VICTORIAN RESPECTABILITY

The 1860s began, MCC was well on its way to its centenary, and
Queen Victoria was almost a quarter of a century into her reign.
Britain was prospering as never before, and the ruling classes, of both
society and cricket, seemed confident that all was well in the world. It
wasn't, but it was all well enough for the time being. There was peace
and contentment throughout the land, at least if you had the money to
afford peace and contentment, and cricket was, comparatively speaking, one of the more democratising influences on society in the middle
years of Queen Victoria's reign.

You could not, however, have readily perceived democracy in action
within the walls of the Pavilion at Lord's, and nor could you have
seen it in the workings of MCC. When George Coventry's year finished,
he handed the Presidency on to another young man, only 22 years old
at the time of his Presidency, by the name of **EDWARD BOOTLE-
WILBRAHAM**, then styled the Second Baron Skelmersdale. With the
towns of Bootle and Skelmersdale in his name, it is not surprising to
learn that the new President was a Lancastrian, born on 12 December
1837, another Victorian baby and, incidentally, the last President born

in Victoria's reign for a further nine years. The portrait of Lord Skelmersdale in the National Portrait Gallery is of a tall man with a long dark beard in the mid-Victorian fashion, a well-made jacket and an earnest expression, but that sketch dates from the 1870s when he was well into his political prime. He could be any important man of the era, a typical member of the social elite, with only his trim figure giving us a clue that he might once have been a sportsman. He was, inevitably, well connected. During his Presidential year, on 16 August 1860, he married Lady Alice Villiers, the daughter of the Fourth Earl of Clarendon, the Whig Foreign Secretary of the 1850s and 1860s and sister of the Fifth Earl, who would take on the Presidency in 1871. He is the only President known to have married during his year of office.

What also happened in his year of office was that the Eyre Estate, who had owned the freehold of Lord's since 1732, put it up for sale at public auction. MCC did not even put in a bid at the auction, and by the end of the day, their new landlord was Mr Isaac Moses, who paid £7,000, a bargain, for the land.

Skelmersdale might once have been a sportsman and a cricketer of social if not national note, being a lifelong member of I Zingari and a vice-president of Lancashire County Cricket Club, but he quickly turned his attention to more significant matters, notably politics. Described in his obituary as 'a Liberal politician' he served three times as Lord Chamberlain from the 1880s, and was indeed Lord Chamberlain in the Conservative government of the Marquess of Salisbury when he died, in 1898. Several other Presidents in future years were also Lords Chamberlain at some stage – notably his brother-in-law the Earl of Clarendon (1871) and the Earl of Cromer (1934).

Skelmersdale was created First Earl of Lathom in 1880, when only 42 years old, but lived only eighteen more years, dying just before his 61st birthday (a lifespan barely two thirds of his great friend the Earl of Coventry). He nominated John, Fifth Earl Spencer as his successor.

JOHN POYNTZ SPENCER, born on 27 October 1835, was educated at Harrow and Trinity College, Cambridge, and succeeded to the Earldom in December 1857. The unusual name Poyntz is also found in the family of the Marquess of Exeter (1838), indicating a family connection here too. Spencer had very briefly been a Member of Parliament before his translation to the Lords, and thereafter remained a very powerful political presence, almost becoming Prime Minister towards the end of his life.

Spencer was known as a leading sportsman of his era, and also as an important figure in society from a young age. Among other offices that he held for many years was the Presidency of Northamptonshire County Cricket Club, the county where the Spencer family home, Althorp, is situated. He was a member of Prince Albert the Prince Consort's household until Albert's untimely death from typhoid in December 1861, just over half way through Spencer's Presidential year. Thereafter Lord Spencer transferred his allegiance to the Prince of Wales, and worked closely with him until 1868, when he was appointed Lord Lieutenant of Ireland.

Spencer retained the Lieutenancy for six years, and what he learnt there made him side with Gladstone in the debates over Home Rule. He had a further stint as Lord Lieutenant from 1882 to 1886, held the post of Lord President of the Council twice in the 1880s, and in 1892 was appointed First Lord of the Admiralty. All these high offices prove how influential a friend he could be to the MCC, and he retained a strong lifelong interest in the Club.

As First Lord of the Admiralty, he worked with Admiral Sir John Fisher, First Sea Lord, in the modernisation of the Navy; it was a process that also involved a subsequent First Lord of the Admiralty and MCC's President in 1908, Earl Cawdor. Between them, from 1894 to 1905 they completely revamped the Royal Navy to face the perceived German challenge. The expenditure, some £31 million at first estimate but inevitably much more once the spending began, was not without strong opposition from both inside and outside the ruling Liberal party, and the rows that erupted led indirectly to Gladstone's resignation as Prime

Minister and leader of the Liberal party. Gladstone wanted Spencer to succeed him as leader, but the Liberals went for Lord Rosebery instead. Rosebery was a racing man rather than a cricketer, although his son Lord Dalmeny captained Surrey from 1905 to 1907 and became President of MCC in Coronation Year, 1953. In 1902 Earl Spencer became leader of the Liberal Party in the House of Lords, but in 1905 he suffered a stroke which left him partly paralysed, and he took no further part in public life. He died just before his 75th birthday, in August 1910.

Spencer is also remembered as the man who introduced barbed wire to Britain, a strange legacy, and for being the several times great grandfather of Prince William and Prince Harry.

E arl Spencer was succeeded by a man just thirteen days older than him, a lifelong friend of the Spencer and of the Beaufort families, **William Philip Molyneux, the Fourth Earl of Sefton.** Like Lord Skelmersdale, Sefton had strong connections with Lancashire. The family seat was at Croxteth Hall near Liverpool and he was Lord Lieutenant of the county for almost forty years from 1858, when he was only 22 years old, until his death in 1897. He was also President of Lancashire County Cricket Club for several years in the 1870s, and his love of cricket was real. As *Wisden* reported in its obituary of Lord Sefton, he was 'a great supporter of cricket and at the time of his death one of the Trustees of the Marylebone Club'.

Sefton's grandfather, the Second Earl (1772–1838), was an early member of MCC and was also known as Lord Dashalong because of his skill at driving a carriage and four. He was a founder member, as we have seen, of the 'Four In Hand Club' along with Lord Worcester (afterwards Duke of Beaufort), Lord Barrymore, Sir John Lade and others. The Club members would dress in blue and yellow striped waistcoats with a black spotted handkerchief protruding from a pocket, and would then drive with as much show as possible from their point of assembly in George Street, Hanover Square out to their chosen destination to dine. The Second Earl was not only a fine carriage driver; he was also a reckless and hopeless gambler. He was described by one contemporary as 'a gigantic hunchback' and a gambler who 'lost largely on all occasions'. So largely did he lose that many of the Sefton estates in and around Liverpool had to be sold to meet his debts. By the time the Fourth Earl inherited the title the coffers were depleted and he had of necessity to live a more proscribed existence than his grandfather had done. He still managed to be President of MCC at the age of 26, and his value to the Britain of his time was acknowledged when he was created a Knight of the Garter in 1885.

Sefton nominated Lord Suffield as his successor. **CHARLES HARBORD, THE FIFTH BARON SUFFIELD**, was the younger half-brother of the Fourth Baron, who had been MCC President in 1836. By this time, Sefton had about 650 fellow members to choose from; MCC, after a period of solid growth, was stagnating in membership and spirit, and its failure to grow beyond something over six hundred members, a figure first attained in 1856, was an indication of the position that the Club had taken up within London society – a good place for the nobility to mix with their social equals on an informal basis, but not really a Club in which the majority of members really cared about cricket. I suppose the same could be said of the Club over a century and a half later, except that the membership roll is about fifty times as great, so the number who do care about their cricket is large enough to fill Lord's to capacity several times a season.

The President of 1863, Charles Suffield, was born on 2 January 1830 so was seventeen years younger than his half-brother and 33 years old when he took on the Presidency. He had been elected in 1855 and remained a loyal servant of the Club right up to his death, at the age of 84, in 1914. He was the first Lord Suffield to survive beyond his forties for some time, as both his father and elder brother had died young. His father, the Third Lord Suffield, who died as a result of a fall from his horse in 1835, when young Charles was only five years old, at least lived long enough to instil a love of cricket into both of his sons. The Third Baron Suffield was the first President of Suffolk County Cricket Club. The family seat, Gunton Park, included a lovely cricket ground where the successive Lords Suffield staged many matches each year.

As *Wisden* remarked of Charles Suffield, he 'played a prominent part in the Club's acquisition of Lord's', although not as great a role as would be played by William Nicholson, still serving loyally on the Committee. Lord Suffield chaired the meeting at which it was resolved 'that the Committee be authorised to make the necessary arrangements by which The Marylebone Club may become lessees of Lord's Cricket Ground for an extended term of 99 years', and then contributed £100 to the purchase of the leasehold, a sum equalled by several members who were ceaselessly pursued by Roger Kynaston for donations. Suffield was also President when a new patron was found for MCC. Thanks in no small measure to the efforts of Earl Spencer, H.R.H. Prince Albert Edward, Prince of Wales, agreed to take on the position in succession to his late father. He also immediately contributed £100 to the Donation fund to acquire the leasehold. Whether his appointment was in any way responsible for the surge in membership over the next couple of years, when 250 new members joined the Club, is hard to tell, but Royal patronage never did any harm, especially at the height of Victorian majesty.

Like many other Presidents, Suffield held strange offices within the farther reaches of their social world. He became Master of the Buckhounds in 1886, in direct succession to Lord Coventry (1859) and several years after the Earl of Sandwich (1866) had held the title. Quite what the Master of the Buckhounds did, or was allowed to do, is rather unclear. It was an office that had its origins in the mid-eighteenth century but was abolished in 1901. No one has suffered from its disappearance, except possibly one or two masterless buckhounds.

Suffield handed the Presidency (but not the Buckhound Mastership) to **WILLIAM WARD, FIRST EARL OF DUDLEY**. This was not, of course, the William Ward who was such a great player half a century earlier and there seems to be no family link between the two men. Lord Dudley was a distant cousin of John William Ward, also confusingly First Earl of Dudley (in a different creation), a Whig politician who was briefly Foreign Secretary in the Duke of Wellington's government in the 1820s. John William died in 1833 and the title died with him, but young William, born in 1817, had a family title of his own: Baron Ward of Birmingham. He married Georgina Moncreiffe, whose mother, Lady Louisa, was the sister of the 1852 President, Viscount Dupplin, who in turn was related by marriage to the Beauforts. The Ward family were very wealthy, thanks to their ownership of coalfields around Dudley, and in 1860 Lord Ward was made First Earl of Dudley (in the second creation). The Wards owned about 200 mines in and around the Black Country, centred on their family home at Himley Hall near Stourbridge. His mines, which were technically very advanced for their time, earned him a reputed annual income of £10,000, so his contribution of a mere £100 to MCC in its time of need seems less than generous.

We note from the Club minutes that 'Mr J. H. Dark parted with his interest in Lord's Ground for a term of 29½ years in 1864 for the sum of £11,000, together with the sum of £1,500 for fixtures. Mr Moses at the same time granted a lease of 99 years at a rent of £550 per annum.' This was a major change in the status of Lord's, and it was hugely significant for the Club that they were now, to a far greater extent, masters of their own destiny. 1864 was a pivotal year for cricket: the sixteen-year-old William Gilbert Grace first played serious cricket and John Wisden published his *Almanack* for the first time. The Marylebone Club's membership grew by one sixth, to 560. Even so, Dudley could not have guessed at the time that in retrospect his Presidential year was one of the most important in the history of the game.

Actually, Earl Dudley was more interested in architecture and creating a beautiful home than he was in cricket. In order to ship his coal to the seaports, he had the Dudley Canal built, with its tunnel and

Lord Ward's Arm, which was completed in 1840 to service the Ward limekilns. Having invested his money wisely in upgrading his distribution network, from the mid-1840s his main interest was in creating a huge palace at one of his other houses, Witley Court. Like many of his moneyed peers who also became President of MCC, he engaged the best architects, builders, decorators and garden designers to create a home which, by the time Dudley died in 1885, consisted of over one hundred rooms and was described as 'a Palladian Palace'. In 1886 *Wisden* did not mention his passing.

D udley, who was 47 in his Presidential year, nominated a man sixteen years older than himself, **ROBERT GROSVENOR, BARON EBURY**, to succeed him. Ebury, at 64, was older than all of his predecessors bar one – the First Earl Verulam, who had been 65 when he took over in 1840. The tradition of young, active Presidents, so heartily pursued by the other William Ward, had finally been laid to rest by a later namesake.

Robert Grosvenor was an outstanding public figure even if he had never been particularly noted for his cricketing skills. He was the third son of the First Marquess of Westminster, and thus related in a cousinly way to the Curzons and thus by marriage to the Dukes of Beaufort. Everyone seems to be related to the Duke of Beaufort: no wonder he became President twice. Grosvenor's wife was a Wellesley, of the family of the Duke of Wellington, and much of his wide range of philanthropic work was with causes also espoused by the Earl of Shaftesbury.

Lord Robert Grosvenor, as he then was, became a Liberal MP for three different constituencies over a period of 35 years from 1822 to 1857, when he was created First Baron Ebury of Ebury Manor. He supported a fine mixture of liberal causes, including Jewish emancipation, opposition to ritualism in the Church of England, and homeopathy. Ebury and the Duke of Beaufort were both early proponents of the merits of homeopathy, so were friends and colleagues if not close blood relations.

Grosvenor was Chairman of the London Homeopathic Hospital from 1854 to 1888, and thereafter President until his death at the age of 92. He was also interested in the weather; he was appointed President of the Meteorological Society of London in 1839, and when that folded, he became a member of the newly-formed British Meteorological Society in 1851. Despite the obviously close correlation between the weather and cricket, Lord Ebury was unique among senior MCC men in his membership of the British Meteorological Society at that time. It would be 150 years before weathermen such as John Kettley proclaimed their love for cricket.

Ebury was an influential, kindly and somewhat eccentric elderly gentleman when he became President. He thereby embodied the image MCC had to the outside world rather more accurately than many of his forbears. He handed the job on to another man who fitted the bill, **JOHN MONTAGU, SEVENTH EARL OF SANDWICH**. Sandwich was 54 years old when he became President and was known more as a soldier than a cricketer. His first wife had been the daughter of the first Marquess of Anglesey, the man who lost a leg at Waterloo, and so by marriage Sandwich was uncle to Lord Uxbridge (1855). In December 1865, at the age of 54, he married for a second time. His bride was the Hon. Blanche Egerton, daughter of the First Earl of Ellesmere and Harriet Greville, sister of Algernon Greville (1828). This marriage connected the Sandwich family with not only the Ellesmeres (the Fourth Earl was to be President in 1920), but also with the Dukes of Richmond and of Sutherland, whose family name was a famous cricketing one: Leveson-Gower. He also became an obscure relation by marriage of Edward Chandos Leigh, the 1887 President. The wedding was well celebrated around Lord Sandwich's home on the borders of Cambridgeshire and Huntingdonshire (of course, nowhere near Sandwich), as we learn from a contemporary document: 'In view of the approaching marriage of the Earl of Sandwich to Miss Blanche Egerton, his Lordship distributed a

liberal supply of meat, bread, beer, tea, tobacco, and snuff, for Christmas merry-making, in the towns and villages around Huntingdon and
Godmanchester.' The men of the towns and villages did fine by the
sound of it, but the women, unless they really appreciated beer, tobacco
and snuff, were less well catered for.

In 1866 and 1867, major changes were taking place in the life of
Lord's too. The MCC minutes record that 'Mr Moses in 1866 sold the
freehold of Lord's Ground to the MCC for the sum of £18,313, being
33 ⅓ years' purchase of the present rent.' This was where men like
William Nicholson helped the Marylebone Club survive, because the
Club did not at this time have anything approaching £18,000 to buy a
freehold without which the Club would have ceased to exist, or at least
have ceased to have its raison d'être: a cricket ground. In 1867, the
Grand Stand was built by a company formed for the purpose, and
called, as one might expect, The Lord's Grand Stand Company, at a cost
of £1,435 5s 4d. This one asset of the company was sold two years later
to MCC for £1,703 6s 8d. More major outlay for the Club, but with the
future of the ground assured, they were more confident.

The 1867 President was **JAMES GRIMSTON, EARL OF VERULAM**, the
first man to be chosen twice to fill the role. By this time Verulam
was a distinguished man of 58, having proved himself a staunch supporter of MCC over the years, as well as a strong voice in the House of
Lords. Although there was no precedent for a man taking on the Presidency for a second time, there was nothing in the rules of the Club to
preclude it, and there is no mention in the minute book either before
or after the Anniversary Dinner of 1867 of this then unique situation.
No one doubts Verulam's suitability for the job, but it seems very odd,
for example, that Verulam's younger brother Robert, a major voice at
MCC for well over twenty years, would have to wait another sixteen
years for his shot at the Presidency while his brother was given an unprecedented second go. Or at least, we assume it was unprecedented. It

is of course possible, if unlikely, that one of the early unknown Presidents held office twice, or that one of the early names that we do know of had been President before. It seems improbable, but if not, why was this unique situation not remarked on at the time?

It seems most likely that Lord Sandwich asked Robert Grimston if he wanted to be President, but for some reason Robert turned him down and suggested his elder brother should have another go instead. As an example of the influence the younger Grimston wielded at Lord's, when a mowing machine was first introduced to the ground in 1868, the year after his brother's Presidency and therefore a time when perhaps his own influence had waned a little, it was said that Robert 'had a great objection to its use, so that when he was in evidence, the machine had to be put in the cart shed'. The Grimston way of doing things harked back to an earlier age of the Marylebone Club.

Verulam handed over to a military man, Lord Methuen. **FREDERICK HENRY PAUL METHUEN, SECOND BARON METHUEN,** was born on 23 February 1818 and thus was fifty years old when he accepted Lord Verulam's nomination. He had been ADC to Queen Victoria in his younger days but by the time he took on MCC's Presidency, he was a Lord in Waiting at the court and, rather more actively, Provincial Grandmaster of the Freemasons in his home county, Wiltshire. There is no evidence that freemasonry was any more firmly established within MCC than within any other London gentlemen's club of the age, but we can assume that many of the members had some connections with the masons, even if they were not as fully involved as Lord Methuen. It certainly never became a requirement that a President be a freemason. Some were and some were not.

During Methuen's year, the building programme for Lord's continued apace. The minute book records that 'the New Tavern was built in 1868–69, contract price £3,983 3s 0d', although there is no indication as to whether this estimate was met.

Methuen's son, also Frederick, who was to outshine his father militarily and become Field Marshal Lord Methuen, married Evelyn, the daughter of Sir Frederick Hervey-Bathurst, the 1857 President. However, if we are looking for connections between families of MCC Presidents, even the Verulams pale beside the Hamiltons, whose first representative on cricket's throne took over from Lord Methuen in 1869.

Henry Charles Keith Fitzmaurice, Fifth Marquess of Lansdowne, was an Eton and Balliol man, and though not born a member of the 'handsome Hamiltons' he married into them. His wife was Lady Maud Hamilton, whose brothers were Presidents in 1874 and 1881, while her brothers-in-law did the job in 1884 and 1888. The 1884 brother-in-law, Lord Winterton, was the son of the 1846 President. Lady Maud's eldest sister was the mother of the Earl of Lichfield, the 1897 President, and another sister was the mother of the Earl of Dalkeith (1913). Yet another became the mother-in-law of the Earl of Pembroke, who was President in 1896, and also grandmother-in-law of Lord Leconfield (1927). Her mother was Lady Louisa Russell, a cousin of Lord Charles Russell (1835), so there were direct family connections via the Hamiltons between eleven Presidents of the Club over 92 years.

The Fifth Marquess was described rather condescendingly as 'not a great Foreign Secretary, but a successful one'. Born on 14 January 1845 (and therefore only 24 years old when he took on the Presidency), he inherited his title in 1866, and in the family tradition (his grandfather had been Canning's Home Secretary in the 1820s) went straight into Whig politics on leaving Oxford. In his Presidential year he joined the government as a Lord of the Treasury, and his rise through the ranks of the Liberal party was thereafter steady if not spectacular. At Lord's the main feature of his Presidential year was the taking on of Guy's Nursery over the bitterly cold winter of 1869/70, to create the extra practice area at what we now call the Nursery End, and Lansdowne was active in all the decisions of his Club during the year. From 1870, his attention turned much more towards the political than the sporting world. He was, like several other MCC Presidents, a colonial Governor General, and spent time in Canada from 1883 to 1888, and then served in India as Viceroy until 1893. He returned to England, by now politically a Liberal Unionist veering towards Conservatism, and almost at once moved into Lord Salisbury's cabinet as Secretary of State for War. He held that post when the Boer War broke out, and he was strongly criticised for the unpreparedness of the British Army for that conflict. However, he showed all the skills of a modern politician by not allowing criticism, however justified, to slow down his career, and in 1900 he became Foreign Secretary, a post he held for five years under two Prime Ministers: Salisbury and A. J. Balfour. The Anglo-Japanese Treaty of 1902 and the Entente Cordiale of 1904 were two of the main achievements of his tenure of office, two agreements that were to have a huge impact on British history in the twentieth century as Britain emerged from her splendid isolation after the death of Queen Victoria. For 'not a great foreign secretary' this was quite a memorial.

Lansdowne's subsequent career revolved around his leadership of the Unionists in the House of Lords and a brief recall to the war cabinet of 1915 as Minister without Portfolio. However, his intransigence over any thoughts of independence for Ireland put him in conflict with his cabinet colleagues and he resigned in 1916. A year later, with revolution breaking out in Russia and civilization as he knew it breaking up around him, he came forward as the leader of a small group of once influential men proposing making peace with Germany. It was the end of his political career. He died aged 82 in 1927, a few days after his great-nephew Lord Leconfield began his Presidential year at Lord's, and 58 years since his own Presidency.

One of the curiosities of MCC Presidential history is why the Marquess of Lansdowne, a pillar of the nobility, related in all directions to the great houses of Britain, should have chosen to nominate as his successor the first commoner to hold that office since 1845. The man he nominated was **JOHN HENRY SCOURFIELD**, Member of Parliament for Haverfordwest, an Old Harrovian and one of the great landowners of Wales at the time, but otherwise so obscure that his contribution to society does not even warrant a mention in the index or footnotes of the history books of the period. So how did Scourfield get the nod? One might have expected the honour to fall upon William Nicholson, who was thanked at the AGM by Lansdowne, who said that 'the Club is still further indebted to Mr W. Nicholson for the accomplishment of its objects.'

The truth is hard to pin down, but John Scourfield, born on 30 January 1808 and thus 62 when he took on the Presidency, had been a member of the Club since 1829. He was always destined for high social position, holding the office of Sheriff of Pembrokeshire as early as 1833, but he never became a peer. He became MP for Haverfordwest in 1852, and remained a Member of Parliament until he died, but never achieved anything approaching high office. He was Chairman of a Parliamentary Committee looking into Railway Deposits, but that seems to have been the peak of his governmental responsibilities. He does not merit an entry in the *Dictionary of National Biography* and although we know he was a major landowner in Pembrokeshire, with about 26,000 acres to his name, he lived as obscure a life as almost any previous or later President. His obscurity is unmasked a little when we discover that until 1862 he was known as John Philipps, and it was because of the death of an uncle that he changed his name to Scourfield by royal decree. His uncle, William Scourfield, had died in 1843 and it took John Philipps nineteen years to get round to changing his name, and thereby securing title to much of his late uncle's estate. Perhaps that was because the name Philipps itself, with that rather unusual spelling, is a well known Pembrokeshire name, the original family being strong Royalists going back across the centuries to Henry V. As Philipps he played a little cricket for MCC between 1830 and 1839, only six games in total. His failure to catch the eye of the selectors more often is perhaps explained by his career batting average: 1.89, which is the lowest of any

President who played in any of the important games of his time. He had a top score of 8 not out, never bowled and took no catches. He was not a good cricketer, but he was a keen club man, and in 1870 he got his reward. He lived only six more years, but in February 1876, four months before his death, he was awarded a baronetcy, so he died Sir John Scourfield Bt., 68 years after being born John Philipps.

Scourfield obviously realised that a title was needed if a man was to be a true President, so he nominated the Lord Clarendon to succeed him. **EDWARD HYDE VILLIERS**, the Fifth Earl, was born in 1846 and inherited his title when his father died in 1870. He was a keen if inactive cricketer who was for many years President of Hertfordshire County Cricket Club (the family seat was near Watford), but probably his main value to MCC was in his connections. His father had been Foreign Secretary at the time of the Crimean War, another man of Whig/Liberal persuasions who served in the cabinets of five different Prime Ministers and alongside men like the Marquess of Lansdowne's father. The Fifth Earl set no such high goals for himself; for a time he was Lord Chamberlain, but he never became as powerful a figure as his father had been. He was also the brother-in-law of Lord Skelmersdale, President eleven years earlier.

Clarendon handed over to a real soldier, one of the few to have reached the Presidency in the nineteenth century. **HUGH RICHARD DAWNAY, EIGHTH VISCOUNT DOWNE**, was described by Lord Clarendon at the Anniversary Dinner of 1872 as likely to be 'no unworthy occupier of the seat I now vacate'. Downe, born in 1844, was just a couple of months away from his 28th birthday when he took over, but was already a professional soldier, commissioned in the Life Guards. He was indeed to prove to be no unworthy occupier of the Presidential seat, and in particular he helped build the links between MCC and the counties through his very strong links with Yorkshire cricket. Lord Downe's family homes were, and still are, at Wykeham Abbey and Danby Lodge, both near Scarborough in Yorkshire. He was from the first a keen supporter of the Scarborough cricket festival, which was the brainchild of men like Lord Londesborough, Sir Charles Legard and C. I. Thornton, and it was a symbol of the importance that county cricket was assuming that MCC should turn to one of its leaders as its President for 1872. Mind you, Downe was also married to Cecilia Molyneux, daughter of the Third Earl of Sefton, and sister of the Fourth Lord Sefton (1862). Downe's mother was daughter of the Fourth Earl of Jersey, and the Seventh Earl (1890) was a second cousin. So he was an MCC insider.

Downe was a good club cricketer, but never had time for anything much more organised than that. On 12 and 13 June 1868, he played for MCC against the first Australian team to tour England. This was the aboriginal team described as 'a fine body of gentlemen' which included such names as Bullocky, Dick-a-Dick, Tiger and Redcap – names that are no odder than some of the nicknames used by Australian Test cricketers today. It was very much a social tour. 'They were every day in touch with lovers of cricket who thought that it was kind to induce them to drink their health and chat with them until the poor fellows got quite helpless', as one contemporary account tells us. Bullocky, for one, was marked down as 'absent' for his second innings as MCC won by 55 runs.

In the seven or eight years since W. G. Grace had first burst on to the scene, cricket had achieved a much higher profile as the young man broke record after record during successive summers. The County Championship was set on a more solid footing and all counties organised themselves into proper clubs. International cricket, such as the aboriginal tour, was getting well under way, with touring teams making their ways to and from America, Australia, South Africa and the Indian sub-continent, beginning a tradition that has reached crazy levels of excess today. MCC needed to change from being a club with a social heritage to a rather more professional, or at least businesslike, body if it were to continue as the heartbeat of cricket rather than as just another smart cricket club. No fewer than 90 new members were elected at the 1872 AGM, but much of the report of the meeting is taken up with an obsequious tribute by Lord Clarendon to the Prince of Wales, who had recently been ill. Was MCC yet a cricket club or still just a gathering of well-born men needing somewhere to let off a little steam?

Change, unfortunately, is not what MCC was known for, and the need for change was hard to see. Perhaps the greatest pressure was beginning to come from south of the river, at Kennington Oval, where Charles Alcock was beginning his long and inventive reign as Secretary of Surrey C.C.C., overthrowing or ignoring traditions that MCC men long held dear. Surrey men have since that time been very rarely appointed as President of MCC. Perhaps the rivalry is too strong. Yorkshiremen, Kent men, Middlesex men of course, Lancastrians, Essex stalwarts, Hampshire men and Sussex men have all been well represented at Lord's, but the Surrey contingent remains surprisingly small. It is still a very long way from Kennington to St John's Wood.

Downe realised that if the Scarborough festival was to prosper, a close liaison with Lord's had to be maintained to ensure that top quality teams and individuals took part in the festival each year. The match between the Earl of Londesborough's XI and C. I. Thornton's XI the year before, on 11 and 12 September 1871, had put Scarborough firmly on the cricket map, and there Downe intended it to stay. Like Londesborough and Legard after him, Downe clearly had some conflict of interest in his Presidency, and he probably took the side of Yorkshire and Scarborough rather than London when it mattered. In retrospect, this would have been a great service for MCC too, opening up their eyes to the world of cricket beyond the Lord's boundary ropes.

D owne, who lived another fifty years and ended up a Major General, handed the Presidency on to his great friend **George Cadogan**, **Viscount Chelsea**. Chelsea, born in May 1840 and educated at

Eton and Oxford without getting into either XI, took over the role as Viscount Chelsea, but his father died during his year, so by the end of it he was the Earl of Cadogan. Despite this personal tragedy, MCC was beginning to pick up speed at this time, along with most cricketing institutions, and during Chelsea's time in the chair, there were 29 resignations and 13 deaths of members, but 228 new members enrolled. The total membership was now up to 1,802, three times the size it had been only a decade earlier. Not that MCC were trying to spread the net too widely – Cadogan's connections were as impeccable as those who went before him. He was son-in-law to the 1841 President, the Second Earl of Craven (which linked him in to the Verulam family) and the Duke of Wellington, whose shadow seems to lurk over many MCC Presidents one way or another, was his great-uncle. In his political career he was an MP until his father's death then served as Lord Privy Seal in Salisbury's Conservative government from 1886 to 1892, and was Lord Lieutenant of Ireland from 1895 to 1902. He died just before his 75th birthday in 1915.

Chelsea handed on to the heir to the Dukedom of Abercorn: JAMES, MARQUESS OF HAMILTON. The Duke and Duchess of Abercorn had fourteen children in 24 years, one of whom died in infancy and another at the age of eighteen. The other twelve, five boys and seven girls, were collectively known as the 'handsome Hamiltons' and they married into most of the noble families of the day. Most of the girls married cricketing men, with only Katherine (who married Lord Mount Edgcumbe) and Albertha (who snared the Duke of Marlborough) letting the side down. Of the boys, James and George both became Presidents of MCC, but Claud, Frederick and Ernest, despite long lives and plenty of opportunity, did not follow their brothers' lead.

James, who was 35 when he took on the Presidency, was no great cricketer, but he did thank his fellow members at the Anniversary Dinner in 1874 for the 'high sense of honour conferred upon me by my election as President of the oldest cricket club in England'. Several things wrong there – it wasn't an election and MCC was not the oldest cricket club in England – but at least he, a man full to bursting with honours, felt happy that MCC had conferred yet another on him. He also pointed out, rather quaintly, that 'cricket is a great social leveller, and long may it flourish, apart from its excellence as a pastime, to bring into happy and healthy connection all classes of the country!' This from the 36th member of the House of Lords to be President in forty years.

At the 1874 Annual General Meeting, the issue of using Lord's for charitable purposes was raised. A Dr Gaye said that he had applied to the Secretary for permission for a band of Clown Cricketers to play at Lord's on behalf of a charitable corporation, but that he had received an answer which he considered 'barely polite'. The Marquess of Hamilton explained to Dr Gaye and the meeting that the Committee 'could not grant permission to any such entertainments' at Lord's. The Secretary (R. A. Fitzgerald) added that 'the Clown Cricketers are a burlesque upon cricket that cannot be tolerated at Lord's.' Fast forward to just over a century later when Colin Cowdrey's final innings at Lord's is against the Lord's Taverners (a 'charitable corporation') in which he is caught Frost (David) bowled Rice (Tim). 'Time to call it a day, I thought' were Cowdrey's words. Whether this was quite the equivalent of the Clown Cricketers of 1874 is hard to tell, but it is gratifying that the committees of recent years do not espouse the same narrow-minded attitude as their Victorian counterparts.

Hamilton handed the Presidency on to the second Scarborough man to hold the office in four years. SIR CHARLES LEGARD BT. was only 29 in his Presidential year, but was described by his predecessor as 'distinguished equally as a politician, a sportsman and a Yorkshire squire'. Sir Charles was an Etonian, but was never good enough to make their cricket XI. All the same, he was a cricket fanatic and deeply involved in the development of the Scarborough Festival. His acceptance speech at the Anniversary Dinner was touching: 'There are occasions when words fail to express the feelings of the heart – this is one of them. When I look at the long roll of illustrious predecessors, my heart fails me.'

One of the issues that arose during Sir Charles' year was the question of cricket and fashion. Lord Harris, a rising star at MCC by this time, was on record as saying that 'there is too much cricket', and the Committee were very concerned that people were applying for membership of MCC just to be able to get tickets for the 'fashionable matches' of the season: Gentlemen v. Players, Oxford v. Cambridge and, especially, Eton v. Harrow. Shades of people joining Notts, Surrey and Warwickshire these days in order to get Test match tickets! 'First class cricket, it is much to be regretted, attracts but few in comparison with fashionable matches,' the Committee noted sternly. 'MCC does not depend on the caprice of fashion,' and they acted to prevent people who did not have the interests of cricket at heart from becoming members. A change in the membership election process was agreed at a Special General Meeting on 2 March 1876, limiting the number of new members to twelve at any one ballot. They added the rider that 'so long as the candidates seek admission to the Club with a view to support cricket and its attendant interests, will their claims be recognised by the electing body, and the future welfare of MCC be placed on a sound basis.'

Given that the Scarborough Cricket Week was rapidly becoming one of the fashionable society events of the year, it is rather surprising that Sir Charles Legard so strongly supported the interests of cricket over fashion, but his main interest was Scarborough. To ensure the continuing relationship between his home town and Lord's, he passed on the Presidency to his friend and ally at Scarborough, Lord Londesborough.

WILLIAM HENRY FORESTER DENISON, FIRST EARL OF LONDESBOROUGH, had been for many years a great patron of cricket in Yorkshire. *Wisden* noted in his obituary that 'the Scarborough

Cricket Week … practically owed its origin to him, and he supported the Festival in most liberal fashion.' The year after his Presidency of MCC, he and Sir Charles Legard were stalwarts of the scheme that enabled Scarborough Cricket Club to purchase its own ground. Like Legard, he was no cricketer himself. 'If proficiency in the game of cricket was a requirement for qualification as President of this Club', he said in his acceptance speech, 'I should have no place here'. He added that he was, nevertheless, extremely fond of the game, which was in his case a great understatement.

He was also, needless to say, well connected. His wife, Lady Edith Somerset, was the sister of the Eighth Duke of Beaufort, who had already been President in 1853, but clearly Londesborough saw no reason to go outside the family when appointing his successor, and remembering the precedent of Lord Verulam, duly gave his brother-in-law the job. It looks as though he was rather unthinking about the whole concept of who should be the next President. Not only did he come up with someone who was related to him and who had already done the job, but he also gave the Duke the wrong date for the Anniversary Dinner. He therefore had to apologise to members, saying that although 'no-one would fill the post more worthily than his Grace', he owed an apology to the Duke who was 'absent from the dinner through having been misinformed by me as to the day'. We get the impression that the Duke was hardly the keenest of members if he did not know the date from other sources than his somewhat scatterbrained brother-in-law, and all in all his Presidency got off to rather a slow start.

The Duke of Beaufort was by now accustomed to being President of cricket clubs, and indeed of inheriting the Presidency from a brother-in-law. He had taken on the Presidency of Gloucestershire County Cricket Club at its formation in 1871 and was to hold the title until he died in 1899. Subsequent Dukes of Beaufort have also held the position in later generations, keeping it in the family. In 1877, Gloucestershire, powered by the three Graces, W. G., E. M. and G. F., were generally reckoned to be the Champion County of the season, a title that they have never won again, either officially or unofficially in the 130 years since.

The Duke's year was eventful in other ways; the death of Sir John Scourfield was noted and a letter of condolence written to Lady Scourfield. The writer of this letter was Henry Perkins, newly appointed as Secretary, and as the Committee minutes noted, 'By the lamented death of Sir John Scourfield and the election of Mr Perkins to the office of Secretary, there became two vacancies on the Committee.' By this time, Committee places were up for election on a regular basis, and no one could hold a lifelong place at the centre of the Club without having to stand for regular re-election.

When the Duke's year was up, he handed the Presidency on to his good friend **FRANCIS WILLIAM FITZHARDINGE BERKELEY, BARON FITZHARDINGE OF BRISTOL**. Although Fitzhardinge himself was 'unavoidably absent from the Anniversary Dinner through being out with his yeomanry', the Duke's nomination was accepted graciously enough. Francis William Fitzhardinge Berkeley was born on 16 November 1826, making him 51 when he took office. His father, Admiral Fitzhardinge Berkeley, had been ennobled, so Francis was only the second holder of the title when he inherited it on his father's death in 1867. His mother was Lady Charlotte Lennox, daughter of the Fourth Duke of Richmond, which means that the Earl of March, the 1842 President, was Fitzhardinge's cousin. Fitzhardinge, a very different man from his cousin, was educated at Rugby School and then commissioned into the Royal Horse Guards where he reached the rank of captain. By 1856 he was out of the Army and into politics, elected a Liberal M.P for Cheltenham from then until 1865. He died childless on 28 June 1896, but his overall contribution to cricket was such that *Wisden* overlooked his passing.

There was one proposal that came before the Committee during Fitzhardinge's year, which could have changed the course of cricket history, or at least diverted it a little. On 17 June 'a letter from Lord

Harris was read proposing that England play the Australian on the first days (of Canterbury Week) at Canterbury, but the Committee suggested that Kent should rather play the Australians on these days.' The chance was thus missed to stage what would have been the first Test Match in England. The Australians, led by Dave Gregory, did play three matches at Lord's and were given a banquet by MCC, but no England versus Australia match took place that year.

Perhaps the best thing that Fitzhardinge could have done was to hand over the Presidency to the man who more than any other deserved the honour, WILLIAM NICHOLSON. In Fitzhardinge's speech in praise of his successor he said that it gave him 'great pleasure to adopt the recommendation of the Committee, who thought this a fitting compliment to pay to Mr Nicholson, as a slight acknowledgement of his liberality in advancing to the Club a large sum of money, required for the purchase of the freehold of Lord's'. The Presidency is not meant to be a Committee recommendation, and this is the only occasion on which we have proof that it was. The timing was precise: on 5 May, a couple of days before he took over as President, 'it was proposed by R. C. Antrobus, seconded by F. Lee and resolved to pay to Mr W. Nicholson £1,500, thus completing the payment of the money borrowed from Mr Nicholson in 1866.' With no money outstanding, MCC could now honour their protector.

William Nicholson made his money from gin, but cricket was his life. He was born on 2 September 1824, so was in his mid-fifties when he took on the Presidency. He was yet another man educated at Harrow and he became a member of MCC in 1845, four seasons after his first match at Lord's, in 1841, at the age of sixteen, playing for Harrow against Eton. *Scores and Biographies* described him as:

height 5'10", weight 11st 7lbs. Has been a most successful batsman for several years, getting his runs exceedingly fast and well in the best matches, especially about 1852, when he was not to be excelled. Is one of the best wicket-keepers in England, standing up pluckily to the fastest bowling.

All in all, he sounds like Adam Gilchrist a century and a half ahead of his time.

Nicholson, well educated and well connected, became a Liberal Member of Parliament, for Petersfield in Hampshire, in 1866. His parliamentary career stuttered when he lost his seat in 1874 and he then changed his allegiance and joined the Conservatives. He regained the seat in 1880, as his time as President of MCC came to an end, but lost it again five years later and moved away from politics. However, despite his great cricketing talent and his political career, it will always be as the saviour of Lord's that he will be remembered. By lending £21,000 to the Club 'as mortgage on a security which the outside public would not take', as *Wisden* noted, 'there is no doubt he saved Lord's from the builders.'

If the crisis had occurred a few years later, in the 1870s rather than the 1860s, when the fashionable Eton v. Harrow and Oxford v. Cambridge matches were bringing new wealth to the Club, Nicholson's bond might not have been needed. By the time Nicholson took on the Presidency of his beloved Club, these matches were already showing signs of a growing popularity. Membership was up to 2,408 and the waiting list now contained 570 names. A stern word of warning had already been issued by the Committee to members taking liberties with their membership rights:

Last year many members were refused carriage tickets owing to want of space; and if the number of applications for carriage tickets goes on increasing, the admission of carriages may have to be stopped altogether. It having come to the knowledge of the Committee last season that carriage tickets were in several cases disposed of to persons who were not members of the Club, the Committee desires to remind members that carriage tickets are not transferable, and that it is most unjust that strangers should have carriage tickets when many members cannot obtain them.

The twin evils of ticket touting and lack of parking space were as prevalent in the 1870s as in the 21st century.

Another tradition was also getting under way at this time. The general healthy state of the Club's accounts was clearly shown by the perennial assaults on them at the Annual General Meetings from the early 1870s by a certain Mr E. C. Willoughby. For several years the minutes record his protests and exchanges with the Committee, usually summarised in the meeting record as 'Mr Willoughby severely criticised the accounts.' By the time Mr Willoughby died, a decade and a half later, he was one of the Club's auditors, in an early example of the poacher turned gamekeeper. Mr Willoughby's successors, 130 years later, still fight their corner.

Nicholson's generosity did not only benefit the Marylebone Club. In the 1890s he bought a piece of land which he presented to his old school, Harrow, as a playing field, to ensure that cricket would always have a high priority and enjoy excellent facilities there. But although he was honoured within the world of cricket, Nicholson died in 1909, aged 84, without a title, and as the only President between Thomas Chamberlayne in 1845 and Vyell 'Teddy' Walker in 1891 to die a commoner.

Nicholson's successor was another Harrow man, Sir William Hart Dyke. Billy Hart Dyke was a great sportsman, but cricket was not the game at which he most excelled. Born in 1837 at the family seat at Lullingstone Castle in Kent, he was elected a member of MCC in 1857 and, as *Wisden* put it in his obituary, 'although gaining little distinction at cricket, he was undoubtedly one of the best rackets players.' He was a brilliant player of rackets, a game invented by the inmates of the Fleet Prison, who devised a ball game using the odd shaped walls of their limited recreation area. As Pierce Egan noted in his *Book Of Sports* published in 1832, rackets is 'one of the most healthful exercises connected with British sports, and the principal Amusement for confined debtors in the Fleet and King's Bench prisons'. Harrow school

built two courts in 1850, and it was here that the young Hart Dyke
learned the game. Such was his brilliance that in 1862 he won the world
championship (admittedly an esoteric world title with a limited field
of contestants) and in doing so became the first man to win the title
who had not learnt the game in Fleet Prison. He was also the first
amateur to win. He used his fame within the game to raise money to
build better quality courts at Harrow, and in January 1865 he played the
first game on the new courts at Harrow, partnering V. E. Walker (Old
Harrovian and MCC President in 1891) in an exhibition match against
two professionals.

Hart Dyke's connections with racket games did not end there. It is
said that in 1875, on the front lawn of Lullingstone Castle, Hart Dyke
and several friends devised the rules of lawn tennis which are broadly
those which are still used today. This claim is open to dispute, because
lawn tennis seems to have sprung up from a variety of different sources
at about the same time. Major Walter Clopton Wingfield is the man
most usually credited with the invention of 'sphairistike', and in 1874,
the year before Hart Dyke and his friends devised things on the lawn
at Lullingstone, Wingfield applied for a patent on his 'New and
Improved Portable Court for Playing the Ancient Game of Tennis'.
But even Wingfield's patent came two years after the establishment of
the Leamington Spa Lawn Tennis Club in 1872. In the end, it was
almost inevitable that MCC was asked to step into the muddle and set
the rules for the game. MCC were of course already custodians of the
Laws of Cricket and also the rules of real tennis and rackets, so in 1875
they were approached to set the rules for lawn tennis. A sub-committee,
led by J. M. Heathcote and including William Hart Dyke, Lord Harris
and Dr Henry Jones of the All-England Club at Wimbledon, set the
new rules, and it seems likely that it was this committee's deliberations
that took place on the lawn of Lullingstone Castle. It is worth a passing mention that one of the men who drew up the rules of Major
Wingfield's version was another Harrovian, Walter Long, who would
become President of MCC in 1906. While it seems unlikely that Tim
Henman will ever be President of MCC, the game of tennis is still

an integral part of MCC life and the influence of MCC over the development of many other 'bat and ball' games should never be forgotten.

Sir William Hart Dyke went on to enjoy a long and distinguished political career. He was an MP for 41 years and 170 days (a year and a day longer than Walter Long), being first elected as Conservative member for Western Kent in 1865, and representing various Kent constituencies until 1906. He was a cabinet minister as Chief Whip from 1874 to 1880, and subsequently as Chief Secretary for Ireland in the mid-1880s, and Vice-President of the Council (minister in charge of education) from 1887 to 1892. He was also President of Kent County Cricket Club in 1884 and a keen member of I Zingari. He is immortalised in a couplet from an IZ poem, which runs as follows:

> The first who dared the ball to strike (full 26 made he)
> Was no one else than Billy Dyke, fresh from the Treasury.

The poet's name was not appended to these lines, and in the interests of literature I have made no attempt to uncover his identity.

Hart Dyke was the son-in-law of the Seventh Earl of Sandwich (1866) and rather more obscurely related to Herbert Jenner (1833) through his grandfather who married one of Jenner's aunts. His great-grandson Tom Hart Dyke broke on to the front pages of the newspapers in 2000 when he was kidnapped with a friend while orchid hunting in Colombia, but released nine months later in the middle of the jungle by the gang who kidnapped them. The gang even gave them 5,000 pesos and told them to get a boat back to civilization, but Hart Dyke and his companion got so lost they met up with the kidnappers again, who this time gave them a map and threatened to kill them if they saw them again. Finally, with the help of a passing park ranger, they made it back to Bogota and safety. Tom Hart Dyke spent his months in captivity planning a world garden to build at Lullingstone Castle. Five years later, his plans were put into action and the garden is now a major attraction at Lullingstone, where once the rules of lawn tennis were discussed.

Billy Hart Dyke handed over to a third successive Harrovian and a second successive Kent man, **LORD GEORGE HAMILTON**. He was the sixth child and third son of the Duke of Abercorn and younger brother of the 1874 President making him, as we have seen, related to a swathe of other Presidents by marriage or blood. He was not a great cricketer, and never made the Harrow XI, but his obituary describes him as 'a hard hitter, an active field, generally at cover slip, and an exceedingly straight and fast underhand bowler'. In 1864, when he was eighteen years old, he did the hat-trick playing for Peripatetics against West Kent at Chislehurst. From 1868 he was a Conservative Member of Parliament for the County of Middlesex, and from 1885 became member for Ealing. His political career culminated in two top cabinet positions: First Lord of the Admiralty under Lord Salisbury from 1886 to 1892 and Secretary for India from 1895 to 1902. He resigned in disagreement with some of Austen Chamberlain's tax proposals in 1903, and gave up his seat in the house in 1906, after four decades at Westminster. He also found time to become chairman of London County Council in 1894, and chaired several parliamentary committees, enquiring into the Poor Laws and the failure of the Mesopotamian campaign in the Great War, among others. A man of many talents and widely distributed favours, he was also Vice-President of Middlesex County Cricket Club from 1876 to 1906, and President of Kent County Cricket Club in 1911. Towards the end of his long life, he was also Captain of Deal Castle, one of his less onerous responsibilities.

Lord George handed over the Presidency to the fourth Harrovian in a row – **HENRY STRUTT, THE SECOND BARON BELPER**. Strutt, the son-in-law of the 1848 President, the Earl of Leicester, was a distinguished politician if rather less distinguished cricketer. He played for Harrow in 1859, when he was already nineteen years old, as a wicketkeeper, and scored 33 against Eton that year. He went up to Trinity College, Cambridge but did not gain a Blue. It was said that he kept wicket well to slow bowling, but lacked the necessary skills to keep to fast bowling. Unlike one of his predecessors in the Harrow XI, William Nicholson, he did not stand up pluckily to the fastest bowling. In his five first-class appearances, between 1862 and 1865, he scored 97 runs at an average of 16.16, but his wicketkeeping was unspectacular: just one catch and no stumpings to show for his efforts.

While studying for his Master of Law degree at Cambridge, he was travelling in Greece with two companions (in December 1865 – were there no lectures he should have been attending at that time of year?) and the group was kidnapped by Greek brigands. The three men each had to pay a £1,000 ransom for their release. This did not seem to slow down his law studies, and by 1867 he was a fully fledged lawyer. The next year he gained election as Liberal MP for East Derbyshire, the constituency that contains the town of Belper, a seat which he held until 1874. He re-entered Parliament in April 1880 as MP for Berwick-on-Tweed, but the death of his father two months later meant that he moved up to the House of Lords.

His father, the first Lord Belper, had made his money and his social position in the cotton trade, as the owner of W.G. and J. Strutt, and young Henry took over the Presidency of the family company in turn. His support of cricket continued throughout his life, with two years as President of Nottinghamshire C.C.C. in 1885 and 1886 to add to his year at Lord's.

Belper handed over to the sixth Harrovian in a row, the **Hon. Robert Grimston**, who took office in 1883. Grimston was already 65 years old at the time he took office, and having been a pillar of MCC for many years, it is odd that he had not been offered the Presidency earlier. We have to assume that he had not been offered it before, as those who have turned it down have often been asked again (Sir Donald Bradman and Doug Insole being further examples of this rule), but it seems odd that a man whose elder brother had been President twice, the first time 46 years earlier, had not taken on the job earlier in his life. As it was, poor Robert Grimston made MCC history by being the only President to die in office.

Grimston was a keen cricketer and fanatically conservative MCC member. He served on the Committee for decades and mainly worked to ensure that nothing much ever changed. He was the second son of the First Earl Verulam (1840) and the younger brother of the Second Earl Verulam (1837 and 1867), and began his cricketing life at Harrow and Oxford, for whom he played in the 1838 Varsity match. All in all, he played over 60 games for Oxford University, MCC and Middlesex, finishing with a batting average just in double figures. He was a barrister by trade, but an MCC potentate most of the time, shaping the Club from the earliest years of Victoria's reign up to his death almost 50 years later. He was strongly against all forms of gambling, and was one of the firmest voices against betting on cricket, which he found anathema. So was the mowing machine when it was first introduced at Lord's in 1868. As we have already noted, whenever Grimston was about, the mower had to be put back in its shed and the sheep brought out to graze.

Grimston's time as President had, through no fault of his own, little impact within the Club. Membership in his year went up by another 92 members to 2,749, a healthy total, but illness prevented him from attending any Committee meeting after 16 July 1883. Thereafter, the other great panjandrum of MCC, Spencer Ponsonby-Fane, took the chair. He finally died on 7 April 1884, a month before the end of his term. The Committee resolved, on 21 April, to send a letter of condolence to his brother Lord Verulam on behalf of the Club. Then:

> the rule of the Club xii (a) relating to a vacancy in the office of President was discussed and it was proposed by Hon. S. Ponsonby-Fane, seconded by Lord Harris and unanimously resolved that Lord Winterton be requested to fill the office of President for the remainder of the year, i.e. up to the Anniversary Dinner on 7 May. Lord Winterton came afterwards and expressed his willingness to accept.

But what about a President for 1884, who must be nominated by his predecessor? Luckily, Robert Grimston, ever the club man, had thought of that. As the minute book also notes, 'Lord Winterton had been nominated to succeed to the office by the late President prior to his death and he nominated himself to that office.' The tributes to Grimston were fulsome and heartfelt:

> His name has been for so many years connected with our national game, as well as with every other manly British sport, that his death must be regretted by all past and present cricketers; but by none so deeply as the members of this Club, with which he has been so long associated, and in which he was so justly esteemed as a true friend, a thorough sportsman and the type of an honourable English gentleman.

CHAPTER FIVE

1884–1913

CRICKETERS AND COURTIERS

By the time MCC neared its century, the Club was in fine form. The difficult years in the middle of the eighteen hundreds were past, and the members and leaders of the Club were confident in the place that they, and cricket, held in society. To this they owed a great deal to factors beyond their control: the emergence of W. G. Grace as the country's greatest sportsman of the era, perhaps of all time; the entrepreneurial spirit of Charles Alcock, the secretary at Kennington Oval, who saw the potential for international sporting fixtures; and the continuing expansion of the British Empire and the civilizing influence that cricket was believed to have on the peoples of the world. MCC had all the while held on to its place as the leading cricket club of the world, partly because of its self-appointed position of arbiter of all that goes on in cricket, and partly because of the reputation of Lord's ground, where all cricketers wanted to play. The power within the MCC was now firmly vested in the senior staff and the Committee. Henry Perkins as Secretary strongly advised the rest of his staff never to listen to anything that may be proposed by the Committee; it was a habit that certainly continued well into the twentieth century as the professional executives just got on with their jobs, regardless of what the amateur committee men wanted. In this, MCC was rather like the government, with 'amateur' politicians nominally running the ministries of government, while the senior civil servants actually got on with the job. The Presidency of MCC was for most holders of the office at this time little more than a prestigious sinecure, which they enjoyed to the full.

The man who took over from the late Robert Grimston was the son of the 1846 President and, having married Lady Georgiana Hamilton, was brother-in-law to the Presidents of 1869, 1874, 1881 and 1888. He was **Edward Turnour, Fifth Earl Winterton**, who like his father had played for his estate, Shillinglee, against the Royal Surrey Militia in 1855 when the Militia were all out for 0. The then Lord Turnour, born on 15 August 1837, was still two days shy of his eighteenth birthday when Shillinglee took on the Royal Surrey Militia who, it is to be hoped, were rather better at fighting than cricketing. Young Edward had just finished a season in the Eton XI with reasonable success, being described as 'a good hard hitter, a fast round-armed bowler and in the field generally cover point or cover-stop'. Winterton was indeed an Eton man, the first to break the run of Harrovian Presidents since the Duke of Beaufort, another Etonian, seven years earlier.

Winterton was 46 years old when he was raised to the Presidency, just a few days before he would have taken on the job anyway. Still, those few days extra made him the President with the longest unbroken term of office until Lord Hawke served all four years of the Great War. His year (and a bit) was notable for one thing in particular – the first Test match ever played at Lord's. Murdoch's Australians were the fourth touring team to come to England from Down Under, but the first to play a Test at Lord's. During the course of the summer, they played four games at Lord's, against MCC and Ground, the Gentlemen of England, Middlesex, and England, and they won only one of these matches: against Middlesex. The game against England was the second of three Tests. The other two, at Manchester and the Oval, were drawn and England thus retained the Ashes, which had been won for the first time

by the Hon. Ivo Bligh's team in Australia eighteen months earlier. Bligh
was no longer in the England team, but four future Presidents of MCC
played for England at Lord's that year – A. G. Steel (the top scorer
for England with a brilliant 148), Lord Harris (the England captain),
Hon. Alfred Lyttelton and Stanley Christopherson, in his only Test
appearance. England won the match by an innings and 5 runs, to set a
precedent for Lord's Test victories which was destined to be almost
impossible to live up to, against Australia at least, almost ever since.

There is not much evidence that MCC understood how momentous
an occasion this would prove to be. The Committee resolved, on
a motion proposed by V. E. Walker, 'to pay the Players in the match
England v. Australia £10 each.' Actually, that wasn't bad for the times,
although we can be sure that the amateur W. G. Grace, who was also
playing, earned a good deal more than that from the game. By the end
of Winterton's year, the Club was able to report 'a new set of dressing
rooms with bathrooms attached, and a new Players' room, have been
added to the Pavilion; hot water has also been laid on.' Things were
looking up for the cricketers at Lord's.

When Winterton's year and a few days were up, he nominated the
Third Baron Wenlock as his successor. BEILBY LAWLEY,
another Etonian, was a young man of 36 when he was appointed President. Although he was one year older than Lord George Hamilton had
been in his Presidential year four years earlier, and older than about 40
of his predecessors, there would not be another President appointed in
his thirties ever again. The only man younger than Wenlock in the years
that followed would be HRH Prince Philip, who was 28 years old in his
first Presidential year, 1949. Wenlock was not much of a cricketer – he
never made the Eton XI nor did he get anywhere near the Cambridge
side during his time there – but he was keen. He became a member
of MCC in 1870 at the age of 21, and took only fifteen years to reach
the Presidency.

Wenlock's family home was in the Yorkshire village of Escrick, between York and Selby. Escrick Park, the Wenlock estate, is now a girls' school, but there is still a beautiful cricket pitch there, where the Yorkshire Gentlemen make their home. Wenlock was a diplomat rather than a politician, and, like many of his fellow Presidents, he was a colonial governor, in his case in Madras. He was very much involved in royal matters, and was part of the Prince of Wales' inner circle. In 1901 he accompanied the Duke and Duchess of York as Lord-in-Waiting on an official tour of Canada, Australia and New Zealand, but it was as Governor of Madras before this that he made his biggest impact on cricket, encouraging the development of local cricket as much as he could. He also played several times with Lord Harris at the Ganeshkind ground which Lord Harris had created while he was Governor of Bombay, though Harris generally made more runs than Wenlock. Harris did, however, consult Wenlock over the dubious action of the Kent player Walter Hedley.

Wenlock handed the Presidency on to one of the great families of MCC history, and of cricket history in general. **CHARLES LYTTELTON, THE FIFTH BARON LYTTELTON**, had a father, four brothers, a brother-in-law, two sons, a nephew and a grandson, all of whom played first-class cricket. The Lytteltons give us one of only two examples of three generations of the same family all being Presidents of MCC, but they go a step or two ahead of the Dartmouth/Lewisham family who have also provided Presidents from three generations, because Charles' younger brother Alfred was also to become President. They were all very good sportsmen. Alfred, President in 1898, played Test cricket for England, but Charles was a rackets player, and was a regular finalist in MCC's tennis and rackets competitions.

The Cobhams were a large clan. As *Vanity Fair* noted in 1904,

Mr. Gladstone was his uncle; Mr Alfred Lyttelton, Secretary of State for the Colonies, is his brother. Another brother was the Bishop of

Southampton, and the Bishop of Rochester is his brother-in-law. Sir Neville, yet another brother, is on the Army Council and the Rev. Edward is headmaster of Haileybury. Lady Frederick Cavendish and Mrs. Talbot, wife of the distinguished MP for Oxford University, are sisters.

Charles himself was the proud father of seven children, three daughters and four sons, the eldest of whom was to become President in 1935.

Much of Lyttelton's year was spent in preparation for the Centenary celebrations of 1887, which would be overseen by his successor, the **Honourable Edward Chandos Leigh Q.C.** 1887 was of course not only MCC's centenary year, but also marked the Golden Jubilee of Queen Victoria, so England's cricketers were in a jubilant mood. Chandos Leigh, born in 1832 at Stoneleigh Abbey in Warwickshire, was not much of a cricketer, but good enough to captain the Harrow XI in 1851 and win a Blue at Oxford for three consecutive years, 1852 to 1854. In 1854, Chandos Leigh played against two future MCC secretaries, R. A. Fitzgerald and Henry Perkins, who were rather better cricketers. Fitzgerald was to become his brother-in-law and a great friend. Eddy Chandos Leigh, as he was always known, scored only 8 runs in his three Varsity matches (although Oxford won all three games by an innings) and there is a story told by Pelham Warner of Chandos Leigh's nephew 'Shrimp' Leveson-Gower, who scored 73 for Oxford in the early 1890s. Chandos Leigh greeted his nephew as he returned from the field to the Pavilion with the cry, 'Well done Shwimp' (he could not get his tongue round the letter 'r'), 'You played just like I used to.'

'Heaven forbid, Uncle Eddy,' replied Shrimp.

Scores and Biographies sums up his cricket by saying that when captain at Harrow he was 'a most excellent and popular one'. His batting style was described as awkward, and in the field at long-stop 'will let a ball go through him rather than by him', which sounds somewhat disconcerting, for the bowlers at least. Much of his adult cricket career was taken up with I Zingari, which he joined very soon after his friends Ponsonby-Fane, Bessborough and Baldwin had formed the Club. He became a lawyer and was always a very clubbable man, counting Robert Grimston and Lord Sefton also among his close associates, and was obviously a hugely popular choice as President in MCC's most significant season. He served them well, and the Centenary Banquet on 15 June at Lord's was his apotheosis. The speakers included the President; the Chancellor of the Exchequer, Rt. Hon. G. J. Goschen; and a slew of past and future Presidents – Viscount Lewisham, Lord George Hamilton, Sir Archibald Smith and Lord Lathom among others. Even the French Ambassador spoke. Viscount Lewisham's speech, toasting 'The Great Army of Cricketers' provoked no fewer than six separate responses, one of which, by W. G. Grace on behalf of 'Medicine', was very brief. Even at this age, just short of his 29th birthday, W.G. had honed his speech-making to a fine and very ruthlessly edited art. Most surprisingly of all, Lord Harris proposed the toast to 'The Press' and 'in doing so bore full and generous testimony to the careful accuracy with which cricket matches were recorded in the papers'. This is not a toast which would be very likely nowadays, even though three men whose careers have included long-term membership of the press corps – Sir Pelham Warner, Tony Lewis and Robin Marlar – have become Presidents of the Club, but only after giving up their season tickets to the Press Box.

The Centenary Week included a match between MCC and England, which England easily won, and a more light-hearted match: 'Eleven Gentlemen of MCC v. Eighteen Veterans of the Club Over Forty'. Edward Chandos Leigh did not play, but enjoyed the spectacle greatly.

Chandos Leigh did a great deal for sport both at Harrow and around the country; he was a founder member of the London Playing Fields Society and in the Midlands, where his family came from, he worked tirelessly to give sporting opportunities to his fellow citizens. He also attended the Canterbury and Scarborough Festivals every year. He was knighted in 1901, at a time when he was counsel to the Speaker of the

House of Commons and also a Recorder of Nottingham, but died in May 1915, just six days after his youngest son Edward was killed in action in northern France. His elder son had been the first Harrovian to be killed in the war, at Mons in August 1914, and the second blow was too much for him. He died, in the same year as W. G. Grace and his great friend Sir Spencer Ponsonby-Fane, of a broken heart.

Edward Chandos Leigh passed the Presidency to yet another member of the extended Hamilton clan, the Duke of Buccleuch, or to give him his full name, **William Henry Walter Montagu-Douglas-Scott, Sixth Duke of Buccleuch**. Born in 1831, he succeeded to the dukedom on the death of his father in 1884, having been known as the Earl of Dalkeith before then. An Etonian, he entered politics as sons of peers were wont to do, and was Conservative MP for Midlothian from 1853 to 1868, and again from 1874 to 1880, when he was defeated by Gladstone after his famous Midlothian campaign. Thereafter, he had more time to devote to his love of cricket.

He married Lady Louisa Hamilton, and thus became brother-in-law to four Presidents, uncle to two more, great-uncle to another and eventually father to yet another. His eldest son, Lord Eskdale, played cricket for MCC from 1881, when he was twenty years old, but died at the age of 25 and thus never inherited the title. His second son became President of MCC in 1913, and a third son, Lord George Scott, scored a century for Oxford in the University match of 1887, and top scored for Oxford, even if he only made 32, in the drawn match in his father's Presidential year. The Duke was not a particularly good cricketer himself, but certainly instilled a love for the game into his sons, and in later years became a trustee of MCC. Before he died in 1914, he presented several eighteenth-century bats to MCC, which are still in the Club's collection.

The Duke handed over to a man who was educated neither at Eton nor Harrow. **SIR HENRY JAMES** was at school at Cheltenham, which can boast a first-class ground as its main cricket square, which neither of the other two schools can do. Young Henry captained his school side in 1844 and 1845, having been born in 1828. So he was already 60 when he took on the job, and was only the sixth man of that age to have become President in the recorded history of the Club. Even up to the Great War there were only four more Presidents in their sixties, but since then the average age has risen appreciably. The first 70-year-old came in 1924, and no one in the 1960s was under 60 when they became President. The appointment of Doug Insole for 2006/07 marked the first time in the Club's history that three successive Presidents have been over 70, and only two men have been made President before their 50th birthdays since World War II – Prince Philip and Lord Cobham. The Club is ageing rapidly if the President is meant to be a symbol of MCC.

Sir Henry was a lawyer and a politician. In late Victorian times MCC seemed to go for politicians as President, perhaps because the Club wished to flaunt its influence by picking highly placed men as their figurehead. Sir Henry was elected firstly in 1868 as Liberal MP for Taunton. He was already just short of his 40th birthday, having established a thriving law practice, and in 1873, after only five years at Westminster, he was appointed Solicitor-General, gained his knighthood and within a few months was promoted to Attorney-General. He lost his job when Disraeli gained office, but when Gladstone swept back into power in 1880, thanks in part to his unseating the Duke of Buccleuch, James was appointed Attorney-General again. Despite being educated at Cheltenham, and on being ennobled taking the title of Baron James of Hereford, Sir Henry was a Surrey man as far as his cricket devotions were concerned, being virtually a lifelong member of the County Club. At least he proves that E. W. Swanton was wrong when he remarked to Tony Lewis that he was the 'first President from west of Watford'.

The 1890 Annual General Meeting was the first one to be held in the new Pavilion, designed by Thomas Verity and built within a year. The meeting congratulated itself on the erection of 'a building worthy of the club' and paid for it in the usual way – by borrowing a bit more from William Nicholson on favourable terms. The new President was another man with a triple-barrelled surname, **SIR GILBERT HENRY HEATHCOTE-DRUMMOND-WILLOUGHBY**, otherwise known as Lord Willoughby de Eresby, and subsequently, from 1892, Earl of Ancaster. Clearly Sir Henry James had been unable to resist the pull of Eton and Harrow, for Lord Willoughby was a Harrovian, originally known as plain Gilbert Heathcote. He was not without all the right connections however: he was the great-grandson of Sir Peter Burrell (Lord Gwydyr), one of the early shapers of MCC and the son-in-law of Lord Strathavon, the very first President for whom we have a definite record. After Harrow, Heathcote went up to Trinity College, Cambridge but never got anywhere near a cricket Blue. From 1852, when he was only 21, he was MP for Boston in Lincolnshire, and from 1856 was elected by the constituents of Rutland, a seat he held until 1867, when he inherited the title of Lord Aveland. His time in the House of Lords was busy if not particularly onerous. For two days short of thirty years, from 24 January 1871 until 22 January 1901 (on the death of Queen Victoria) he was Deputy Lord Great Chamberlain, and while in office he firstly enlarged his name to Heathcote-Drummond-Willoughby, in 1872, and then was appointed Privy Counsellor in 1880. He succeeded to the title of Baron Willoughby de Eresby in 1888 and was created Earl of Ancaster in 1892. The confusion in his names was carried on by his children, one of whom became Earl of Ancaster in due course, two of whom used the full three surnames, one just called herself Heathcote-Drummond and the youngest son settled for plain Willoughby. He, like the sons of Eddy Chandos Leigh, was killed early in the Great War, but by then his father had died, aged 80, on Christmas Eve 1910.

Lord Willoughby's chosen successor was, finally, a cricketer of real note. **VYELL EDWARD WALKER**, known as Teddy, was born on 20 April 1837 and was one of the Walkers of Southgate, a famous family if not quite so ermine-soaked as most of his predecessors. There were seven Walker brothers, all Harrow educated, of whom John, the eldest, Teddy, Isaac and Russell were the best cricketers. In the custom of the day, they were invariably known by their initials – V.E., I.D. and R.D. Only John got away with being known by his first name. Probably the best cricketer was I.D., who died at the comparatively young age of 54 in 1898. As *Wisden* noted in its special article on I.D., 'it is perhaps a fair criticism to say that V.E. was the finest all-round player, and I.D. the best bat.' Most of the brothers involved themselves in Middlesex cricket, (apart from John, who played for Surrey before Middlesex came into being) and were instrumental in the formation of the County Club. V.E. was captain of Middlesex from 1864 until 1872 and was treasurer from 1897 until he died in 1906. He was President of the Club in 1869, while also captain (a feat that Lord Harris also pulled off at Kent), and again from 1898 until his death. Without him, Middlesex could not have prospered in the way they did. The Walker Trust ground at Southgate, founded by John Walker in 1859, is still being used by Middlesex and was the scene of a stand of 372 for the first wicket between Mike Gatting and Justin Langer in 1998, against Essex.

As a cricketer, he achieved a feat that has only once been equalled. In 1859 he took all ten wickets in an innings for England against Surrey at the Oval, and also scored 108. Twenty-seven years later W. G. Grace equalled Walker's effort, for MCC against Oxford University, by taking all ten wickets and scoring a hundred, but since 1886 no one, not Sobers, Miller, Botham or Flintoff, has matched these extraordinary efforts. That century was, incidentally, the only one that Walker ever scored in first-class cricket, but in 1865 he again took all ten wickets with his underarm slows, for Middlesex against Lancashire. For a few seasons Walker was considered the best all-rounder in the world, but when W.G. came along he had to forfeit his pre-eminence.

For the first time in sixty years, MCC in 1892 was led by a second successive commoner, as Walker handed over to **WILLIAM DENISON**, another man, like Lord Wenlock, whose enthusiasm for the game outstripped his ability. Denison was a distant cousin of his namesake Lord Londesborough, who had been President in 1876, and he had uncles who were powerful and distinguished men – a Bishop of Salisbury, a speaker of the House of Commons and an archdeacon who instigated Harvest Festival services. Denison was born in Woolwich in 1843, but spent much of his childhood in Australia. His father was Governor of Tasmania from 1846 to 1854 and of New South Wales from 1854 to 1861, and was very much involved in the establishment and development of what is now the Sydney Cricket Ground. By this time, however, young William had been sent to Eton and thus did not accompany his father to Madras when he was appointed Governor General there in 1861. After Eton, Denison joined the Army, played a great deal of cricket for the Royal Artillery and retired in 1878 with the rank of captain. By the time he left the Army he had already been MP for Nottingham for four years, so one must assume either his Army duties or his parliamentary duties were not particularly taxing. He never got very far either soldiering or as a parliamentarian, so one must assume that his heart was not really in it.

His cricketing connections were with Nottinghamshire, and in 1888 he was President of the County Club. His service with MCC began in earnest in 1882 when he joined the Committee, and he remained a committee man for the better part of the next twenty years. In 1891, the year before his Presidency of MCC, he became President of the Cricketers' Fund Friendly Society, in succession to Lord Harris who had gone to govern Bombay. This was a charity in which Teddy Walker was very closely involved, and the connection between the two men seems to have been through their work for the Cricketers' Fund.

Denison handed over to **WILLIAM HENEAGE LEGGE, SIXTH EARL OF DARTMOUTH**. Dartmouth was another Eton man, but eight years younger than Denison. His family connections with MCC were strong and would get stronger with the generations. He was the son-in-law of the Earl of Leicester, who had been President in 1848 and his uncle on his mother's side was the Earl of Aylesford, who as Lord Guernsey had been President in 1850. Lord Dartmouth was, like Denison before him, keen but no more than average as a cricketer, failing to make the XIs at either Eton or Oxford. He played a great deal of cricket for MCC, I Zingari and the Lords and Commons, and claimed to have represented Shropshire, Staffordshire, Warwickshire and Cheshire in the early days of these county clubs' existence. As he described it in an early edition of the *Cricketer* magazine, 'from the finish of the Eton and Harrow match until the end of the season, we used to wander from house to house playing in cricket weeks.' He was MP for West Kent and then for Lewisham from 1878, when he was 27 years old, until he inherited the earldom in 1891. In 1888 he was President of Kent C.C.C. and for forty years until his death aged 84 in 1936, he was President of Staffordshire C.C.C. He only played one first-class match, for MCC against Hampshire, but scored 5 not out and 25 not out, so retired with a batting average of infinity.

The nephew of Lord Guernsey nominated the Earl of Jersey as his successor for 1894, keeping the Channel Islands connection strong. Lord Jersey, or **VICTOR ALBERT GEORGE CHILD-VILLIERS** to give him his full baptismal name, was born in March 1845 and was better known as a runner than as a cricketer. He was another Eton and Oxford man, but like many other Presidents before him, failed to catch the selectors' eye at either place. As a long distance runner, however, he was pretty good. In the Varsity match of 1865 he came second in the mile to R. E. Webster, who in years to come would be ennobled as Lord Alverstone and take on the MCC Presidency in 1903. We cannot be certain, but that is probably the only important mile race in history in which the first two places were taken by future Presidents of MCC. In the two-mile event, which Webster won again, Lord Jersey could only come fourth.

Lord Jersey succeeded to the title when he was only fourteen years old, so he never had a spell as an MP. He did, however, take an active role in the Lords, and was Paymaster-General briefly between 1889 and 1890. He was then appointed to be Governor General of New South Wales, following in the footsteps of Denison's father thirty years on, and he returned just in time to take on the MCC Presidency.

Jersey handed over to one of the great men of Victorian cricket, **George Robert Canning, the Fourth Baron Harris.** Lord Harris, born in Trinidad in 1851, was the first Test cricketer to become President of MCC, seventeen years after his Test debut. Harris was everything in Victorian cricket, except the greatest cricketer of his age. He was very good indeed, but everybody else had to admit second best to W. G. Grace. His enthusiasm for cricket was as unbounded as his energy. In 1875, at the age of 24, he was President, secretary and captain of Kent County Cricket Club, and he retained the captaincy and the secretaryship for another four years. Oh, and he joined the MCC Committee for the first time in 1875 as well. As *Wisden* said of his efforts in 1875, 'Lord Harris, as President, Hon. Secretary, Captain of the County Team, greatest aggregate and highest average scorer for the county, must have been head and hands full of Kent in 1875.' 'It would be difficult, if not impossible, to over-estimate the amount of good his lordship has done for Kent cricket', says his own *History of Kent CCC,* but, if that is a biased opinion, *Scores and Biographies* agrees. 'No cricketer, perhaps, ever did more for a county, if his Lordship's merits and performances as a batsman are considered in conjunction with his ability as a general manager of the Kent XI.' He was also a fast round-arm bowler of mixed success (he did take W.G.'s wicket at Canterbury in 1876, but only after the doctor had scored 341) and a brilliant fielder, at point or just backward of square.

It was not only Kent that owed its life's blood to Lord Harris. He captained (and virtually selected) the XI for the first Test Match played in England, at the Oval in 1880, and, but for his efforts, the match might never have happened. He was also a staunch defender of the Laws of Cricket. 'Rules are made to be broken, Laws are made to be kept' was his motto, and in 1885, for instance, he cancelled Kent's return match with Lancashire because he felt that two of Lancashire's bowlers were chuckers. But although he was an autocrat, he did a very great deal for the players who turned out for him, and they were devoted to His Lordship.

He also dabbled in politics and stepped rather more deeply into colonial waters. From 1885 he was appointed Under-Secretary of State for India, and the next year he became Under-Secretary of State for War. In 1890 he was appointed Governor of Bombay, breaking a family tradition, for his great-grandfather, great-uncle and father had all been governors of Madras. In his five years in India, he built his own cricket ground at Ganeshkind, near what is now Pune, and he attracted the same loyalty from his Indian cricketers as he had from his Kent and England XIs. 'He was our guru' was the opinion of Framji Patel, one of his Bombay cricketers. It was at Ganeshkind that he played several games with Lord Wenlock, then Governor of Madras. He played cricket at club level until quite late in life, but it was MCC where his heart truly lay. 'My whole life has pivoted on Lord's,' Lord Harris once said. He died in 1932, aged 81.

Lord Harris was bound to be a hard act to follow, especially as His Lordship remained on the MCC Committee, checking up on every little detail within Lord's as though it were his own fiefdom. He passed the buck to **SIDNEY HERBERT, FOURTEENTH EARL OF PEMBROKE** and Eleventh Earl of Montgomery, who was another man to have married into the Hamilton family. His wife was Lady Beatrix Lambton, daughter of the Earl of Durham and Lady Beatrix Hamilton, who was sister and sister-in-law to half a dozen Presidents. Lord Pembroke's family was also related by marriage to Henry Howard's family, taking the Presidential connections back sixty years, and his successor was his cousin-in-law.

Apart from the fact that he married into a clan that based its life around cricket, there is no evidence that Sidney Herbert himself took much of an active role in the game. He was not a cricketer at Eton, did not gain a Blue at Oxford, and his obituary in *Wisden* merely records the fact that he died in Naples. His claim to the Presidency was based on his political standing rather than on his cricketing skills. Herbert was the second son of the Twelfth Earl, so had no great expectations. His family ensured he was elected as a Liberal Unionist MP for Wilton in Wiltshire in 1877, when he was 24, but he then managed to lose his seat in the 1885 general election. This would not be unusual were it not for the fact that Wilton was the seat of the Earls of Pembroke, and his family virtually owned political opinion in Wiltshire. He finally struggled back into the Commons as MP for Croydon in 1886, and switched his allegiance to the Conservatives. He remained as MP for Croydon until he inherited his brother's title in 1895, the year before he took on the MCC Presidency. He never really rose very high in the political world, being appointed a junior whip and to a junior Treasury post. He was probably best known at the time as being the handsomest MP of his generation (this was before women were allowed to vote or become members of Parliament, so we can assume it was a male opinion being voiced), but good looks never made much of a difference in politics. If you have a good head of hair, you will get elected. Lose your hair and the public lose confidence: it is an immutable law of politics. Herbert had a good head of hair.

Perhaps the most exciting event of Pembroke's year was the visit of the Australians under Harry Trott. The first day of the Lord's Test attracted a crowd of about 30,000, well above normal capacity, and as *The Times* reported next day, 'Lord's has scarcely ever been the scene of so much noisiness and rowdyism.' Lord Harris, displaying the sense of his own importance that an ex-President is allowed, wrote later that 'it was a dreadful sight for those who love the strictness of first-class cricket played at Lord's.' The Committee were charged with ensuring that there could never be a 'repetition of a scene so deplorable'. And, of course, there never has been.

Pembroke's successor was the **EARL OF LICHFIELD**, a second-generation Hamilton through his mother, Lady Harriet Hamilton. The Earl of Pembroke was his cousin's husband. Lichfield, a Harrovian, did manage to make the first XI during his time there, being then known as Viscount Anson, but failed to gain a Blue during his time at Trinity College, Cambridge, where he was a contemporary of several Lytteltons and Ivo Bligh, among others. He, like his two predecessors, was elected to MCC in 1871 (when he was only fifteen) and played an active role in the Club's affairs for much of his life.

The main business of his Presidential year was a Special General Meeting on 28 February 1878, when a successor to Henry Perkins, the Secretary retiring after 22 years in the post, was chosen. The meeting was held in the Queen's Hall, Langham Place and, as *Wisden* reported, 'fully 1,500 members were present'. It hardly seems a sensible way to choose an applicant for a job, especially one as important as this, but the meeting was only really necessary because there was no unanimous choice. Or, at least, the Committee had a unanimous recommendation: Mr F. E. Lacey of Cambridge University (where he played alongside Lord Hawke (1914) and Sir Kynaston Studd (1930)) and Hampshire. The problem was that one of the unsuccessful candidates, a Mr J. S. Russell, refused to accept the Committee's decision. He therefore provoked the meeting, which attracted members from far and wide – 1,500 attending out of a total membership of 4,287 at the end of Lichfield's year is a huge turnout and a sign of the importance of the issue. In the end, it was all a bit of a damp squib. Mr Russell withdrew his objection

Above: 1912, Victor
Cavendish, Ninth Duke of
Devonshire

Above right: 1911, William
Grenfell, First Baron
Desborough

Right: 1913, John Montagu-
Douglas-Scott, Earl of
Dalkeith

Above: 1914–18,
Martin Bladen, Seventh
Baron Hawke

Left: Lord Hawke in
old age

1937, Col. The Hon. John J. Astor. President in the 150th year of the Club's existence.

Above: 1919, Henry William, First Baron Forster of Lepe

Below: 1923, James William Lowther, First Viscount Ullswater

Above: 1922, Frederick Thesiger, First Viscount Chelmsford

Below: 1934, Sir Rowland Baring, Second Earl of Cromer

1935, John Lyttelton, Ninth Viscount Cobham

1938, Rt. Hon. Stanley, First Earl Baldwin of Bewdley

1939–45, Stanley
Christopherson

1946, General Sir
Ronald Adam Bt.

Above: 1947, Rt. Hon. Wykeham, Second Baron Cornwallis

Below: 1949, HRH Prince Philip, Duke of Edinburgh

Above: 1948, Alexander Hore-Ruthven, First Earl of Gowrie, V.C.

Below: 1950, Sir Pelham Warner

1951, William Findlay

Below right: 1953, Harry
Primrose, Sixth Earl of
Rosebery

Below: 1952, Henry Somerset,
Tenth Duke of Beaufort

before the meeting began, and the recommendation that Francis Lacey get the job was passed *nem. con.* The Committee took the opportunity to rewrite the rules so that they alone had the right to hire and fire the Secretary, and Lichfield's tact as chairman was praised in all quarters.

The Earl of Lichfield also earned his own little niche in the Club's history by becoming the only President to be shot dead. This was not a crime of passion by an outraged husband, mistress or secretarial candidate, but a tragic accident on the moors near his seat at Shugborough Hall. He died in July 1918, just before the end of the Great War, at the age of 62.

His successor was his contemporary at Trinity College, Cambridge: ALFRED LYTTELTON; an Etonian took over from a Harrovian again. Alfred's elder brother had already been President, and he was thus the second Lyttelton and the second Test player, after Lord Harris, to be President. Alfred was the youngest of twelve children, eight of whom were boys, of the Fourth Baron Lyttelton, so never had any hope of inheriting the title. His sporting skills were such that he became the only double international ever to take on the Presidency: he earned one cap at football, when he played for England against Scotland at Kennington Oval in March 1877, and scored England's only goal in a 3-1 defeat. His brother Edward also won a football cap in the same fixture one year later. As a cricketer, Alfred is remembered as a fine wicketkeeper and the man who shed his gloves and took four Australian wickets for 19 runs in a Test bowling underarm lobs, as the tenth bowler tried as Australia passed 500 for the first time in a Test. That was at Kennington Oval, too, making Lyttelton pretty certainly the only man to score an international goal and take a Test wicket on the same ground anywhere in the world. He was also, for good measure, a wonderful rackets player and amateur champion at real tennis from 1882 to 1895.

Apart from being a friend of his predecessor from university days, Lyttelton, a lawyer, had also been legal private secretary, or 'Devil', to the then Attorney-General, Sir Henry James (1889), in the mid-1880s. In 1895 he entered Parliament as a Liberal Unionist MP for Warwick and Leamington, and after the Boer War was sent out to South Africa to chair the Transvaal Concessions Commission, charged with restructuring the country. By the end of his political career he had served as Colonial Secretary and was a firm supporter of women's suffrage. He died quite suddenly in 1913, having been hit in the stomach by a cricket ball, which created an abscess. His death at the age of only 56 was widely mourned. *Vanity Fair* had described him in 1884 as 'an excellent young man of good manners and of good report', and Lord Curzon wrote that 'no boyish hero was ever quite such a hero.'

Even the Prime Minister, Herbert Asquith, was moved to say in the House of Commons that Alfred Lyttelton 'came nearest to the mould and ideal of manhood which every English father would like to see his son aspire to'. Lord Darnley, in his appreciation in *Wisden*, wrote of a man who had a 'tall, vigorous, muscular athletic grace characteristic of every movement, the merriest eye, the most engaging smile that ever gladdened the heart of a friend – were there ever so many brilliant and attractive qualities blended in one youthful person?'

The Lytteltons raised an XI of family members in 1867 when Alfred, the youngest player, was just ten years old. Father, two uncles and eight sons beat the might of Bromsgrove School, but they were not to be the only Presidential family who could raise a cricket team on their own. Stanley Christopherson, who held office for longer than any other President throughout the Second World War, was one of ten brothers who, with their father, played plenty of matches against local sides in Kent in the 1880s.

Lyttelton handed over to another Cambridge man, and another lawyer, but one of an earlier generation. **Sir Archibald Levin Smith** – Lord Justice Smith to give him his official title – was born in 1836, making him the last President born before Victoria came to the throne. Smith had been a member of MCC since 1861 and played occasionally for them in matches in the sixties and seventies. He also played for Gentlemen of Sussex quite regularly and in 1862 scored 95 against Midland Counties Diamonds at Brighton. *Scores and Biographies* described his bowling as 'fast underhand with a curious "windmill" delivery'. He was never, however, selected for the full Sussex County XI.

He was up at Cambridge from 1857 to 1859 but concentrated at that time on rowing. He won his Blue in all three years, with mixed success. In 1859 the Cambridge boat sank, and Smith was the only member of the eight who could not swim. He was saved from drowning by an umpire, who threw him a lifebuoy. His law career was rather more successful than his rowing one: in 1883 he was appointed a High Court judge, and in 1892 became a Lord Justice of Appeal, the rank he held during his Presidential year. The following year he was appointed Master of the Rolls, in succession to Lord Alverstone, who would be President of MCC in 1903. His interest in cricket was shown by his contribution of a chapter to the book *The Walkers of Southgate*, about Teddy Walker (1891) and his family. His chapter 'Reminiscences, by an Old Friend of the Walkers' was not necessarily the stuff from which best-sellers are made, but the book stands the test of time. It was advertised on line in 2006 by an American bookseller who wanted $150 for a good copy, but who also noted that 'it might as well be in Sanskrit for all it means to me.'

Archibald Smith's death in 1901 echoed his efforts in the Boat Race. On a family fishing trip on the River Spey, his wife was swept away and drowned, while Smith, still a non-swimmer, was unable to help. He died eight weeks later, probably of a broken heart.

Sir Archibald's nomination as President for 1900 was one of the great names of English cricket, the man for whom the Ashes were made, the **Hon. Ivo Francis Walter Bligh**. An indirect descendant of General 'Skirmish' Bligh of the early years of the Marylebone Club and nephew of E. V. Bligh who won a cricket Blue for Oxford in 1850, 'Nellie' Bligh was born in 1859, making him just 41 years old when he took on the Presidency. He was educated at Eton and Cambridge, at both of which establishments he was captain of cricket and an outstanding competitor at rackets and tennis. Cricket was his first love, and at 6ft 3in he was an imposing sight at the crease when he drove with the full swing of the bat. He took a team to Australia in 1882/83 to win back the Ashes, and did so. At the same time he won the hand in marriage of the Australian lady who presented him with the tiny but now priceless Ashes urn. This urn, given to MCC by his widow when Bligh died in 1927, is now the single most famous trophy in cricket and, indeed, perhaps the most famous trophy in British sport, which is why the name of Ivo Bligh will always be remembered. However, the Ashes urn is not really a trophy. It is just a symbol of the contests between England and Australia. The actual trophy is the modern Waterford glass urn, several times the size of the original on which it is modelled.

Seventeen years after his triumphant Australian tour he was made President of MCC. In the October of his Presidential year, his elder brother died so by the time he stepped down he was the Eighth Lord Darnley. His was a bad year for deaths in high places, for just three months after his brother's death, Queen Victoria, never much of a cricket follower, although she did once enquire after WG's health, also died, and her son, once patron of MCC, ascended the throne as Edward VII.

Unlike many of his immediate predecessors, Bligh never felt a burning urge to go into high politics, preferring the life of a stockbroker and wine importer, as well as that of country gentleman on his estate at Cobham Hall, near Gravesend in Kent. His connection with Kent cricket was as strong as with Lord's, and he was President of the County Club in 1892 and 1902. His health was never the strongest, but he lived until he was 68, and when he died he was mourned as 'one of the most genial and kind-hearted of men'.

Bligh handed over the reins of the Club to a man who had been his near contemporary at Eton, the Fourth Earl Howe. RICHARD GEORGE PENN CURZON-HOWE was born on 28 April 1861, and thus was a few days past his fortieth birthday when he took over at Lord's. The Annual General Meeting at which his succession was announced was taken up largely with a debate about proposed changes to the LBW rule. The debate was led on one side by Alfred Lyttelton, who felt that batsmen were scoring too many runs – the sort of viewpoint that a wicketkeeper and occasional bowler would take – and that limits must be imposed on their freedom to score. In this debate, he was up against the 1892 President, William Denison, whose main argument seemed to be that the Law should not be changed because there were objections to it. In the end, he had his way, but only just. The proposal for change, to a law which would have read: 'If with any part of his person (except the hand) which is between wicket and wicket he intercept a ball which would hit his wicket – Leg Before Wicket', was carried by 259 votes to 188, but, as it needed a two-thirds majority, it fell short by about 40 votes and was thus not put into effect. The debate raged on for years, of course. It still rages.

Lord Howe inherited the title in the year before he took over at Lord's, so he was somewhat in limbo, no longer able to be a Member of Parliament, which he had been for fifteen years, and still looking for a proper job. His interest in cricket was genuine, dating back to the time two decades earlier when he had been in the XI at Eton, and he had been President of Leicestershire C.C.C. in 1886, in the days before that county held first-class status. He had the family qualifications for MCC also. His father's half-sister married James, Marquess of Hamilton (1874) to link his family to the Abercorn clan, which he further bonded with by marrying the daughter of the Duke of Marlborough and Lady Albertha Hamilton. He eventually got himself a full time job, becoming Lord Chamberlain to Queen Alexandra from 1903 to 1925. He died in 1929.

Lord Howe handed over to a man who was a lawyer, a Test cricketer and an active participant in the great LBW debate of 1901 on the side of the status quo. What's more, he was not educated at either Eton or Harrow. **ALLAN GIBSON STEEL** was a Marlborough man, where he excelled at cricket. According to one of his teachers there, 'Steel was never a better bowler than during his last year at school.' In the Cambridge XI of 1878, generally reckoned to have been the best university side to that time, he was seen as the star. In that season, his freshman year, Cambridge won all their matches and beat Oxford by an innings, and Steel topped their batting and bowling averages. He also topped the national bowling averages with 164 wickets at 9 runs apiece. He hardly needed any change in the LBW law to help him take wickets. He was considered the natural successor to V. E. Walker as the second best all-rounder in England after W.G. However, as batsmen got used to his bowling, slow leg-breaks on a perfect length, it became less effective, and in later years he changed his mind about the LBW law, to become a leading proponent for change. However penetrative his bowling may have been, his chapter on 'Bowling' in the *Cricket* volume of the Badminton library was immediately regarded as a masterpiece when it was first published, and is still referred to as a classic piece of cricket writing, lucid and instructional.

He was no Adonis in the Lyttelton mould, being rather short and a little short-sighted, but he was a very effective sportsman, playing a number of different sports extremely well. He played thirteen times for England at cricket, captaining his country in the 1886 series against Australia, but by that time he was a batsman rather than a bowler.

A Lancashire man, he trained as a barrister and for many years had a good practice based in Liverpool. From 1904 until his death ten years later, at the age of only 55, he was Recorder of Oldham. As his great friend Bob Lyttelton (yet another Lyttelton brother) noted in his tribute in *Wisden* after Steel's death, he 'was always cheery and he never made an enemy. Nothing made him lose his temper and many a young cricketer was helped by him.'

Steel handed over in 1903 to another lawyer, and another man who went to neither Eton nor Harrow, and another man whose sporting credentials were impeccable. **RICHARD EVERARD WEBSTER, FIRST VISCOUNT ALVERSTONE** had been born on 22 December 1842, so was 60 when he took office. He had been educated at Charterhouse, a school which would provide more Presidents in future years, and Trinity College, Cambridge, Alma Mater of most of the Lytteltons, the Earl of Lichfield, Ivo Bligh, Lord Willoughby de Eresby and several others. He played cricket for Charterhouse ('is a good long field'), but did not gain a Blue at Cambridge, preferring, as we have seen, to run for Cambridge and beat all comers at one and two miles. Nevertheless, he maintained his own cricket ground in later years at his home, Winterfold, near Cranleigh in Surrey.

Off the games field, he led an amazingly busy life. In 1868 he qualified as a barrister and within ten years was appointed Q.C. In 1885 he was elected for the first time to the House of Commons as Conservative MP for Launceston, in Cornwall, and was immediately appointed Attorney-General. The next year the Conservatives were out of office and Webster switched constituencies, to the Isle of Wight, a seat he held until appointed to the House of Lords in 1900 as Lord Chief Justice, a title he held when he was President of MCC. He was also Lord Chief Justice when he co-edited *Surrey Cricket* with Charles Alcock, one of the great early books on English cricket. Webster was a Surrey man right through, but like that other Charterhouse boy, Peter May the best part of a century later, he made it to the top at the rival headquarters in St John's Wood. He was actually President of Surrey and MCC at the same time, a double that has been pulled off by county Presidents before and since, but not often by a Surrey man. To add to his duties, he was the first President of the Amateur Football Alliance between 1907 and his death in 1915, and from 1909 was a trustee of MCC. He also served on some odd legal bodies, representing Britain in the international arbitrations on the Bering Sea and Venezuela, and he was President of the 1903 international court appointed to decide the boundaries of Alaska. No doubt several Presidents have in their time arbitrated on the boundaries of cricket fields around the world, but no MCC man apart from Lord Alverstone has decided on the boundaries of a place as big as Alaska.

The 1904 season was notable for the return of the first MCC team ever sent abroad to play Test matches, with the Ashes. The side, under Pelham Warner, had been sent under the auspices of MCC somewhat experimentally, and there was still opposition within the Club to the idea that they should sponsor England's tours abroad. However, the whole thing worked so well that for the better part of the twentieth century all Test playing tours were MCC tours. Lord Alverstone had to report a loss on the tour of about £1,500 to the Annual General Meeting, but this did not prevent the membership approving the accounts 'after a few queries had been answered', according to *Wisden.*

After the meeting at the Anniversary Dinner, Lord Alverstone nominated the Marquess of Granby as his successor. **HENRY JOHN BRINSLEY MANNERS**, heir to the duchy of Rutland, was born on 16 April 1852 and was yet another lover of cricket who was 'not in the eleven either at Eton or Cambridge' as *Wisden* put it. If the truth is told, he was not really someone who excelled at anything very much. In his public life, his career was overshadowed by that of his father, the Seventh Duke of Rutland, who as Lord John Manners was a key political figure in the middle of the nineteenth century, a prominent member of the cabinets of Lord Derby and subsequently holding high office for most of the forty years from the early 1850s. He was also a noted writer and a pillar of the Victorian establishment, which made him a very hard act to follow. It seems Henry did not really try to live up to his father's brilliance, contenting himself with the Lord Lieutenancy of Leicestershire for the first 25 years of the new century, in succession to Earl Howe (1901), and throwing himself into the London social scene, of which his wife was a leading figure. His family seat at Belvoir Castle was a principal concern of his, and he spent a great deal of his time developing and improving the castle and its grounds, which his family had owned since the time of Henry VIII. His father was still alive, aged 86, during Granby's Presidential year, and he did not inherit the title until two years later.

Granby handed over to **CHARLES GREEN**, although he did this in spirit rather than in person, as he had to leave after the Annual General Meeting of 1905 and did not attend the dinner. Green was an entirely different type of man: middle class, comfortably off rather than landed gentry, and a fine cricketer who was the driving force behind the development of one of the less fashionable county clubs, Essex. Green, an Uppingham and Cambridge man, had been born in 1846, and won his Blue at Cambridge four years in succession, from 1865 to 1868. He was described as 'one of the most brilliant batsmen of his day', but had actually first won his Blue for his fast round-arm bowling. He batted at number ten in 1865, and took four wickets opening the bowling in Oxford's second innings, but Cambridge still lost. By 1866, he had moved up to number seven, and bowled first change. Oxford won again. In 1867, he batted at number nine in the first innings, but was promoted up the order in the second innings as Cambridge successfully chased victory, by five wickets. He only bowled eight balls (two overs) in the match. In his final year, he captained Cambridge and hit 44 and 59 batting at number six, and became the first man ever to total 100 runs in the Varsity match. He did not bowl at all, Cambridge won easily and his cricket destiny was set.

Green played all of his cricket before Essex was considered first class, and he played mainly for Middlesex and Sussex. Despite being described as one of the most brilliant batsmen of his day, it must have been a short day, because he never scored a first-class hundred. His finest hour as a batsman was probably in the 1871 Gentlemen v. Players match at the Oval, when the Gentlemen were set 144 to win in 105 minutes. Green hit 57 not out to win the match with three minutes to spare, the final 27 runs coming in seven hits.

He joined Essex in 1882, some years after first coming on to the MCC Committee, and was instrumental in helping move the head-quarters of the infant club from Brentwood – too far from London – to Leyton, to a ground owned by the Lyttelton family. He was appointed captain in 1883 and held the position for five seasons. A few years after he retired as a player, in 1895, Essex were accepted as a first-class county, and by 1897 the club was thriving, with over 1,500 members and third place in the Championship, its highest position until 1978, when they came second. Green was chairman of the club throughout this time, giving up the post in 1912 under rather acrimonious circumstances. As *Wisden* reported it, 'The financial position being very unfavourable a special meeting was called in December at which it was unanimously decided to go on with the club.' Green told the meeting that he was resigning from the chairmanship of the club, saying he was 'bitterly disappointed at the lack of support accorded to the club', and that 'frankly speaking, he was tired of the whole thing'. However, despite washing his hands of the management of the club, he gave Essex £400, which was enough to cover all their debts and enable them to begin 1913 unencumbered. Green was rewarded with the Presidency in 1913, and a year in which the club broke even off the field despite less promising results on it.

To earn the money he was able to give to Essex, he was a partner in the family firm of F. Green and Co., and also a director of the Orient Steamship Company. It was said that he was even keener on hunting than on cricket, and that he was Master of the Essex Hunt and was out with them at least four days a week during the season for many years. When he died, towards the end of the Great War, he left a cup and a bat in his will to MCC. He wrote,

> to the Marylebone Cricket Club I bequeathe the large Gold Cup which was presented to me by the County of Essex on behalf of the County Cricket Club and also the bat which was presented to me by the MCC after the University match of 1868. I should like both the cup and the bat to be placed in the Pavilion, at Lord's, where I have so very many

happy associations, and as a small acknowledgement of the many kindnesses I have received during the year 1905 when I had the honour of being
President of the Club.

Many happy associations and many kindnesses are still sensations
enjoyed by Presidents a century later. Some things at Marylebone (some
would say most things at Marylebone) never change.

By the time that the Golden Age of cricket and the splendours of the
Edwardian Age were in full bloom, the Marylebone Cricket Club
was the true hub of world cricket. Only in Australia and to a lesser
extent South Africa was the game being played on a full time basis, and
England's cricketers were the best in the world (including in their
number, as they did, such Englishmen as Ranjitsinhji). MCC ruled
world cricket and they knew they did. It was a glorious time to be
English and a cricket lover, and with enough money to cover the £2 a
year's cricket at Lord's cost.

The connection between the rulers of cricket and the rulers of Britain
was strong. In 1906, MCC had **WALTER HUME LONG**, subsequently
Lord Long of Wraxhall, as their President. Walter Hume Long, born
on 13 July 1854, was another Harrow man, and he played for Harrow
against Eton at Lord's in the 1873 match. He made 36 and 17, as Harrow
won by five wickets. He was known as a 'good, free hitting batsman' as
his *Wisden* obituary recorded, and in later life also played for Devon and
Wiltshire. He completed his education at Christ Church, Oxford but
did not win a Blue.

His family had a long history of government. Both his father and his
maternal grandfather were members of Parliament, and Long himself
was first elected as Conservative member for North Wiltshire in 1885,
but in a parliamentary career of 40 years and 169 days (almost as long as
Billy Hart Dyke's stint at Westminster), he represented seven different
constituencies, ranging geographically from Wiltshire to Liverpool,

from London to Bristol, and on to Dublin. His career in Parliament was unspectacular but generally successful, as he became a lesser pillar of successive cabinets. In 1895 he was appointed President of the Board of Agriculture, a post he held until 1900, when he was made President of the Board of Local Government for another five years. In 1905, he was appointed to his highest post, Chief Secretary for Ireland, but the government were defeated shortly thereafter and he was out of office for the next ten years. He was still influential and well connected in all the right places, and just the sort of man MCC needed as their President. In fact, when Balfour retired as leader of the Conservatives in 1911, Long's name was put forward as a possible successor, but he was not chosen. In 1915, in the wartime coalition government, he returned as Local Government man once again, and in 1916 was given the Colonial Office. In 1919, after the war had ended, he was given his one military appointment as First Lord of the Admiralty, but in 1921, aged 66, he resigned and was ennobled as Baron Long of Wraxall. His eldest son, heir and namesake, Brigadier General Walter Long, was by this time dead, having been killed in Greece in 1917, one of the higher ranked casualties of the Great War. Baron Long died in 1924.

Long appointed in his place another political heavyweight, a political opponent but a cricketing ally. **ROBERT THRESHIE REID**, universally known as Bob, was in 1907 the Liberal Lord Chancellor, and on being given the job in 1905 had been created the First Baron Loreburn. Reid, educated at Cheltenham and Balliol College, Oxford, was a great sportsman in his younger days. Born in 1846, in Corfu, one of the handful of Presidents born outside Britain, he was in the Cheltenham College XI from 1862 for three summers. At Oxford he gained his cricket Blue in three years, 1866 to 1868, playing against Charles Green each year. Strictly speaking, he only played two and a half games, because for the final innings of his third game he was absent, an absence that was not explained in any of the reports of the match. He was a wicketkeeper, and a very good one at amateur level, but after university he found little time to play serious cricket, apart from a few games for Kent, whom he probably represented on the basis of it being the county closest to his place of birth. He had also, at Oxford, won his Blue for rackets and was known as a very fine sprinter in those early days of amateur athletics.

He became a barrister, and was called to the Bar in 1882. Two years earlier he had been elected Liberal Member for Hereford, but he lost the seat in 1885. In 1886 he was back again at Westminster, representing Dumfriess-shire, and in 1894 gained his first senior office as Solicitor-General. This involved him in the Venezuela boundary dispute as a colleague of Lord Alverstone (1903). In 1905 he was made Lord Chancellor by Prime Minister Campbell-Bannerman, a post that he held until 1912. He clearly did a first rate job as Lord Chancellor, because in 1911 he was promoted from Baron to Earl. In his retirement, towards the end of the Great War, he linked up with the Marquess of Lansdowne (1869) in trying to secure peace with Germany, which marked the end of his public career.

Loreburn was also President of Kent C.C.C. in 1907, but he seems to have been quite capable of performing two cricketing and one governmental job at the same time. Lord Harris, in his *Recollections and Reminiscences* says that Reid played one game against the Yorkshire Gentlemen (quite probably at Escrick Park, Lord Wenlock's home) and had his finger broken by a reverend gentleman called Carter. 'Years later', wrote Harris, 'when Reid, then Lord Loreburn, became Lord Chancellor, he wrote to Carter offering him the living of Thring, and added, "You see, I bear no malice for that finger of mine you broke ever so many years ago."' A long memory is obviously a necessity if you intend to become Lord Chancellor.

Loreburn passed the Presidency on to **FREDERICK ARCHIBALD VAUGHAN CAMPBELL, THIRD EARL CAWDOR**. The Earl had been Loreburn's contemporary at Oxford, although they were at different

colleges. Cawdor's Eton and Christ Church implies greater social standing and less academic brilliance than Loreburn's Cheltenham and Balliol,
and Cawdor was not reading law, so their paths may well not have
crossed. He was also not known at all as a sportsman, failing to play for
either institution at any known sport. On coming down from Oxford,
Cawdor, a Scottish peer, went to Westminster as Conservative member
for Carmarthenshire from 1874. He was a Welshman at heart, taking a
great interest in local affairs in Pembrokeshire and Carmarthenshire,
and was for ten years chairman of the Great Western Railway Company.
His interests were in transport of all kinds: when he was President of
MCC, he was also President of the Institute of Naval Architects.

His highest government post was as First Lord of the Admiralty
under Balfour before the First World War, when he and the First Sea
Lord, Sir John Fisher, introduced major changes to the Royal Navy,
with a view to facing up to German rearmament. The fleets were reor-
ganised and redistributed, from now on based in Malta, Gibraltar and
the U.K. ports, and the plans for a new class of battleship, the Dread-
nought, and battle cruiser, Invincible, were laid. Cawdor did not live
to see the fruits of his labours, however, as he died in 1911, five days
before his 64th birthday. Although he had been President of MCC just
three years earlier, *Wisden's* obituary merely recorded his death, making
no reference to cricket (or anything else) other than his year as President.

Cawdor was the first cousin of the Third Earl of Ellesmere, so the
1920 President, the Fourth Earl, was Cawdor's first cousin once
removed. The family connections continue. In nominating his successor, Cawdor went for a highly connected courtier, whose ancestor had
been President in 1839. The Tenth Earl of Chesterfield was not a direct
descendant of the Sixth Earl who was the 1839 man, as the Chesterfield
line had a habit of dying out at regular intervals. In 1871, when the
Seventh Earl died of cholera caught at a house party at Lord Londesborough's home, at which the Prince of Wales, MCC's patron, was

present, the line transferred to a distant cousin, who also died childless twelve years later. An even more distant cousin was handed the title, and it was his son, **Edwyn Francis Scudamore-Stanhope**, the Tenth Earl who took on the Presidency in 1909. He was 55 years old. It has to be admitted that the Tenth Earl was hardly a better President than the Sixth Earl. He had no known cricketing qualifications, but as a past Captain of the Yeomen of the Guard (yes, the title really existed) and a past Captain of the Gentlemen-At-Arms (sounds like a cricket team, but it isn't), to say nothing of his role as Master of The Horse, he was a man with all the right connections.

The Chesterfield connection with Lord's actually goes back to before the birth of Thomas Lord. Until 1732 the family of the Earls of Chesterfield owned the land on which Lord's now stands. It was the Fourth Earl, the one who wrote the famous *Letters To His Son* and who was a major figure in Whig politics in the early part of the eighteenth century, who sold the land on his return to England in poor health after a period as ambassador at The Hague. He sold it to Henry Samuel Eyre, and when Lord originally took on the lease, it was still part of the Eyre Estate. The freehold was bought at auction in 1860 by Isaac Moses, who sold it on to MCC six years later for almost three times what he had paid for it – £18,313 6s 8d for a £7,000 outlay. It was to be many years before MCC honed its business instincts.

Chesterfield handed over to one of the second-generation Presidents, **William Denison, Second Earl of Londesborough**, and the son of the 1876 President. The Denisons were closely associated with the Scarborough Festival, and the Second Earl, who was 45 when he took office, was as keen as his father to keep the Festival as a central event in the English cricket season. It was at his family home (when he was only six years old) that cholera had threatened the life of the Prince of Wales, so it was perhaps inevitable that he would be President of MCC when the Prince of Wales, by now King Edward VII, did

actually die. However, MCC did not lack a patron long. After a respect-
ful interval to mourn the previous patron, King George V, a man with
absolutely no known interest in cricket whatsoever, was installed as the
Club's patron. Denison was not particularly known as a cricketer himself, though his passion for the game is well documented, but he shared
an interesting connection with his nominated successor, Lord Desborough. The similarity of their surnames apart, and the fact that they
were both christened William, both Londesborough and Desborough
were closely related to famous war poets. Londesborough's sister, Lady
Ida Denison, married Sir George Sitwell, and their three children
gained great literary distinction for the family. Dame Edith Sitwell and
Sir Osbert Sitwell were the elder two, but it was the youngest,
Sacheverell Sitwell, who was probably best known for his poetry of the
First World War. Lord Desborough's son, Julian Grenfell, wrote 'Into
Battle', one of the most evocative poems of the Great War, and he was
killed in 1915 at the age of 27.

Lord Desborough, born William Grenfell on 30 October 1855, has a
strong claim to be considered the greatest all-round athlete of his
generation (a generation that includes C. B. Fry), as well as a major
political figure of his day. It is hard to imagine that a more versatile man
has ever been a member of MCC, let alone occupied the Presidential
chair. He was educated at Harrow, and played in the XI in 1873 and
1874, but when he went up to Oxford, he did not get a cricket Blue. He
did however, gain Blues for athletics (as a fine three-miler) and rowing
(in the Boat Race in both 1876 and 1877, the latter being the famous
dead heat). He was also a fine fencer, and among his other accom-
plishments was the feat of swimming across the basin of the Niagara
Falls (twice, four years apart), climbing the Matterhorn three times and
teaching the writer Frank Harris how to operate a punt. He first entered
Parliament as Liberal MP for Salisbury in 1880, but resigned two years
later to become a war correspondent in the Sudan, when, working for
the *Daily Telegraph*, he once confronted an advancing enemy alone,
armed only with an umbrella. He lived to tell the tale and was back in
Westminster in 1885, but out again in 1886, before being returned for

Hereford in 1892. That only lasted a year, but he was elected as MP for Wycombe in 1900, a seat he held until his elevation to the peerage in 1905. He held many other posts in his time in national politics, from the first Chairman of Thames Conservancy to chairman of the organising Committee for the 1908 Olympics, which were held in London. He was President of the Amateur Athletic Association, the Lawn Tennis and Croquet Association and the Royal Life Saving Society (and if anybody was qualified for the job, a man who had swum Niagara Falls surely was).

In 1920 he made a speech to the Empire Club of Canada in Toronto, in which he said that:

> I was President of the Marylebone Cricket Club, which is *the* cricket club in our country, and we had the pleasant duty of sending out an XI to Australia. I have to say that that XI did very well, and brought back what is called 'The Ashes', though I have never quite known exactly what that meant. However, they got on a great deal better than the Australians at that time considered at all possible, and they rather fancy themselves at cricket.

He could have been speaking 85 years later, and the words would still ring true.

In the same speech, he referred to his time working on the 1908 Olympics.

> There is much to be said against the Olympic Games, as they are very often carried out on much too big a scale … yet, on the whole, they have increased the spirit of true sportsmanship among the nations that have joined in.

He might have been pleased that the 2012 Olympics would plan to include archery at Lord's.

He lived until he was almost ninety, but many years before that Desborough was upset to find his obituary printed in *The Times*. It was Lord Bessborough, heir to the I Zingari founder, who had died, and

Desborough telephoned to protest. The story goes that Desborough told the editor, 'Look here, you've published my obituary this morning,' to which the editor replied, 'I'm sorry, my Lord. Where did you say you were calling from?'

During 1911, the Club purchased the freehold of numbers 2 and 4 Grove End Road, expanding their influence a little further, and also lent £1,000 to Desborough's old school, Harrow, to purchase extra land for cricket pitches. Almost inevitably, his successor was an Old Etonian.

D esborough was rumoured to have turned down the position of Governor General of Canada, but his successor at MCC did not. Indeed, he was Governor General when Desborough made his speech in Toronto, and if Desborough was offered the post, we can assume it was the Duke of Devonshire who made the offer. **Victor Cavendish, Ninth Duke of Devonshire**, had married the daughter of Lord Lansdowne (1869), another Governor General of Canada, and two of their daughters married aides-de-camp to the Duke while he was in Canada, so clearly romance was in the Ottawa air. Another daughter married Harold Macmillan, the future Prime Minister, and their younger son married Fred Astaire's sister Adele.

The Duke was an Eton and Trinity, Cambridge man, but not particularly a cricketer. Born in 1868, he inherited the duchy from his uncle in 1908, but before that had been Member of Parliament for West Derbyshire from 1891, when his father, the previous incumbent, died and Lord Victor Cavendish, as he then was, inherited the seat unopposed. He remained in Parliament until 1908, reaching the fringes of power as Financial Secretary to the Treasury from 1903 to 1905. His Presidency of MCC happened in the years between leaving the Commons and taking on Canada, and it featured the only summer for almost seventy years in which two Test teams toured England. The Triangular Tournament of 1912, between England, Australia and South Africa, was not a success and has never been repeated, but by the end of the century, it was routine for two touring teams to visit England each summer, even if they did not play Test matches against each other.

The summer of 1911 had been exceptionally dry, so when that was followed by a dry spring in 1912 (early signs of global warming, no doubt) the outfield and wickets began to show signs of real wear and tear. The summer itself was exceptionally wet, and playing three Tests at Lord's in 1912 merely added to the pressure on the ground staff. By the end of the summer, it was decided that 'special treatment would be required', as the minute book tells us, and the decision to overhaul and enlarge the drainage system was taken.

The Duke of Devonshire was a farmer at heart and he was no doubt pleased to have an issue of real interest to him that he could get his teeth into. In Canada, he was to get himself very much involved in the development of agriculture across the breadth of the country, but also kept up his interest in sport, even if cricket did not come into the picture very much. At Rideau Hall, the official residence of the Governor General, he built tennis courts, and held skating and toboggan parties during the winter. He was also very interested in ice hockey, but there is no evidence that he ever got involved in cricket on ice, which had been played even in Britain's milder winters in the late nineteenth century, and which still is played in Estonia.

The Duke of Devonshire, as one of the grandest men in Britain, might have struggled to find a man worthy to be his successor at Lord's, had he not turned to another man whose father had been President before him. The man he nominated was **JOHN CHARLES MONTAGU-DOUGLAS-SCOTT, EARL OF DALKEITH**, and son of the Duke of Buccleuch (1888) who had married, inevitably, one of the 'handsome Hamiltons', Lady Louisa. Born in 1864, he was 49 years old when he took on the Presidency, having already enjoyed a career in the Royal Navy and as a Member of Parliament. He represented Roxburghshire as a Conservative between 1886, when at the age of 22 he merely fulfilled his obligations to the family by taking over the seat his father had held until he inherited his title, and 1906, when he stepped down. He was never seen as a political high flier, and was content to be known as a benign landowning nobleman, a dying breed as the Great War loomed.

He was not helped in his Presidential year by the severe illness that struck Francis Lacey, the Secretary, but happily Mr Lacey recovered, to carry on in his post for many more years. In the interim, the secretarial duties were carried out by John Shuter, the former Surrey captain. There were also issues of personal conduct exercising the minds of the Committee and their legal advisers. At a Special General Meeting following the 1914 Annual General Meeting, at which Dalkeith stepped down, the proposals of the Club were put to the membership. They proposed a new rule which stated, in best legalese:

> In case the conduct of any member, either within or out of the Club shall, in the opinion of the Committee or of any twenty members of the Club, who shall certify the same in writing to the Committee, be injurious to the character and interest of the Club, the Committee shall be empowered, after enquiry, to recommend, in writing, such member to resign.

The Club had moved a very long way from the devil-may-care attitude of a century earlier, and no doubt many of the stalwarts of the Club in the first decades of the nineteenth century would have been excluded from the Club by this rule, but this was the apogee of MCC's self-satisfaction, the dying embers of a certainty that being a member of the Marylebone Club was the highest honour a man could wish for.

The rule, which was carried by the meeting, went on to confirm that:

> if the member so recommended shall not comply within fourteen days from the date of such recommendation, the Committee shall then call a Special Meeting, and if such Meeting, at which there shall be not less than twelve members present and voting, calls for the expulsion of such member, he shall cease to be a member of the Club; his name shall be

erased from the list; but his subscription for the current year shall be returned to him, and he shall be forever after ineligible for election or for admission as a visitor of the Club.

Such a draconian rule makes one wonder who had caused the issue to arise in the first place. It looks like a very large and expensive sledge-hammer to crack a comparatively small nut, but the rule remained and even today in a variant form is still there.

CHAPTER SIX

1914—1945

BETWEEN THE WARS

Lord Dalkeith did not know it, but when he handed over the Presidency to one of cricket's most powerful men, it would be for five years, not just one. The Great War was imminent, and cricket would have to lower its profile for the duration. MCC, along with the rest of the establishment of Britain, would have to turn its energies towards winning the war, or as it was put at the time, 'greater battles than are fought with bat and ball over twenty-two yards'.

It was a stroke of supreme good fortune for MCC that Dalkeith chose MARTIN BLADEN HAWKE, SEVENTH BARON HAWKE as his successor, for Hawke, who had been a committee man at MCC for many years, was, like Lord Harris at Kent, a man who ruled his County Club with a rod of benevolent iron. Hawke was a Yorkshireman, although he was not actually born in the county he captained, managed and strove for all his life. In an era when Yorkshire prided itself on only fielding men who had been born in the county, Hawke was the exception, born in 1860 just across the border in Gainsborough in Lincolnshire. He was educated at Eton and Magdalene College, Cambridge, hardly the pedigree for a true Tyke, but by 1892, when his portrait appeared in *Vanity*

Fair, he was a Captain of the Third Battalion of the Princess of Wales' Own Yorkshire Regiment, as well as captain of Yorkshire C.C.C. Interestingly, Hawke was described in the same article as 'the only amateur player who has regularly captained the County Eleven'. He has subsequently, and rather unfairly, been portrayed as the man who did all he could to make sure that no professional would ever captain England, or, by extension, any county side and yet the true facts are that he was not against professional captains, certainly not against professional cricketers, and equally certainly devoted to the cause of a successful Yorkshire county team. It was during his years in charge of Yorkshire that the idea came into focus of a strong Yorkshire side meaning a strong England side. His years in charge were extensive: he was captain of Yorkshire for 28 years from 1883 to 1910 and President for 40 years until his death in 1938. Like Harris at Kent, he combined the job of captain and President with little difficulty.

It is hard to overestimate the role that Hawke played for MCC, Yorkshire and English cricket throughout his life, but during the war years he came into his own. He had not expected to be President for so long when he took office, but there seems little doubt that he was quite happy to retain the title for as long as the war might last. In 1917, the minutes of the Annual General Meeting show that 'owing to the continuance of the War, the Anniversary Dinner again cannot be held. Lord Hawke has accordingly been invited by the Committee to remain in office, and has consented.' The use of the word 'accordingly' is intriguing. Just because a dinner cannot be held does not mean that the incumbent President cannot nominate a successor, but clearly Lord Hawke was very happy not to, and the Committee were equally happy for him to continue. There seems no sense of an unwelcome precedent being set or of a tradition for one-year Presidents being set aside. The war was a desperate time, and desperate times provoke desperate reactions. A four-year Presidency was just one of those reactions.

Hawke certainly enjoyed his Presidency, despite the difficulties of the times. He began it with a sick Secretary, Francis Lacey, and in 1915 lost his Treasurer, Sir Spencer Ponsonby-Fane. Sir Spencer was replaced by none other than Lord Harris (who had briefly stood in for Francis Lacey before John Shuter took on the job slightly more permanently), so their two lordships stood firm at the helm of the Club through the dark years of war. Hawke held at least one official post at Lord's, apart from being a Committee member, for 24 years, from 1914 when he became President, until his death in 1938. He was President from 1914 to 1918, a trustee from 1916 to 1938, and Treasurer from 1932 to 1937.

No major matches were played at Lord's in the war years, and no professional playing staff was retained. After the dinner, in June 1914, to celebrate the centenary of the present (third) Lord's ground, there was little to cheer MCC members over the next four years. There were no anniversary dinners, no Oxford v. Cambridge or MCC versus touring teams, no Test matches, nothing that was not directed towards the war effort. As Lord Hawke said in his speech to the 1915 Annual General Meeting, 'You will note with pleasure how our ground has been used for military purposes.' Subscriptions were suspended for members serving in the armed forces, and, as a result, MCC suffered four years in which its financial strength was eroded. The number of members involved in the war effort was hard to put an exact figure to, but Lord Hawke said the number 'seems to be 2,112' in 1915, of whom 69 had already been killed. By 1918, the Roll of Honour included 290 names. By the end of the war, membership, which had been 5,352 in 1914, was up to 5,403. This was an increase of 459 over the previous year, so numbers had been falling, not surprisingly, during the war years. At the 1916 Annual General Meeting, Lord Hawke noted that 'the membership of the Club is no less than one sixth below the maximum which was fixed in 1910, at 6,000, and the numbers have fallen abnormally since 1912, when there were 5,343 members. The Committee believes it would be in the best interests of the Club to increase numbers by exceptional arrangements.' As the Long Room was at the time being used 'for making hay-nets for horses for the Army' it is perhaps not surprising that membership should have slipped a little, but in 1916, for example, there were still over one hundred matches, between schools and military units, played at Lord's.

The Club also supported the government's efforts to finance the war effort. As Lord Hawke also stated at the 1916 meeting, 'The Committee, feeling that an Institution so important as MCC should not hesitate to respond to the appeal of the government to subscribe to the 5 per cent War Loan, arranged with the London and South Western Bank to take up £50,000 stock on behalf of the Club.' MCC was now an important institution, in its own eyes at least, and also, quite remarkably, a reasonably rich one.

Lord Hawke, who died in an Edinburgh hospital after an operation at the age of 78, lived to see Len Hutton, the Yorkshireman who would become England's first professional captain, score his 364 against Australia at the Oval, and his life bridged the gap between the golden late Victorian and Edwardian age of cricket, and the more modern era of bodyline, Bradman and Test matches against India, West Indies and New Zealand as well as the old guard of Australia and South Africa. Lord Hawke had been heavily involved in expanding cricket around the world, having led teams to Argentina, the United States and Canada, India (where he played with Lord Harris and Lord Wenlock and stayed with Sir Stanley Jackson), the West Indies, Rhodesia, South Africa, and all over Australasia. As Sir Stanley Jackson said of him, 'he had a long innings, played it well and enjoyed it.'

When finally the Great War ended and Hawke was accordingly able to hand over the reins of power, he nominated the **RT. HON. HENRY FORSTER** to succeed him. Forster, who emulated Viscount Chelsea in 1873 by being ennobled during his Presidential year, had been educated at Eton and New College, Oxford, and played in the Varsity match in 1887, 1888 and 1889. He played in the first match as opening bowler (despite bowling slow left-arm spin) and number eight batsman, and distinguished himself by scoring 60 not out, his career best, in Oxford's first innings, as Oxford won by seven wickets. A year later he had been promoted to number six, but was now only second-change bowler. He made only 1 run, and took two wickets in a rain-interrupted draw. In his final year he was opening the batting and the bowling but was unable to prevent Oxford from losing by an innings. Among his contemporaries at Oxford were the Hon. Frederick Thesiger, who as Lord Chelmsford was to become MCC President in 1922, and M. R. Jardine, Douglas Jardine's father.

After his cricketing career with Oxford, he played a number of games for Hampshire, mainly under the captaincy of Francis Lacey, who by 1919 was well into his time as Secretary at Lord's. Although Forster played for Hampshire on and off until 1895, his political career was launched in 1892, when he was elected as Conservative MP for Sevenoaks. Henry Forster's parliamentary career was reasonably successful but for a big man he kept a low profile. He was a Treasury Commissioner from 1902 to 1905, and in 1915 he was appointed financial secretary to the War Office in the wartime coalition government (responsible for the War Bonds to which MCC had subscribed £50,000), and in 1917 he was appointed a Privy Counsellor. He remained at Westminster until December 1919, towards the end of his Presidential year, when he resigned and was created Baron Forster of Lepe. Six months later he accepted the post of Governor General of Australia.

He never lost his interest in cricket, and did much to encourage the growth of the game throughout the Empire, as it was then. He enjoyed entertaining the MCC teams that came to visit Australia during his five years there, even though England lost nine of the ten Tests played in Australia in that time. His period as Governor General marked a definite move away from the strong and proactive role earlier incumbents had played, towards the modern symbolic role of head of state in lieu. He made no real attempt to influence the politics or politicians of Australia and was content to open new buildings, attend big sporting events (he loved racing and golf as well as cricket, and is one of only two men to have been Captain of the Royal and Ancient as well as President of MCC), make stirring patriotic speeches and unveil war memorials. Both his sons were killed during the war, and he built a monument to the memory of his elder son within a church in Newcastle, New South Wales, during his time there.

Forster handed over, a couple of months before he set sail for Australia, to the Fourth Earl of Ellesmere, better known in cricket circles as Lord Brackley, the title he used before inheriting the earldom. JOHN FRANCIS GRANVILLE SCROPE EGERTON, to give him his full set of baptismal names, like many titled cricket lovers of his generation, enjoyed taking touring teams overseas, and in 1905 took a side, under the auspices of MCC, to West Indies for three months. They played twenty matches in that time, winning eleven, drawing six and coming second in three. They were of good club standard, with some fine players, including Capt. Wynyard, G. H. Simpson-Hayward the lob bowler and two professionals, E. G. Hayes and G. J. Thompson. Brackley himself was a batsman and occasional wicketkeeper of no great pretensions, but he was well liked by all his team-mates.

Apart from his cricketing interests, Lord Ellesmere, who inherited the title in 1914, was well connected to all the right people. His wife was the daughter of the Fourth Earl of Durham, and thus niece of the 1896 President, the Earl of Pembroke. Her sister married the Thirteenth Earl of Home, whose son, better known as Sir Alec Douglas-Home, became President in 1966. Ellesmere's younger brother Thomas married Lady Bertha Anson, daughter of the 1897 President and granddaughter of the 1848 President. They were also connected to the Leveson-Gower family and the Dukes of Sutherland. One way or another, Ellesmere was fairly closely related to at least eighteen other Presidents.

Ellesmere was, as his title suggests, a Lancastrian: he had been President of Lancashire C.C.C. during the war years and vice-president for many years afterwards. He handed over the MCC title to one of the great Yorkshire cricketers of his time, COL. THE HON. AND RT. HON. SIR STANLEY JACKSON. Jackson was born in 1870 as the seventh child of the Rt. Hon. W. L. Jackson, who became Lord Allerton after a long political career. Although Sir Stanley was 50 when he took on the Presidency, the memory of his cricketing feats was still fresh in the memory. He was educated at Harrow and Trinity College, Cambridge, a well-trodden path for Presidents to take. At Harrow, his brilliant all-round skills gave his side victory in 1888 over Eton by 156 runs, one of the bigger margins of victory in that series. At Cambridge, he won his Blue four years in a row, from 1890 to 1893, and while never setting any match records, he was on the winning side three times out of four. As captain of Cambridge in 1893, he employed a tactic that was to lead to a change in the Laws. At the end of Oxford's first innings, the last-wicket pair were overheard discussing whether to get out deliberately, so that the follow-on would have to be enforced, meaning that Cambridge would have to bat last on a disintegrating wicket. In those days, the follow-on was not optional. Jackson immediately instructed the bowler, C. M. Wells (later to become a rugby international and Eton housemaster), to bowl deliberately wide so that Oxford would go past the follow-on target. Wells bowled a wide and a no-ball, both of which went to the boundary and the crisis was averted. Three years later, after a similar incident in the 1896 match, the law was changed to empower the leading captain with the choice of whether to enforce the follow-on.

Jackson then played for many years for Yorkshire and England, and, on his nomination to the top MCC post, became the fifth England captain to become President. He rarely captained Yorkshire, because that position was firmly taken by Lord Hawke, but he was captain of England in one of their most successful Ashes series, in 1905, when England beat a very strong Australian side 2-0, with three matches drawn. Jackson won all five tosses in that series, scored 492 runs at 70, including two centuries, and took thirteen wickets at 15 apiece with his right-arm fast-medium cutters. By coincidence he was the exact twin of his Australian counterpart, Joe Darling. Both men were born on 21 November 1870.

Jackson followed his father's footsteps into Parliament in 1915, as Unionist member for Howdenshire in Yorkshire until 1926, the year before he was appointed Governor of Bengal. He became chairman of the party, but his main claim to fame is in the story of how Winston Churchill, his fag at Harrow, introduced Sir Stanley to Lloyd George in the Palace of Westminster. Lloyd George's response to the introduction was effusive: 'I have been looking forward to meeting the man who gave Winston Churchill a hiding at school.' Jackson went on to become chairman of the Test selectors in 1934, the year of Bradman's second tour of England, and in 1943 was appointed to chair a special Committee set up by MCC to consider the structure of post-war cricket. Their recommendations were, to our eyes sixty years on, hardly revolutionary. They felt that any division into two leagues 'would spell financial disaster for those in the lower half of the table'. They were unanimous in recommending that cricket on Sundays should not be introduced. They were relaxed about the duration of the cricket season, the conclusion of which could 'be deferred to the second week in September'. They also abandoned the eight-ball over experiment of 1939, suggested the introduction of new balls every 55 overs and were in favour of some sort of knock-out competition, 'should a satisfactory scheme be evolved later in which all matches are played under the Laws governing three-day cricket'. They were not really looking to make major changes: they just wanted to get back to playing cricket as soon as possible after the war ended. This Committee sat in 1943 and published its findings in March 1944, over a year before the war actually ended and still three months before D-Day. The Marylebone Club was obviously supremely confident of the outcome of the war.

Jackson was almost assassinated in India by a young woman who fired five shots at him at close range while he was at a meeting in Calcutta. The shots all went wide, giving Jackson another two decades of active life.

Jackson handed on the Presidency to the man who had captained Oxford against his Cambridge side in 1890, the HON. FREDERICK THESIGER, who by 1922 had become Viscount Chelmsford. His father, from whom he inherited the title, was General Lord Chelmsford, the man who had been in command of the British forces massacred at Isandhlwana by the Zulus in 1879.

Thesiger, two years older than Stanley Jackson, was in the Winchester XI for three years, and was so promising that he even played for Worcestershire (then a minor county) at the age of sixteen. On going up to Oxford, he was a fixture in the university side from his freshman year. He actually only played two and a bit Varsity matches: in 1889, his second year, he was unable to play because of a family illness, and in 1891, his final year, he injured his hand while fielding on the first day, and was replaced for the entire match by T. B. Case. He was a brilliant scholar as well as a cricketer, and, between all these traumas on the cricket field, Thesiger was earning himself a First in jurisprudence. He was then elected a Fellow of All Souls, and eventually, in 1932, became Warden.

After Oxford, Thesiger played only a little cricket, for Middlesex. He was too busy building, like Jackson, an outstanding political and administrative career. In 1905 he was appointed Governor of Queensland, and in 1909 became Governor of New South Wales until 1913. He was back in England in time to enjoy the MCC dinner on 23 June 1914 to celebrate the centenary of the present Lord's Ground, 'in every way a memorable gathering', at which he added to the overall enjoyment of all by pointing out that he had sat at the bedside of two grievously ill England captains in Australia, namely A. O. Jones in 1907/08, and Pelham Warner in 1911/12. At the beginning of the Great War, he joined the Dorset Regiment as a Captain, despite his age – 46. By 1916 Chelmsford was governing again, this time as Viceroy of India, a post he held until 1921. On his return to Britain, he took on the Presidency of MCC, but shortly after completing his year he surprised the conservative cricket establishment by taking the post of First Lord of the Admiralty under Ramsay MacDonald's first ever Labour government. He died in 1933 at the age of 64.

Lord Chelmsford nominated as his successor another politician, VISCOUNT ULLSWATER OF CAMPSEA ASHE. Viscount Ullswater had, until two years earlier, been the Rt. Hon. James Lowther MP, Speaker of the House of Commons from 1905. On his retirement, at the age of 65 in 1921, he took the title of Viscount Ullswater, and devoted much of his years of retirement to his great love: cricket. He was a Lowther, a descendant of Colonel Henry Lowther who had played such an active role in the early years of MCC, and the head of a cadet branch of the Earls of Lonsdale, whose passion was boxing rather than cricket. Ullswater, born in 1855, had played cricket for Bedfordshire in the 1880s, but never gained higher cricketing fame. He was a bowler rather than a batsman, but at Eton and Cambridge did not distinguish himself greatly, never earning a Blue. He played plenty of matches for Campsea Ashe in Suffolk, his home for many years, a place that he included in his title, but he never aspired to anything greater than that. For him, cricket was to be enjoyed.

He trained as a lawyer and was called to the Bar in 1879, but it was not long before he sought a full time political career. In 1883 he briefly became Conservative MP for Rutland, but he soon lost that seat again. He was back in Parliament in 1886 as the member for Cumberland, and in 1895 he was appointed Deputy Speaker. In 1905 he was elected as Speaker, and held the post in succeeding parliaments until he retired in 1921, a much longer tenure as Speaker than most. A man with a splendid goatee beard, he presided over the House of Commons with firmness but also with humour and, reportedly, never let his strong Conservative feelings impinge on his impartiality. These were perfect qualifications for his role as President of MCC.

One of the more remarkable features of Lord Ullswater's life was the very length of it. He lived until he was 94, the longest lived of all MCC Presidents, and when he died in 1949 his eldest son and his eldest grandson were both already dead, his grandson having died at the age of 32 in the Second World War. He was therefore succeeded in the title by his great-grandson, then a boy of seven; this was one of only a handful of examples of a boy succeeding his great-grandfather in a peerage.

Ullswater chose a political colleague, and a good cricketer, to succeed him. **BARON ERNLE OF CHELSEA** had, as Rowland Prothero, played cricket for Hampshire almost fifty years before, as a right-hand bat and right-arm medium-pace bowler. Born in 1851, he was already 72 years old when he took on the Presidency, and had retired from Parliament by then. After schooling at Marlborough College, and playing in their first XI in 1870 and 1871, Prothero went up to Balliol College, Oxford in 1872. In 1875, on graduation, he was elected a Fellow of All Souls, sixteen years before Lord Chelmsford achieved the same honour. While he could match Lord Chelmsford's academic achievements, he could not match his sporting ones: he never received his cricket Blue. His first-class career consisted of six matches for Hampshire in the 1870s, in which he scored 190 runs (including one innings of 110) and took ten wickets at 18 runs each.

Prothero was a multi-talented man. He was a lawyer and an authority on agriculture, and a writer who was from 1894 appointed editor of the *Quarterly Review*, a position he held for five years. In 1914, he was elected a Member of Parliament for Oxford University, and was almost immediately recruited into the wartime coalition government as President of the Board of Agriculture. His only son was killed in the war, a tragedy that he shared with many other distinguished men of his generation, but he continued at Westminster until 1919, when he was created Baron Ernle. The books he wrote were well received and influential works in their day, but their titles do not set the pulse racing a century on. *Pioneers and Progress of English Farming* and *The Life and Correspondence of Dean Stanley* were two of his better known works. Ernle was, incidentally, the son of a clergyman, one of the few Presidents with a close family connection to the Church of England. He retained a strong faith throughout his life, and the impression one gains of him at this distance is of a brilliant, rather severe man who would not have been known for his sense of humour. When he died in 1937, the title died with him.

In 1925 the mantle passed to **SIR JOHN DE ROBECK**, an Irishman of Swedish stock, who was born on 10 June 1862. He was a sailor, ultimately reaching the rank of Admiral of the Fleet, having entered the Royal Navy at the age of thirteen in 1875. This made him one of the very few Presidents to that point who had not been educated at public school (notably Eton or Harrow) and Oxbridge. He was not a first-class cricketer, but all his life he was an avid club cricketer. He joined MCC in 1898, and played many games for the Club, as well as for Devon, I Zingari and in countless Navy games. He was a useful batsman who averaged 34.50 in his first season playing as an MCC member, when he was already 36 years old. He joined the MCC Committee some years before his nomination as President, and was a great believer in the diplomatic benefits of playing cricket around the world. He was recorded as pointing out at the 1923 Anniversary Dinner that he had played in most parts of the world and wished to emphasise 'the enormous influence for good any English, and especially an MCC, team carries to whatever part of the Empire they may go'.

He had also fought naval battles in most parts of the world. At the outbreak of the Great War, he was a Rear-Admiral, and was soon given the responsibility, as deputy to Admiral Carden, for the East Mediterranean Squadron, who were given the task of carrying out the expedition to capture the Dardanelles Straits. Admiral Carden soon fell ill, leaving de Robeck in sole charge of the operation, which proved disastrous. They sailed right into a Turkish minefield, which sunk five Allied ships, and prompted de Robeck to refuse to continue the operation until Allied troops had been landed and could capture the high ground dominating the straits. His refusal to continue, even under pressure from Winston Churchill as First Lord of the Admiralty, made many feel that de Robeck thereby doomed the whole venture to failure, but in his view it would only have been an even greater failure if he had risked more of his fleet without any defensive protection. Eventually, the attempt to land troops was made, but that too failed. By the end of 1915, de Robeck had earned high praise for his role in evacuating Gallipoli, to bring to an end the whole Dardanelles campaign which had proved so humiliating for the Allied forces. By the end of the war, he had been promoted to the rank of Vice-Admiral and collected a bucketful of honours. He was now a baronet, a G.C.B. and a G.C.M.G., with a grant of £10,000 from a grateful nation for his efforts (though quite what the nation had to be so very grateful for is not altogether clear). From 1919 to 1920 he was back in Turkey as British High Commissioner at Constantinople. He retired from the Navy in 1924 with the rank of Admiral of the Fleet, and a G.C.V.O. to add to his collection, and almost at once took up his MCC role. He died suddenly, at the age of 65, in 1928.

Sir John chose **Thomas Brand, Third Viscount Hampden**, as his successor, and in doing so gave the extraordinary Hamilton clan yet another President. Hampden, whose mother was a Cavendish and a relative of the Duke of Devonshire (1912), was born in 1869, making him 57 when he took on the Presidency of MCC. His wife, Lady Katharine, was the daughter of the Sixth Duke of Buccleuch (1888) and Lady Louisa Hamilton, and was the sister of the Earl of Dalkeith (1913). Together they produced eight children, including four sons, but remarkably none of them became President of MCC in their turn. Hampden was, like Sir John de Robeck, a military man, who ended his career as a Brigadier General with as impressive a set of initials after his name as the Admiral himself.

Hampden, then merely Hon. Thomas Brand, was educated at Eton, where he played in the XI from 1884 to 1887, as a slow right-arm bowler of some distinction. He was in the same XI as, among others, the son of Lord Cadogan (1873) and members of the Hervey-Bathurst and Coventry families, Presidential pedigrees all. He captained the 1887 side to a five-wicket victory against a Harrow side that included both Archie MacLaren and Stanley Jackson, and was given great credit by *Wisden* for all three aspects of his game – batting, bowling and captaincy. He went up to Cambridge, but, despite appearing in a Freshman's match, did not gain a Blue.

He went into the Army, and would have had the chance to travel when his father was appointed Governor of Australia from 1895 to 1899 (in the years before the Australian states joined forces to form the Commonwealth of Australia in 1901, the title was just plain Governor, not Governor General). He was President of Hertfordshire C.C.C. in 1920 and a member of MCC since early manhood, but otherwise does not appear to have been very much involved in cricket, except as a spectator. He was Lord Lieutenant of Hertfordshire for 37 years from 1915 to 1952, and Colonel of the 10th Royal Hussars from 1935 to 1939, a position that Viscount Downe (1872) had held from 1912 to 1924, but these duties were largely unrelated to cricket. All the same, 1926 was to prove a momentous year for MCC, Lord's and the President.

The new Grand Stand and the cantilever stand at the north end of the Mound Stand, both of which had been committed to a few years earlier, were now due for completion, and had it not been for the General Strike, which began on 5 May 1926, they would have been completed and opened exactly on time. As it turned out, the General Strike only lasted a week and the delays proved minimal. The new Grand Stand was open for business in time for the Lord's Test on 26 June, and such was the interest in the new stand (and in the visiting Australians) that the total attendance for the match exceeded 70,000 and the gates had to be shut on the Saturday – an unusual event in those days. As Viscount Hampden said at the Annual General Meeting in 1927, 'the total cost of the works, exclusive of the seats, fittings and fees, should not exceed about £47,500, towards which the sum of £40,000 has been received as a result of the election of 200 Life Members.' Now there was a bargain – life membership of MCC in 1926 for £200. The new Grand Stand received generally good notices, although there was noted at the AGM the fact that 'the view obtained from these stands, except in the case of a few seats in the corner of the Grand Stand, gave, it is believed, general satisfaction.' Pelham Warner, rather later, noted less enthusiastically that 'never in the history of cricket has so large a stand held so few people,' but the Grand Stand, with the Father Time weathervane on top, remained for over seventy years until replaced by the present Grand Stand, completed in 1998.

Even more significant for the Club than the new stand was the retirement of the Secretary, Francis Lacey, after twenty-eight years in the job. Much to everybody's pleasure, he was knighted on his retirement, the only Secretary of MCC yet to have received such an honour, and the difficult job of replacing him was given to William Findlay, who a quarter of a century later would emulate Benjamin Aislabie by completing the double of Secretary and President.

After such a momentous year, one in which England regained the Ashes as well as everything else, 1927 was always likely to be rather more subdued. MCC membership was actually down on the previous year, by sixteen to 5,604. The tourists were the New Zealanders, for the first time, but not with Test status, and the President of MCC was Lord Leconfield. **Col. Charles Henry Wyndham, Third Baron Leconfield**, was one of those Presidents of whom it could have been written (and in his case, was written) that he 'has always been interested in the game, though he never obtained note as a player'. He was the nephew by marriage of his predecessor Lord Hampden, although he was only three years his junior. He was also nephew by marriage to the Presidents of 1896, 1897, 1912 and 1913, and on the other side of his family was first cousin to the then Lord Dalmeny, the former Surrey captain who would himself be President in Queen Elizabeth's Coronation year, by which time he was the Earl of Rosebery. The Club pedigree was secure, and, after thirty years as a member, it was no doubt his turn to be President.

Lord Leconfield, a Sussex man who had already been President of Sussex County Cricket Club, was the latest owner of the family seat, Petworth House. He may not have guessed it in 1927, but he would be the last Leconfield to own the House and adjoining estate, because those two unavoidables, death and taxes, would take them away. In fact, the need for liquidity had forced Leconfield to sell several valuable parts of his collection from well before his death: he sold the Great Book of Thomas Trevilian, a stunning manuscript dating from Shakespeare's time, at Sotheby's in 1928; sixty years later the book came back to Britain and into the collection of another cricket lover, the late Sir Paul Getty. Lord Leconfield, who lived until he was eighty and died in 1952, was forced by his post-war circumstances to hand over Petworth House to the National Trust in 1947, but when he died five years later, there were still heavy death duties for his nephew and heir, John Wyndham, to have to meet on the vast art collection of at least seven hundred paintings that remained in the family. The taxman eventually settled by taking over many of the most valuable items in the collection, giving them a value of £500,000. Art experts at the time were outraged by the government's cavalier attitude, as they knew these particular works were worth at least double the official estimate, but the Leconfield family had to accept the valuation. The entire estate then passed into state ownership, managed by the National Trust. Petworth House is today one of the Trust's most popular attractions.

To read the *Cricketer* from 1928 is to realise how little the sub-editors had to change the reports of MCC Annual General Meetings each year. 'At Lord's last week the Earl (sic) of Leconfield, the retiring President, nominated the Fifth Earl of Lucan as his successor. The latter, although always fond of cricket, never gained note as a player.' A year earlier, the new President had been 'interested in' cricket rather than fond of it, but still equally noteless as a player. BRIGADIER GENERAL GEORGE CHARLES BINGHAM, FIFTH EARL OF LUCAN, PC, GCVO, KBE, CB, TD, was born on 13 December 1860, so at 67 was one of the oldest men to date to have been nominated President. He was educated at Harrow, where he did not make the XI, and then went into the Army and Sandhurst, where again he failed to impress the cricket selectors. Soldiering was in the Lucan blood, of course. His grandfather the Third Earl was in command of the cavalry division during the Crimean War, and was held responsible for, among other things, the charge of the Light Brigade. If, in the words of Lord Tennyson, 'someone had blunder'd', the view of many of his colleagues, notably Lord Raglan, was that the someone was Lucan. The hapless general returned to Britain where he successfully defended himself in the House of Lords. His military career may have been over at that point, but in 1887, at the age of 87, he was promoted to the rank of Field Marshal. Perhaps this was the origin of the nickname 'Lucky' Lucan.

His grandson, who was elected a member of MCC in 1884, remained a devoted member of the Club for the rest of his long life. He was also a keen golfer, which occupied much of his adult spare time. He was captain of Laleham G.C. near Chertsey for ten years before the First World War, and was President from 1913, when he gave up the captaincy, until he died in 1949. It was a family job – the Sixth and Seventh Earls in their turn were Presidents of Laleham G.C. as well. The Seventh Earl, the infamous one and grandson of the Brigadier General, retained his Presidential title for nine years after his disappearance, which makes one feel that this was not the most burdensome role in sports administration. The Fifth Earl served MCC well as President in a comparatively quiet year, at least as far as major changes to the look or style of Lord's were concerned. He nominated as his successor another soldier, Viscount Plumer of Messines.

HERBERT CHARLES ONSLOW PLUMER was born in March 1857, so at 72 was the second-oldest man, after Lord Ernle in 1924, to take on the Presidency. He was a very distinguished soldier but there is little evidence of any skill at, or participation in, cricket. He did not make the XI at Eton, and was certainly not the right shape for too much sport, being short and squat, always immaculately turned out, yet with a red face, a pot belly and a thick moustache; but as a leader of men he was superb. He began his military career in 1876 as a sub-lieutenant in the 65th Foot, and forty years on was given command of the Second Army, who were dug in around Ypres. He was cautious and thus spent a great deal of time planning his battles, and was very popular with his troops, who nicknamed him 'Daddy'. His colleagues called him 'Plum' and some of his junior officers during the long winters on the Somme called him 'Drip', because of his constantly runny nose.

His generalship brought his country one of the few decisive victories of the war, when he attacked at Messines Ridge in 1917. 'Gentlemen,' he said before the attack was launched, 'we may not make history tomorrow, but we shall certainly change the geography.' On 7 June 1917, he launched his offensive with an explosion of nineteen vast mines at dawn – the loudest man-made noise ever heard. It was so loud that Lloyd George said he heard it in Downing Street, and if the Prime Minister heard it, it seems likely that those living in and around Lord's would have heard it too. After the war, Plumer was given a viscountcy and from 1919 to 1924 was Governor of Malta.

It was noted in the annual report that Dr Lawson Williams had attended to 'the many accidents and cases of illness that have occurred on the ground, in the pavilion and amongst the staff'. In more litigious times, such a report might signal the impending bankruptcy of the Club as the victims of these accidents and illnesses eagerly queue up to sue. For many years, virtually the same lines, thanking Dr Williams for his care, appeared in the report. Lord's was obviously a dangerous place.

Lord Plumer broke with tradition, and established a new one, by nominating his successor at the Annual General Meeting, rather than at the dinner afterwards. His nominee was SIR JOHN EDWARD KYNASTON STUDD, BT. OBE, known universally as J.E.K., except to his mother, who called him Kynaston. Born in 1858, he was, like his predecessor, already in his seventies when he became President. He had been virtually Plumer's contemporary at Eton, and with his younger brothers G.B. (George) and C.T. (Charles) was a pillar of one of the strongest Eton sides ever seen. Kynaston was never on the losing side against Harrow or Winchester, and he hoped to take his winning ways with him to Cambridge. Both his younger brothers preceded him at the university, and in 1879 only G.B. was in the side, when Cambridge won by nine wickets. In 1880, G.B. and C.T. both played (Cambridge won by 115 runs), but in 1881, when the three brothers all played under the captaincy of Ivo Bligh, Cambridge lost by 135 runs. In 1882, once again all three brothers played, this time under the captaincy of G.B. and this time Cambridge triumphed, by seven wickets. G.B. made a century and C.T. took seven for 54 in Oxford's first innings, but J.E.K. had a quiet game. Lord Hawke and C. A. Smith, both future England captains, were also in the Cambridge XI. That was the year in which Cambridge beat the touring Australians by 7 runs, thanks in great part to the Studd brotherhood: J.E.K. made 6 and 66, G.B. made 42 and 48, and C.T. scored 118 and 17 not out.

In 1883, with C.T. in charge, Cambridge won once again by seven wickets. C.T. took eight wickets in the match (to Aubrey 'Round The Corner' Smith's nine) and J.E.K., opening the batting, had another quiet game. In 1884, J.E.K. was captain and, sadly, Cambridge lost by seven wickets, thus spoiling the family record. C.T. and G.B. both went on to play Test cricket for England, but J.E.K. never did. He was a member of MCC from 1878, when he was just 20 years old, but played little first-class cricket after finishing at Cambridge. The record of three brothers captaining Cambridge in successive years might have seemed impossible to equal, but 39 years later the three Ashtons did the same thing, and one of them, Sir Hubert, went on to become President of MCC as well. In the address at J.E.K.'s funeral in 1944, Canon Frank Gillingham, cricketer, cleric and orator, said that Kynaston realised after his time at Cambridge that 'games were only a preparation for sterner duties.' These sterner duties included helping his brother Charles prepare for his life's work as a missionary in China, and in his educational interests as head of the Polytechnic Institute (originally called the Young Men's Christian Institute, now the University of Westminster). In this role, he took over from Quintin Hogg, father of the 1933 President, Viscount Hailsham. Sir Kynaston was also appointed Lord Mayor of London in 1928, and given a baronetcy at the end of his year. In his mayoral year, he gave banquets both to I Zingari and to the triumphant England team after their Ashes victory of 1928/29, and when the Australians toured England in his MCC year, he gave a banquet for them at Merchant Taylor's Hall, one of the more sumptuous cricketing occasions of the inter-war years.

Sir Kynaston Studd nominated Viscount Bridgeman as President for 1931, which he did, following Lord Plumer's example, at the Annual General Meeting. **William Clive Bridgeman, First Viscount Bridgeman of Leigh** was born on the last day of 1864, a grandson of the Second Earl of Bradford. He was another Etonian, just a few years behind Studd at the college, and another Trinity, Cambridge man. At Eton he played in the XI in 1884, and at Cambridge gained his Blue in his final year, 1887. His batting average for Cambridge that summer was 34, including one innings of 162 not out against Sussex, which *Wisden* described as 'a superb 162, batting for nearly six hours without making a mistake'. He did not play much first-class cricket after coming down from Cambridge, but did play a number of games for Staffordshire, and was, as the *Cricketer* put it, 'eminently successful in country house matches'.

Politics were Bridgeman's love and his career. He began as private secretary to the Colonial Secretary, Lord Knutsford, in 1889, and by 1895 was fulfilling the same role for the Chancellor of the Exchequer, Sir Michael Hicks-Beach. He started working his way up the electoral ladder from a low rung: in 1897 he became a member of the London School Board (where he would have come across J. E. K. Studd), and in 1904, when he was already almost forty years old, he was elected a member of the London County Council. In 1906, he finally made it to Westminster, as Conservative MP for North Shropshire. He held that seat, or its redistributed successor Oswestry, until he retired in 1929. From 1911, 'Willie' Bridgeman held official posts in Parliament, beginning as an opposition whip, and when Lloyd George created his coalition government in 1916, Bridgeman was appointed Parliamentary secretary, firstly to the Ministry of Labour and then at the Board of Trade. In 1922, after the collapse of the coalition government, he was appointed Home Secretary in the administrations of Bonar Law and Baldwin, the latter being not only another future President of MCC but also one of Bridgeman's closest political friends. With the victory of the Labour party under Ramsay MacDonald in 1924, his career might have been at an end, but in November that year he was back in a new Baldwin government as First Lord of the Admiralty, a post which he held until his retirement from politics in 1929. On his retirement he was appointed Viscount Bridgeman, and he kept active by serving on countless committees and, in 1931, by becoming President of MCC. He was appointed chairman of the governors of the B.B.C. in 1935, but died within a year of taking office.

Willie Bridgeman chose Viscount Lewisham to take on the Presidency in 1932. **WILLIAM LEGGE, LORD LEWISHAM** was the first President whose father and grandfather had also held the position. His father, the Sixth Earl of Dartmouth, had been President in 1893, and his mother's father, the Earl of Leicester, was President in 1848. His uncle was the Earl of Lichfield (1897), and he married the grand-daughter of the 1863 President, the Fifth Baron Suffield. There were plenty of relations to tell him how to do the job. Legge, born on 22 February 1881, was no great shakes as a cricketer, although like many of his predecessors, and many of his successors, he was keenly interested in the game throughout his life. He involved himself in all sports, and partly as a result of being Member of Parliament for West Bromwich for several years, but more because the family seat was at Patshull House in Wolverhampton, he was President of West Bromwich Albion F.C. until his death in 1958. He was also, from 1928 until 1936 when he inherited his father's title, Lord Great Chamberlain, a title which co-incidentally had been held almost 150 years earlier by Sir Peter Burrell, Viscount Gwydyr, one of the most active of early MCC members.

It was Lewisham's misfortune to be President during the bodyline tour of 1932/33, when cables between St John's Wood and Australia caused deep rifts in Anglo-Australian sporting and diplomatic relations. However, Lewisham certainly did appreciate the significance of the actions of the England team, sent as ever under the aegis of MCC, and knew that a great deal of subtle diplomacy would be required if England ever wanted to play Australia again. Pelham Warner, the manager of the MCC team, was proving to be a weak man in the face of unprecedented pressure from the government of Australia and the media from both sides of the world, so the Committee of MCC needed a strong and influential man at the helm in 1933 to help pick up the pieces and try to put them back together again.

Lewisham made an inspired choice in nominating **DOUGLAS McGAREL HOGG, FIRST VISCOUNT HAILSHAM**, a lawyer and politician who had reached the heights of Attorney-General and Lord Chancellor and who could bring considerable influence to bear on all sides. Hailsham, born on 28 February 1872, was the son of Quintin Hogg, the only non-footballer whose statue in London includes a football. Quintin Hogg was an educationalist and sports enthusiast whose influence on his son was strong in all areas, and his son, a close associate of Sir Kynaston Studd, took his father's values into Conservative politics. He had been appointed Attorney-General in 1927 and Lord Chancellor in 1928 during Stanley Baldwin's government. By 1934 he was playing a less central role in national politics, but was still a powerful man with powerful friends, exactly the kind of man MCC needed when they found themselves thrashing about in the diplomatic quicksand.

The bodyline crisis, initially caused by the tactics of the MCC captain and his bowlers, quickly spun (or, more correctly, bounced) out of control, and MCC alone was not able to handle the public reaction, in both Australia and England, which threatened to overshadow everything that happened that summer, which turned out to be one of the sunniest for many years, on the field at least. By the time that Hailsham took office, although Australia had drawn back from the implication in the first flurry of cables that the English tactics were 'unsportsman-like', there was still a very real doubt as to whether the proposed tour of 1934 by the Australians to England would take place. MCC formed a committee of investigation, chaired by Lord Hailsham, and they summoned all the principal suspects to give evidence. By 12 June, barely six weeks after Hailsham had taken up residence on what was once the woolsack of cricket, but which now must have felt like a sack of thorns, MCC were still trying to protest their innocence. 'The term "bodyline" would appear to imply a direct attack on the batsman,' they wrote. 'The Committee consider that such an implication implied to any English bowler in Australia is improper and incorrect.' They went on to complain about the behaviour of the Australian crowds, which they suggested had unfairly whipped up public antagonism towards the MCC tourists. 'The Committee, while deeply appreciative of the private and public hospitality shewn to the English team, are much concerned with regard to barracking, which is referred to in all the reports, and against which there is unanimous deprecation.'

On re-reading the correspondence between MCC and the Australian Board, one can only wonder at the diplomatic skills of Lord Hailsham and his team. The MCC side used tactics which, while not strictly illegal, were clearly against the spirit of the game at the time, and yet rather than take responsibility for the rumpus it caused, they and their Committee managed to win both the Ashes and the diplomatic exchanges afterwards. What is more, they did it without promising anything more than that they would continue to disapprove of un-sportsmanlike cricket, and even that might have been overstating the case. MCC wrote on 9 October 1933 that 'your team can certainly take the field with the knowledge and with the full assurance that cricket will be played here in the same spirit as in the past,' a double-edged promise if ever one was written down. The Australians had quite specifically been objecting to the spirit in which cricket was played in Australia, yet here was a promise that could be interpreted as MCC's intention to do more of the same. The Australians responded rather weakly that they 'assume that such cable is intended to give the assurance asked for in our cablegram of September 22'. MCC's retort was brief: 'You must please accept our cable of October 9th, which speaks for itself, as final.'

On the basis of this exchange of cables, the Australians agreed to tour in 1934. Of course, the 1934 tour in the event went very well (apart from the fact that Australia regained the Ashes) and the wounds were healed, but MCC were still, quite clearly, the rulers of world cricket. It is impossible to imagine quite such a supine attitude being taken by any national cricket board towards MCC these days, but, in 1933, Britain was still the centre of the Empire, and still considered 'home' by the vast majority of Australians. This psychological factor undermined the Board's position, even though they held the moral high ground. Nowadays, things would be very different: one need only look at the debates over the West Indian fast bowling attack from the 1970s to the 1990s, or international attitudes to Muralitharan's bowling action.

Lord Hailsham may not have been much of a cricketer, but he certainly did a fine job for MCC. When his year was up, just as the Australians were flexing their muscles at Worcester, Leicester and elsewhere, Hailsham handed over to the Earl of Cromer. Born on 29 November 1877, SIR ROWLAND THOMAS BARING, SECOND EARL OF CROMER, was another Etonian who failed to make the college XI. He became a diplomat, courtier and member of the board of the family bank, Baring Brothers, including a spell as managing director just before the First World War, when he joined the Grenadier Guards. He was ADC and/or Equerry to King George V, the Duke of Connaught, the Prince of Wales and the Viceroy of India, and collected a massively impressive collection of initials after his name. GCB GCIE KCVO GCStJ PC ADC, not to mention the Order of St Anne of Russia (Second Class) and the Royal Victorian Chain, require quite a large business card to do them justice. He was also Lord Chamberlain for sixteen years from 1922 to 1938, during which time he gained notoriety for his thoroughly disapproving attitude to the comedies of Noël Coward, and towards the allowing of nude performances at the Windmill Theatre (permitted on the understanding that the ladies did not move while on stage). It was for this decision that he was recently portrayed in the film, *Mrs. Henderson Presents*, by the actor Christopher Guest, who off screen is Lord Haden-Guest, and the son-in-law of Tony Curtis. The real Lord Cromer's connections were just as stellar. His wife, Lady Ruby Elliot-Murray-Kynynmound, was the daughter of the Earl of Minto, and her sister married both the son of the Marquess of Lansdowne (1869) and, subsequently, Col. J. J. Astor, who would be President in 1937. This puts Lord Cromer onto the fringes of the Hamilton family, along with a score of other Presidents.

Lord Cromer's diplomatic skills helped ensure a happy Australian tour in 1934, and he had the privilege and pleasure of being the only MCC President to oversee an English victory against Australia in the twentieth century – a victory won mainly by the weather and the bowling of Hedley Verity. At the end of his year, Cromer handed over to the scion of a family who had as strong a claim as any to be the most powerful cricketing family in Britain, John Cavendish Lyttelton, Ninth Viscount Cobham.

JOHN LYTTELTON was born on 23 October 1881 and was educated at Eton, where he did not play in the XI. His younger brother George did, even while John was still at school, but despite the pedigree of grandfather, father, four uncles and two brothers who all played first-class cricket (as did Lord Cobham himself, briefly), he never matched the cricketing achievements of most of his family. He was MP for Droitwich from 1910 to 1916, but was more at home as Lord Lieutenant of Worcestershire, a post that he held from 1923 until his death in 1949. He was the first county President since the time of Lord Hawke and Lord Harris to play for his county. In 1924, when he made his debut, he was not President, but he took over for 1925, when he played twice

more, and then became chairman. At the time of his death he had
reverted to the Presidency. Worcestershire in 1925 was not the youngest
team on the county circuit. Lord Cobham was already 43 years old, his
good friend Lord Somers, who was almost a regular in the County side,
was 38 that summer, but they were mere spring chickens in comparison with Rev. R. H. Moss, who played his one and only first-class
match, for Worcestershire against Gloucestershire in May that year, at
the age of 57. This represents, as far as is known, the oldest first-class
debut in English cricket history. Worcestershire would not have been
the nimblest side in the field that season.

Lord Cobham, despite his modest achievements on the field, was a
popular and successful President of MCC, and in later years as Treasurer,
a role which he filled from 1938 until his death. When he had to decide
who should succeed him, he turned to his near neighbour in the west
Midlands, and former county colleague in the Worcestershire side,
Lord Somers.

L IEUTENANT-COLONEL THE RT. HON. ARTHUR HERBERT
   TENNYSON SOMERS-COCKS, SIXTH BARON SOMERS, was born
on 20 March 1887, and was educated at Charterhouse. He was a good
schoolboy cricketer, a right-hand batsman who scored 115 not out for
Charterhouse against Westminster in 1904, and finished the season top
of the school batting averages. *Wisden* described him that year as 'a cool
and determined player at a crisis'. Lord Somers, who inherited the title
in 1896 at the age of nine, became a professional soldier in the First Life
Guards, and had a good war. He was never the most robust of men, his
cricket career being limited to seventeen first-class matches, sixteen for
Worcestershire in 1923 and 1925, and one against them, for MCC, in
1906. He had a highest score of 52, at an average of 13.44, and only
bowled two overs to little effect in his entire career. He spent some time
in Australia, firstly as Governor of Victoria and then as acting Governor General of Australia between October 1930 and January 1931. On

his return to England, he became a vice-president of Worcestershire, but could not oust his old friend Lord Cobham from the Presidency. As a consolation, he was awarded the plum job at MCC for 1936.

In that year, membership of the Marylebone Club increased by 90 to 6,656, but perhaps the most important event of the year was the change in the LBW law. In 1936, an experimental Law 24 had been introduced, which for the first time allowed batsmen to be out LBW if the ball pitched outside the off stump. The experiment was such a success that it was virtually unanimously agreed that the new law should be incorporated fully into the Laws, which it was at a special meeting held after the 1937 Annual General Meeting. The LBW Law has not changed in any fundamentals, despite endless discussion, since that time. Its number has changed, and the rider about whether or not a stroke was being played has been added, but basically the Law passed when Lord Somers was President is still in force.

Somers failed to marry into any of the noble families of cricket (although his sister married the son of the 1871 President, the Earl of Clarendon), but he did have an uncle, also called Arthur Somers-Cocks, who was for many years headmaster of Harrison College in Barbados, the Alma Mater of the young Pelham Warner. Towards the end of his life, Lord Somers was appointed Chief Scout in 1941, in succession to Lord Baden-Powell. He held that title for barely three years, before he died, aged only 57, at home in Eastnor Castle on 14 July 1944.

Somers nominated **COL. THE HON. JOHN JACOB ASTOR** as his successor. Astor was certainly the first MCC President born in the United States. He was the fourth child of William Waldorf Astor, and was five years old when the family left New York City in 1891 to live permanently in England. He was educated at Eton, and by the time he got there he had shaken off his American past to such an extent that he played for two years with distinction in the college XI. *Wisden* said he 'played very sound cricket, and should be heard of at Oxford', but the prediction proved incorrect. Astor went up to New College, Oxford, but did not get a Blue, but later on did play a few games for Buckinghamshire. He then went into the Life Guards, having been ADC to Lord Hardinge, Viceroy of India, before the outbreak of the First World War. He was seen by many as more American than British (the Americans knew him as John Jacob Astor V), but made up for it by involving himself in many quintessentially British institutions. He was actually a British citizen, and proved it by winning a gold medal for Britain at the 1908 Olympic Games in London, in the rackets doubles. He was Member of Parliament for Dover from 1922 to 1945, for some of that time alongside his sister-in-law Nancy Astor, the first woman to take her seat at Westminster. His wife had previously been married to the son of the Marquess of Lansdowne (1869), and had during her marriage been sister-in-law to the Duke of Devonshire (1912). He held directorships in the Great Western Railway Company, Hambros Bank, Phoenix Insurance and Barclays Bank among others. He was Deputy-Lieutenant of Kent for a quarter of a century and Lieutenant-Colonel of the City of London Home Guard from 1940 to 1944. He also bought *The Times* on the death of its proprietor Lord Northcliffe in 1922, and retained it until 1966 when he sold it to the even less English Lord Thomson of Fleet. Certainly, it is as a journalist and press baron that Astor will be remembered.

However, the most English of all the institutions he allied himself to was MCC. He was a keen member, and served on the Committee for many years, using his money and influence where needed for the good of the Club. His Presidency in 1937, MCC's 150th anniversary year, was popular and well deserved. To celebrate the 150th anniversary, MCC organised two matches at Lord's in late May, one a Test trial match billed as North v. South, and the other the MCC Australian XI v. The Rest. In the trial match, Hutton made a century for the North and Hammond one in reply for the South, while Farnes and Verity, two casualties of the coming war, took the most wickets. The MCC Australian XI beat the Rest quite easily, but not before Alf Gover took seven for 44 for the Rest. In all, almost 28,000 people attended the games, despite poor weather at the start of the week, and the added complication of a bus strike. The Celebration Dinner was not held until 15 July, at the Savoy, with over 400 people present. Col. Astor presided, the Duke of Gloucester, the King's brother, attended and read a telegram of congratulation from King George, but Sir Pelham Warner was very disappointed in the speeches. Lord Hawke was one of the speakers, as the only man there who had also played in the Club Centenary match in 1887 and been present at the Ground Centenary dinner, but when Col. Astor concluded the evening with a speech in which he paid tribute to the Lord's staff – that must have had them all standing and cheering – Sir Pelham realised that no one had even mentioned the names of Lord Harris or W. G. Grace, the only two men to whom there were at that time memorials at Lord's. A frightful faux pas is what Warner called it, but no one else took such umbrage. Astor redeemed himself, if he ever needed to, by getting *The Times* to publish a special edition to commemorate the 150th anniversary. This was reprinted in book form and presented to MCC. Whether Col. Astor presented it as Chairman of *The Times* or whether he received it as President of MCC is not recorded. In January 1956 he was created Baron Astor of Hever (Hever Castle having been his home since his father died in 1919) and in 1971 he died in Cannes at the age of 85, the first President of MCC known to have been born and to have died outside Britain.

To prove the strength of his connections, Astor nominated as his successor his erstwhile boss **STANLEY BALDWIN**, the first former Prime Minister to become President of MCC. Baldwin, now the First Earl Baldwin of Bewdley, was Conservative Prime Minister from 1923 to 1924, and again from 1924 to 1929 and from 1935 to 1937. Baldwin was known for his contempt of most press barons, whom he accused of wanting 'power without responsibility – the prerogative of the harlot throughout the ages', so it was quite a tribute to Astor's powers of persuasion that he was able to nominate Baldwin as his successor.

Born on 3 August 1867, and therefore already 70 when he took over at Lord's, Stanley Baldwin was the only son of a wealthy industrialist, the owner of an ironworks in Wilden, just south of Kidderminster. His mother, Louisa MacDonald, was the daughter of a Methodist minister, and one of her sisters married a man called John Lockwood Kipling. Their son Rudyard was Baldwin's first cousin. Another of Baldwin's aunts married the pre-Raphaelite artist Edward Burne-Jones; and a third married Edward Poynter (1836–1919), at the time a better known and better appreciated artist than Burne-Jones, and who ultimately succeeded Sir John Millais as President of the Royal Academy, becoming in the process first a knight and then a baronet. Young Stanley Baldwin's connections were quite different from those of most MCC Presidents, but equally impressive.

Baldwin was educated at Harrow and Trinity College, Cambridge; it was a route to success followed by many others, but he did not play representative cricket at either institution. After university, he joined his father's ironworks, quickly if unsurprisingly rising to the rank of financial director, and it was not until 1908, when he was already over 40, that he first entered Parliament. Even then, he was merely stepping into his father's shoes as Conservative member for Bewdley, having two years earlier contested and lost the seat of Kidderminster. His political beliefs were radical for Conservatives of the time, as in his view the rich ought voluntarily make donations to help repay the nation's wartime debts, but he was an eloquent, sensitive and clubbable man, if rather cautious, and seemed to rise in the party's ranks almost without trace. He was broadly popular within the Conservative Party, but, as a later Tory Prime Minister, Harold Macmillan, pointed out, he was 'respected and almost loved by the Labour Party'. This may have been partly because he was the leader who called the General Election of January 1924, which gave the Labour Party their first taste of government, but it was also because he was so determined to see the downfall of the Liberals that he was prepared to encourage the rise of the Labour Party.

Baldwin was a strange mixture of energy and lethargy. He took two months' holiday every summer in Aix-les-Bains, yet at times of crisis, such as the General Strike of 1926 and the Abdication Crisis ten years later, he was an indefatigable pillar of strength. Lloyd George once said that 'to try to make any impact on Baldwin is like trying to cut a cushion with a sword.' The feeling was mutual: Baldwin called Lloyd George 'the Goat' and thoroughly disapproved of both his personal lifestyle and his political beliefs. His friends were loyal to him and he was true to them. Lord Bridgeman (1931) was one of them; Baldwin appointed him as Home Secretary in his first government in 1923. The Duke of Devonshire (1912) was also in Baldwin's first cabinet, as Colonial Secretary, and his second cabinet from November 1924 also included Sir Douglas Hogg, later Lord Hailsham (1933), as Attorney-General. The political strings that MCC pulled between the wars were tied together by Stanley Baldwin, the dominant political figure of the two decades between the wars.

These days, we think of him mainly as the Prime Minister who effectively forced King Edward to abdicate rather than contemplate a morganatic marriage, his strong Methodist principles combining with his personal feelings towards the King, which were unenthusiastic at best. However, he had to deal with the rise of Fascism and Nazism in Europe and to address the problems of rearmament after the war which should have ended all wars. He was a natural peacemaker, and was temperamentally ill-equipped to take on the European dictators, who were not interested in peace. He resigned in May 1937, and left Downing Street with the words, 'I am a gentleman at large now.' Almost exactly a year later, he became President of MCC.

Cometh the hour, cometh the man. The Presidents of MCC between the two world wars were almost exclusively courtiers, military leaders or politicians who had an interest in cricket (or 'a love of cricket', depending on which words came that year to Pelham Warner as editor of the *Cricketer*). There had not been a Test cricketer, or even a man known first and foremost for his cricketing skills, since Sir Stanley Jackson in 1921, and even he had built a very public post-cricket career. MCC was in danger of forgetting what it was there for, of drifting backwards into its past glories and being content with existing as just another pillar of the establishment – an establishment which had already been rocked by one world war and which was about to be changed forever by another. It was time for the Club to focus on cricket once more.

It is not clear by what arcane process Lord Baldwin came up with the name of his successor, but we must assume that, as he had not been the most hands-on of Presidents, he took the advice of his Committee in choosing **STANLEY CHRISTOPHERSON**. Or maybe he thought that a shared Christian name was as good a reason as any. The death of Lord Hawke in 1938 meant that for the first time in over fifty years, he was not on hand to have a say in the selection process. It is the prerogative of the President to nominate whomever he likes, but in practice the opinion of the Committee and perhaps of past Presidents is taken into account, even if the final decision is for the President alone. Of course, it is possible that the nominee will turn down the offer; this has happened on many occasions. All of these refusals went officially un-recorded, but inevitably some have come out into the open. If this happens, the President has to find another candidate. It is said that in one post-war year the outgoing President spoke to five or six men before finding one who would agree to take on the job, but in most years the first man asked has leapt at the chance. Stanley Christopherson, who was a Committee member of long standing, would have been seen as a safe pair of hands by the Committee, but there is no evidence of any particular friendship between him and Lord Baldwin which leads us to believe that this was a personal decision by the outgoing President.

However the decision was reached it was a fortunate one. In May 1939 the clouds of war were certainly gathering. The meeting at Munich between Hitler and Chamberlain had happened eight months earlier, but peace in our time was no more likely. It was entirely possible, but at the same time unthinkable, that whoever was to take over the Presidency in May 1939 might have a long stint ahead of him. Stanley Christopherson was already 77 years old when he took office, at that time the oldest man ever to take on the job, and by the time he actually stepped down, in May 1946, he was 83, a record that still stands. Christopherson was born in Kidbrooke, at the metropolitan end of Kent, on 11 November 1861, one of ten brothers who all played cricket at club level and above. Together with their father, they regularly fielded a family XI towards the end of the nineteenth century, mainly against school teams. Stanley was the best cricketer in the family, a fast-medium bowler in an era when amateurs usually left the bowling to the professionals. He played fairly regularly for Kent during the 1880s, bowling off a long run which ended in his classically pure high-arm delivery, and in 1884 met with such success that he played not only for the Gentlemen against the Players, but also in the Second Test against Australia, at Lord's. This was the first ever Test at Lord's, and England won by an innings and 5 runs. Christopherson made 17, batting at number eleven, but only took one wicket, and was never selected to play for England again. An injury to his arm in 1886 effectively finished his career.

The 1939 season was a memorable one for the cricket played at Lord's. George Headley became the first man to score a century in each innings in a Test there, and in what was for many people the highlight of the season, Harrow at last beat Eton, for the first time since 1908. A crowd of some 8,000 people watched the climax of the match, and after the Harrow captain, A. O. L. Lithgow, hit the winning runs and had been carried off the field in triumph, they cheered outside the Pavilion for twenty minutes. As *Wisden* put it, 'there followed a free fight for top hats.' It was as if everybody knew that this might be the last match at Lord's for some time. The release from conformity was exhilarating. Only six weeks later, Europe was at war.

Stanley Christopherson was a financier, who had enjoyed a long and successful career in the City. He was a tall man of great charm, and in his youth very handsome. The team photograph of the Lord's Test of 1884 shows a serious looking young man sitting cross-legged on the ground at the feet of Lord Harris, his cap too small for his head. Alongside him in the team are three other MCC Presidents of the future, Lord Harris, Allan Steel and Alfred Lyttelton, making this side the only one to contain four future Presidents. There have been three future Presidents in a Test team often enough, but never four, apart from that first ever Test at Lord's, a century and a quarter ago.

During the long war years, the Committee annually asked Christopherson whether he would agree to stay on as President, and annually he said yes. He was deprived of the services of both the Secretary, Lieut. Col. R. S. Rait Kerr, and the assistant secretary, Ronnie Aird, for the duration, but into their shoes stepped two men steeped in Lord's history – the recently retired Secretary William Findlay and the grand old man of Lord's, Sir Pelham Warner. They supported Christopherson throughout the war years and were ultimately rewarded with Presidential years of their own once peace was restored. It was said that Christopherson, despite his busy schedule in the City as, among other things, chairman of the Midland Bank, never missed a Committee meeting and visited Lord's practically every day. Remember, he had his eightieth birthday in 1941, to become the first ever octogenarian President. He was a truly indefatigable man, whose strength of purpose and devotion to MCC kept the Club going during the war. He missed his last Annual General Meeting, in 1946, through ill health, but by then the crisis was past. MCC was back up and running, top class cricket was being played at Lord's again, and a bright new future beckoned. Christopherson was appointed a trustee of the Club in 1946, along with Sir Pelham Warner, 'in recognition of their signal services to the MCC since 1939'. He died only three years later, aged 87, and it is a great pity that he died without the knighthood that he most certainly deserved for his services to MCC, Lord's and cricket in general throughout his life. As his *Wisden* obituary put it, 'in all walks of life he always played the game.'

CHAPTER SEVEN

1946–1966
POST-WAR, RESISTING CHANGE

The end of the war came in June 1945 in Europe and in August in the Asian theatres. In June 1945, Stanley Christopherson had just been confirmed in another year in office, so it was not until 1946 that a new President could be inaugurated and the post-war era at St John's Wood begin. This being the first year of full cricket after a war in which the whole country, indeed the whole Empire, owed its salvation to the fighting spirit of the Allied forces, it was perhaps not surprising that Stanley Christopherson nominated a general to succeed him. Not that **GENERAL SIR RONALD FORBES ADAM BT**. was an ordinary general – he was an organiser who had been Adjutant General to the forces for most of the war – the man who kept the Army supplied and the men fit and armed to fight.

Ronald Adam was educated at Eton and then at the Royal Military Academy, Woolwich. He served with distinction in Flanders and Italy during the First World War, but if his subsequent career is anything to go by, he was more suited to be an organiser of the fighting than a participant. By 1936, when Britain's rearmament was politically unpopular but actually urgent, he was Deputy Director of Military Operations at the War Office, and by 1939 he was Deputy Chief of the Imperial General Staff. His main claim to the gratitude of the nation was his role as Adjutant General to the Forces from 1941 until 1946. He was the man who oversaw the training and supply of Britain's conscript Army, and his success was an achievement that even the more optimistic of his supporters had hardly expected. He was the man who thought up the Home Guard, he was the man who organised prisoner of war camps (from which only one German prisoner ever escaped) and he was also closely involved in post-war defence planning. He stepped down from active service shortly after the war ended, which gave him the opportunity to take on the MCC Presidency, but was still involved for many years with several national and international organisations. He was Chairman of the British Council from 1946 to 1955, and was its director-general for most of that time, from 1947 to 1954. He was Colonel Commandant of the Royal Army Dental Corps from 1946 to 1951 and a member of the Miners' Welfare Commission from 1946 to 1952. Most importantly, he was a member of the Executive Board of UNESCO from 1950 to 1954, being its chairman for his last two years. He was also, by the time he died, the oldest member of I Zingari, a club he had joined in 1935. Cricket was an integral part of his life, not merely another organisational project. All the same, when he stepped down in 1947, he was asked to chair a standing sub-committee 'to examine the implications of the Town and Country Planning Bill 1947'. The right man in the right place once again.

At the 1946 Annual General Meeting at which Sir Ronald took over, the grateful thanks of MCC for its deliverance, along with the rest of Britain, were expressed by the election to Honorary Life Membership of several of the Allied war leaders. Field-Marshal Lord Wavell, Admiral Lord Cunningham, Admiral Lord Fraser, Field Marshal Lord Alanbrooke, Field Marshal Lord Alexander of Tunis, Marshal of the R.A.F. Lord Tedder and Marshal of the R.A.F. Lord Portal were all elected, along with Field-Marshal Lord Montgomery, Winston Churchill and General Dwight D. Eisenhower. Not many American Presidents have been elected to honorary life membership of MCC, and there is little evidence that Eisenhower had any idea of the game or of the honour he was receiving, but he accepted it just the same. When he attended a Test match in December 1959, between Pakistan and Australia at Karachi, during his Presidency (of the United States, not MCC) he was not seen to be wearing his MCC tie and clearly had little idea what was going on. Two of those new life members did have some idea of what was going on, though. Both Lord Alexander and Lord Portal would become Presidents of MCC in their time. Lord Alexander was a renowned schoolboy cricketer, but Lord Portal had fewer pretensions to cricketing talent.

Sir Ronald nominated as the next President a man who played cricket to a good standard, if you count captaining Kent in the 1920s as playing to a good standard. **WYKEHAM STANLEY CORNWALLIS, SECOND BARON CORNWALLIS**, was born at Linton Park in Kent on 14 March 1892, and was educated at Eton, where he was a contemporary of Dick Twining (1964) and Hon. Lionel Tennyson among others, but he did not play for the college. He completed his education at Sandhurst, and became a regular soldier, eventually reaching the rank of captain in the Royal Scots Greys. After service in the First World War, Cornwallis began playing sporadically for Kent, as an opening bowler who on occasions could be genuinely quick. Unfortunately, he had played virtually no cricket since leaving school, apart from a few country house games before the war, and he was not physically fit enough to withstand the rigours of bowling through a county season. His appearances for Kent were infrequent, and even in the years 1924 to 1926, when he led the side, he was by no means a regular player. In 1924, for example (when Stanley Christopherson was President of Kent), he took only 25 wickets and scored 178 runs all summer. He had to be carried from the field at Canterbury when he tore a ligament fielding on 4 August, and did not play again that year. All in all, he took 118 wickets in a 106-match career spanning eight seasons, but as a captain he was very popular with his players and he kept Kent in the top five of the County Championship in each of his three summers in charge. It has to be said that any team with Frank Woolley and Tich Freeman as its backbone has a pretty good chance of doing well, but beyond those two consummate cricketers, Kent was a team that relied heavily on the availability of talented amateurs.

After he retired from cricket and the Army, Cornwallis became active in business and in public life, in Kent and elsewhere. He was for many years Lord Lieutenant of Kent and was a staunch member of the county cricket club, and of I Zingari. In 1948, he was for a few months President of both Kent and MCC – neither the first nor the last man to hold another Presidency during his MCC year. When he died in 1982, a couple of months before his 90th birthday, he was mourned as one of the last of that breed of amateur cricketers who, lacking any outstanding cricketing talent, nevertheless did such outstanding work for their county clubs.

Cornwallis nominated the Earl of Gowrie as the President for 1948, an apt choice for an Australian touring year. **ALEXANDER GORE ARKWRIGHT HORE-RUTHVEN, FIRST EARL OF GOWRIE**, was born on 16 July 1872, making him almost 76 years old on becoming President. He was the second son of the Eighth Lord Ruthven and, like so many Presidents before him, was educated at Eton. This was, in effect, his local school as he had been born in Windsor, but he was withdrawn from the school early because of his poor eyesight. This did not stop him joining the Army, and going to North Africa to take part in the Sudan campaigns as a captain in the Highland Light Infantry. On 22 September 1898, during fighting at Gedarif in eastern Sudan, he saved the life of a wounded Egyptian officer who was lying in the path of charging Sudanese rebels. This is not the place to argue the rights and wrongs of British Imperialist policy in the Anglo-Egyptian Sudan in the late nineteenth century, and Hore-Ruthven did not stop to consider whether or not the Sudanese had the right to want foreigners out of their homeland. He ran forward to pick up the injured man and carried him, under heavy fire, back to British lines. For his bravery, he was awarded the Victoria Cross, one of 37 Etonians to win that award for valour, but the only one to gain the Presidency of MCC as well.

Much of Gowrie's subsequent career was linked to Australia. In 1908, he went to Australia as military secretary to the new Governor General, Lord Dudley (another cricket follower, whose father had been MCC President in 1864). He was still a soldier at this time and after two years in Australia, Hore-Ruthven was posted to India. In the First World War, he fought in France and at Gallipoli, where he was badly wounded. By the time the war ended, he was a Brigadier-General, and he was appointed commander of British forces in Germany from 1919 to 1920. In 1928, he left the Army and was appointed Governor of South Australia, a post he retained for six years. During this time, the Third Test of the 1932/33 series was played in Adelaide, a match described by *Wisden* as 'probably the most unpleasant ever played'. England won by 338 runs, but feelings boiled over on the issue of bodyline bowling. Hore-Ruthven was by lucky chance in England at the time, and it was his meetings in London, advising the Secretary for the Dominions J. H. Thomas, which helped keep diplomatic relations between the two countries open in the face of a barrage of telegrams from Australia.

In 1934, he was appointed both Baron Gowrie and governor of New South Wales, a post he kept for two more years before in 1936 he was appointed Governor General of Australia, in succession to the controversial Australian Sir Isaac Isaacs. Gowrie was a quiet success in the top post. He had little power, but had to intervene twice in domestic politics: firstly when firstly Prime Minister Joseph Lyons died suddenly in 1939, and then in 1940 when a general election produced no clear winner. He remained in Australia until 1944, just over a year after he learned that his only son had been killed in Libya on Christmas Eve 1942. He was created Earl of Gowrie on his return, and for 1948, the year of the first post-war tour by an Australian side, he was a happy choice as President of MCC. He died in May 1955 and the title passed to his grandson, who became a Conservative politician and the first cabinet minister to undergo a heart transplant.

Gowrie, who in 1948 was Lieutenant-Governor of Windsor Castle, broke with all precedent by nominating as his successor a member of the Royal Family, **H.R.H. PRINCE PHILIP, DUKE OF EDINBURGH** and consort to Princess Elizabeth, then heiress presumptive to the throne. The Duke was only 28 years old, and the youngest President since Viscount Downe in 1872. He was also the first President to be born in the twentieth century. The appointment was greeted with huge pride and satisfaction by the Club and its members, but it took the new President himself by surprise. He was a serving naval officer at the time, and did not expect to have time to attend all the Committee meetings and Test matches that a President was expected to. However, he allowed himself to be persuaded by Lord Gowrie, largely because he had a great interest in cricket, and in all team sports as well as in the development of sport for young people. He had been in the second XI at Cheam prep school, but captain of the 1st XI at Gordonstoun and, although his opportunities to play the game with any degree of seriousness were restricted by his military and royal duties, those who saw him play at school believed that, given the chance, he would have been able to play to good club standard. He was an off-spinner and hard-hitting batsman at school, and played one or two charity matches in the 1940s and 1950s. The 1950 *Wisden* shows a picture of him bowling the first ball at a new ground in Oxfordshire. Even in a tie and brogues, the action is pure and the concentration unwavering.

Probably the most important issue that MCC addressed during Prince Philip's year was that of the status of professional cricketers. Since the end of the war, there had been the first signs that the old distinction between amateurs and professionals was becoming anachronistic, and the borders were being blurred. Even before the war, Walter Hammond had switched from professionalism to amateur status so that he could be appointed captain of England, and men such as Bill Edrich of Middlesex did the same thing to captain their counties. Paul Gibb, the idiosyncratic Yorkshire wicketkeeper, became the first Oxbridge Blue to play cricket as a professional, but it was not until 1949 that MCC first offered Honorary Cricket Membership to a handful of great professional cricketers of the past. This was the thing of which Prince Philip was most proud, and it was the first hesitating step that MCC took towards equality among all players, which was still a decade and a half away. Among the 26 professionals offered honorary membership were such great players as Jack Hobbs, Herbert Sutcliffe, Maurice Tate, Harold Larwood, Frank Woolley, Patsy Hendren, George Hirst, Wilfred Rhodes, Maurice Leyland and S.F. Barnes. It was, if not the beginning of the end, at least the end of the beginning for amateurism.

Again in 1949 a committee, under the chairmanship of Harry Altham (1959), was set up to look into the future of English cricket, with particular reference to cricket in schools of all types and for all ages. This was another issue close to the President's heart, tying in with his presidency of the National Playing Fields Association, and anticipating by one year the birth of the Lord's Taverners in 1950, a charity of which Prince Philip has been patron and 'Twelfth Man' from the start, and which raises money for youth cricket and to give other sporting chances to young people. MCC has always devoted a great deal of time to planning its future, both by crystal ball gazing to see how the game will develop and by architects' plans to work out how Lord's will develop, but over the years there had been comparatively little time and effort devoted to the cricketing ambitions of those too young to become MCC members. Yes, there were plenty of schools matches at Lord's and fixtures such as Lord's Schools v. The Rest were a sign of the interest that the Club took in youth cricket, but it had always been aimed at the public schools, bringing the new generation of suitable young men into the arms of the Marylebone Club. The 1949 initiative was the first really inclusive youth cricket initiative taken by MCC, and it owes a great deal to the determination of the President to make sure that it happened. Now, over fifty years on, MCC plays a major role, not only in schools and university cricket, but also in inner-city cricket, girls' and women's cricket, and cricket for the blind and the disabled. Much of this eagerness to be involved can be traced to the Altham Committee and the 1949 President.

The Duke of Edinburgh nominated as his successor the one man who more typified Lord's than any other, possibly in the entire history of the Club. **SIR PELHAM WARNER**, born in 1873, was 48 years older than his predecessor when he took office in May 1950, and after so long a wait for the very top job, it was perhaps fitting that he had one of the longer terms of office – seventeen months rather than the normal twelve. This was because it had already been decided that from now on the term of office should run from 1 October to 30 September each year rather than from AGM to AGM, May to May. Pelham Warner, as the first beneficiary of this new ruling, held office from May 1950 to the end of September 1951. The idea was, and still is, that the name of the new President is announced at the AGM, but the cricket season immediately ahead is the responsibility of the incumbent. That makes planning for the season far easier for MCC, knowing who their President is, than if they discover at the last minute that the new man has an active business or political career and might not be available for Committee meetings or Test matches starting in a matter of weeks or days. The new system seems to work, and has been operating for almost six decades without serious mishap.

Sir Pelham Warner, known affectionately throughout the world of cricket as 'Plum', had done everything in cricket, almost always with great success. Born in Trinidad in October 1873, he was educated at Rugby and made his debut at Lord's as a fifteen year old in 1889, playing for Rugby against Marlborough. He scored 3 and 16, but in the second innings hit his first boundary at Lord's. 'I can feel her on the bat now,' he wrote in his history of Lord's. 'An idle and perhaps improper boast, but what would life be without its memories?' After that first sweet hit, Warner's long life was inextricably linked with Lord's. He went up to Oxford, where he was a contemporary of C. B. Fry and H. D. G. Leveson-Gower, and played in the Varsity matches of 1895 and 1896 without particular success. He went on to captain England and play for Middlesex for over 20 years, finishing in 1920 at the age of 46 by leading his beloved county to the Championship after a thrilling final match against Surrey. He then turned to administration

1955, Harold,
Field Marshal
Earl Alexander
of Tunis

1956, Walter, First
Viscount Monckton
of Brenchley

1957, Bernard Marmaduke Fitzalan-Howard,
Sixteenth Duke of Norfolk

1963, George O. B. 'Gubby' Allen

Left: 1958, Charles, Marshal of the RAF Viscount Portal of Hungerford

Below: 1959, Harry S. Altham

Below: 1960, Sir Hubert Ashton

1961, Col Sir
William Worsley, Bt.

1962, Terence, Lt Col.
Lord Nugent of Harline

1964, Richard H.
Twining

1965, Lt General
Sir Oliver Leese

1966, Rt. Hon. Sir
Alec Douglas-Home

1967, Arthur E. R. Gilligan

1968, Ronald Aird

1969, Maurice J. C. Allom

1970, Sir Cyril Hawker

1971,
Frederick
R. Brown

Below
right:
1972,
Aidan M.
Crawley

Below:
1973,
Harold,
Lord
Caccia

and journalism, a difficult but heady mixture, founding the greatest of all cricket magazines, the *Cricketer*, in 1921, and becoming heavily involved in MCC's affairs as committee man, England Test selector and, as we have seen, Deputy Secretary during the Second World War. He was also President of Middlesex C.C.C. from 1937 to 1946. There is a remarkable souvenir of his Test selector days hanging on the wall of the Committee Room at the St Lawrence Ground, Canterbury. In Sir Pelham's handwriting is the team list for the Lord's Test of 1926 against Australia. The full team is written out, but there is an interesting error, which shows Warner's age. Instead of 'M. W. Tate', Warner has written 'F. W. Tate', Maurice's father, who played one fateful Test in 1902. Even in the 1920s, Warner was of a different generation.

He also managed tours abroad, including the 1932/33 tour to Australia, which must rank as the low point in his career, and the 1947/48 team to West Indies, his original homeland. By the time he took office as President at Lord's, he must have thought his time had been and gone, perhaps imagining himself another victim of the supposed bias against journalists that was then supposed to be rife at Lord's. However, when his name was announced at the 1950 Annual General Meeting (by Lord Cornwallis, in the chair in place of the Duke of Edinburgh, who was on naval duties) the room erupted in a most un-Long-Room-like burst of cheering, which lasted for some minutes. He was, incidentally, chronologically the last of the many MCC Presidents who have been caricatured in *Vanity Fair*. His portrait had appeared in September 1903.

It was, of course, a West Indian summer in 1951, and Sir Pelham, who had been knighted for his services to cricket as long ago as 1937, enjoyed himself enormously, despite the fact that West Indies, with the three Ws and Ramadhin and Valentine, proved far too strong for England. That winter, while still President, he was Chairman of Selectors picking the touring team to Australia, making him the only man to have been President of MCC at the same time as being an England selector. He had two summers in charge, and the 1951 tourists, South Africa, obliged by losing the series to England.

In 1953, MCC gave a dinner in his honour to celebrate his 80th birthday, and on 7 May 1958, he opened the new stand between the Grand Stand and the Pavilion, which was named in his honour the Warner Stand. This was the first permanent stand at Lord's to be named after any individual, and though it has now been followed by the Allen Stand and the Edrich and Compton Stands, the honour remains with Warner as the first man to be so honoured. Sir Pelham died in 1963, aged 89.

No doubt very much aware of the honour the Presidency conferred on those who had worked for many years at Lord's, Sir Pelham chose as his successor an old comrade from the Committee room, WILLIAM FINDLAY. Findlay, born on 22 June 1880, was a Lancastrian, but his parents sent him to Eton for his education. He captained the college XI in 1899 and then went up to Oxford, and won his Blue in three consecutive years, from 1901 to 1903, captaining the team to victory in his final year. He was a wicketkeeper and a good enough batsman to open the innings for Oxford, but not for Lancashire, for whom he played on and off over the next four or five seasons, helping them win the Championship in 1904. In August 1906, when Kent played Lancashire at Canterbury and won by an innings and 196 runs, Findlay was not playing, but that did not stop him becoming a leading figure in one of the most famous cricket paintings of all time, Albert Chevallier Tayler's aptly titled 'Kent v. Lancashire 1906'. The painting was commissioned by the Kent club to celebrate their first ever Championship title, and Lord Harris, ever the benign dictator, told Tayler that the painting had to be, in photographic terms, an action shot including all the Kent XI, and that the bowler had to be Colin Blythe. Tayler had no trouble in persuading all the Kent XI to sit for their portraits, and he scarcely needed to work with John Tyldesley, the Lancashire batsman facing Blythe in the painting, as it is mainly his rear view that is shown. But he found it very difficult to persuade any of the rest of the Lancashire XI to come and sit for him in London, especially Harry Makepeace the opening batsman, whom he wanted to portray at the non-striker's end. The solution was to ask Findlay to sit for him. Findlay retired from playing cricket at the end of the 1906 season to take up the position of secretary at Surrey after the death of the great Charles Alcock, and so was in and around London all winter. The painting was duly completed, and William Findlay is thus immortalised as part of a match he never played in. In 2006, it was put up for auction by Kent C.C.C. at Sotheby's, and reached a hammer price of £600,000, a record for a cricket painting.

Findlay became a professional cricket administrator of the highest order. After several years at Kennington Oval, he moved to Lord's as assistant to 'Ben' Lacey, and took over from the great Sir Francis when he retired in 1926. He remained as Secretary for ten years until 1936, but after that was always at the heart of some Committee or another. The 1937 Findlay Commission was charged with looking into the financial and other difficulties facing counties taking part in the County Championship, a subject which probably needs a permanent commission. The issues may change but the problems do not. Findlay's commission was in particular keen to see brighter play, but the real trouble with county cricket was that it did not fit in easily with modern life. As the rest of our lives got more professional and more hectic, there was little time or sympathy for the nineteenth century style of county cricket, sport for sport's sake and leisure for the leisured classes, with the professionals doing the hard work for meagre pay. Test cricket still had great support, but even in the 1930s, there were signs that county cricket was losing its grip on the public imagination. It is a tribute to men like Findlay and his successors, and to the determination of the great British public to enjoy living in the past, that the County Championship still exists, seventy years on from Findlay's commission.

Findlay was a very popular man at Lord's, with scores of references to his never-failing courtesy and his diplomatic manner. Lord Plumer, the 1929 President, made perhaps the most famous, and most condescending, remark about him: 'If Findlay had been a soldier, I should like to have had him on my staff.' Findlay died in June 1953, a few weeks before England regained the Ashes.

Findlay nominated as his successor a man who had little direct experience of first-class cricket, **Sir Henry Hugh Arthur Fitzroy Somerset, Tenth Duke of Beaufort**. Sir Henry was the grandson of his namesake, the 1853 and 1877 President. He was born on 4 April 1900, and was educated at Eton and Sandhurst. He was lucky enough to be just too young to fight in the First World War and spent much of his adult life in the comparative quiet of his home, Badminton House, which he looked after and developed with great devotion. His father died in 1924, so the Tenth Duke was still a young man when he inherited the title. He was very well connected: he married Princess Mary of Teck, the daughter of Adolphus, Marquess of Cambridge, who was both a grand-niece of Queen Victoria and niece of Queen Mary, King George V's consort. Clearly the Royal Family had forgiven the Beauforts for their efforts to prove that they, not the Hanoverians, were the true royal line of Britain. Anyway, it was Coronation year, and Queen Elizabeth II, not King Henry IX, was riding in the golden coach.

Horses were his great sporting love. He was known as Master not merely because he held the title of Master of the Horse from 1936 until 1978, but because like his father and grandfather before him he was Master of the Beaufort Hounds and it was during his time that the Badminton Horse Trials grew to become one of the major three-day events in the world calendar, but cricket was certainly a strong secondary interest. He was a member of both I Zingari and the Free Foresters for many years, and, though there is little evidence of his playing skills, he also hosted many matches at Badminton House, on the ground developed by his grandfather a century earlier. He was also, like his forbears, President of Gloucestershire County Cricket Club for many years. It was a pity so few members of Gloucestershire's side were involved in the wonderful regaining of the Ashes that summer. Only Tom Graveney featured in any of the Tests.

The Duke nominated as his successor his great friend from the racing world, the Sixth Earl of Rosebery. The Earl was better known in cricketing circles as Lord Dalmeny, his title when as a young man he captained Surrey. **ALBERT EDWARD HARRY MEYER ARCHIBALD PRIMROSE, LORD DALMENY**, born on 8 January 1882, was the son of the Liberal Prime Minister Lord Rosebery, the only Prime Minister so far to own a Derby winner while in office (these days such extravagance and lack of concentration on the job in hand would be the kiss of death for any politician). Educated at Eton, he was in the XI the year after William Findlay, and scored 52, 'by fearless hitting' said the reports, in a narrow one-wicket defeat against Harrow at Lord's in 1900. After Eton, Dalmeny took the well-trodden path to Sandhurst and was then commissioned in the Grenadier Guards. He managed to combine several careers, because by 1906 he was not only still an Army officer, but also captain of Surrey County Cricket Club and a Liberal Member of Parliament. He was only captain of Surrey for three seasons, from 1905 to 1907, and only an MP for four years, from 1906 to 1910, but he was a significant success as the former, if less so as the latter. Quite how good a job he could have done for his constituents in Scotland while at the same time playing for Surrey is uncertain, but Surrey members were not unhappy. In 1905, he awarded Jack Hobbs his county cap after only two games, and, from 1906, he renewed a happy association with William Findlay that had begun at Eton, when Findlay was appointed Secretary of Surrey. Dalmeny was also responsible for approaching Surrey's landlord at the Oval, the Prince of Wales (later King George V), to get permission to use the Prince of Wales feathers as the club crest.

Harry Dalmeny's father died in 1929, making him the new Earl of Rosebery. By now, at the age of 47, his interests lay far more in the parade ring than within the boundary ropes, and while he never won the Derby like his father, Rosebery was an important and successful racehorse owner between the wars. In 1945, when Churchill's wartime coalition government broke up and it was clear there would soon be a general election, Churchill formed an interim administration in which, to everybody's surprise, Lord Rosebery, a well known Liberal, was appointed to the cabinet as Secretary of State for Scotland. Since 1929 he had been Lord Lieutenant of Midlothian, and so was rather more qualified for the job than during his cricketing days. The position did not last long, though, as Churchill and his Conservative party were roundly beaten in the 1945 election. Rosebery went on to become President of the Liberal Party from 1945 to 1957, and, in October 1953, he took over as President of MCC.

In 1954, the new President was Lord Cobham. COL. THE HON. CHARLES JOHN LYTTELTON, TENTH VISCOUNT COBHAM was a member of the Lyttelton family, the son and grandson of former Presidents. His father, the Ninth Viscount, had held the position in 1935, and his grandfather, Baron Lyttelton, had done so in 1886. He was one of the most enthusiastic cricketers ever to have held the Presidency, but was not ever as gifted at the game as many of the rest of his family. Born in 1909, he was educated at Eton but never challenged for a place in the XI there. However, he was a most diligent student of the game, and by force of hard work and persistence, he made himself good enough to play for Worcestershire in 1932, a few years after his father had stepped down as captain of the county. Worcestershire were not the strongest county in the inter-war years, and Cobham would have struggled to make the Yorkshire XI, for example, but despite his family connections he was not in the side for his name alone. He toured Australia and New Zealand in the winter of 1935/36 as vice-captain to Errol Holmes on a tour aimed at healing the rifts caused by the bodyline tour three years earlier. The side was of no more than county standard, including as it did eight amateurs, but it succeeded in its main purpose, of making MCC teams welcome once again in Australasia. It also gave him his first extended look at New Zealand, the country where he would return as Governor General in 1957, after his stint as MCC President. Cobham was a man of boundless enthusiasm, whose cricketing philosophy was that attack is the best form of defence, and he spread that message with gusto wherever he went. In his Presidential year, he hosted a dinner at the Guildhall in Worcester to welcome the South Africans, who were playing their opening match in Cobham's home county, as was becoming traditional for all touring teams. He was outspoken in his criticism of post-war cricket:

> I do not think people will follow cricket much longer unless the game is reborn, but reborn it will be, and I think there are signs that the players will again hit the ball hard, high and often. Can we get rid of those awful bores who prod doubtfully at half-volleys and let every long hop pass by? They are the ones who are emptying our cricket grounds.

When an MCC team toured New Zealand in 1960/61, Cobham showed he was still as good as his word. Playing for his own Governor General's XI at the age of 51, and batting at number ten against an attack made up of Larter, David Smith, David Allen, Don Wilson and Bob Barber, he hit 44 in 21 minutes, including two sixes. Hitting hard, high and often was the way Lord Cobham lived his life.

During Cobham's Presidency, there was another problem vexing the Committee. By the end of December 1954, membership stood at 7,900, at the upper limit of the Club's capacity. However, the waiting list had grown to such an extent that it was stated at the AGM that 'some candidates might soon have to wait forty years for election.' This was when the proposal that 'A' Stand be developed as an extension to the Pavilion was put forward, so that membership could be increased from a maximum 8,000 to 11,000 once it was finished. 'A' Stand became the Warner Stand, and membership was increased. It did not solve the problem entirely, however. The waiting list for membership is now less than 40 years, but non-playing member candidates can still expect to wait 20 years or more for acceptance.

Lord Cobham nominated Field Marshal Earl Alexander of Tunis as his successor. Lord Alexander, born **HON. HAROLD RUPERT LEOFRIC GEORGE ALEXANDER** on 10 December 1891, was educated at Harrow, where he played in the first XI. He was a member of the Harrow XI in 1910 that lost so narrowly to Eton in what has become known as Fowler's Match when the Eton bowler took eight for 23 in Harrow's second innings, to give Eton victory by 9 runs when Harrow were only chasing 55 to win. Alexander had the ignominy of being last man out, but at least he did not fall victim to Fowler. Alexander was a bowler, not a batsman, and he did his bit for Harrow, taking five for 40 in the match. It was not enough.

After Harrow, Alexander, who was a great-grandson of the Earl of Verulam (1840), went to Sandhurst and played little further cricket apart from club and services matches. He joined the Irish Guards and was almost immediately on active service. He was wounded twice during the First World War, won an M.C. and a D.S.O. and was a brigadier by Armistice Day. Between the wars he married Lady Margaret Bingham, daughter of the Earl of Lucan (1928), and was briefly ADC to King Edward VIII in 1936. By the start of the Second World War, he was a Brigadier-General. The war started badly for him, as he was involved in the retreat of the British Expeditionary Force from Dunkirk. He was the last soldier to leave. His main successes were as Commander in Chief in the Middle East, where, as Harold Macmillan later wrote, 'If Montgomery was the Wellington, Alexander was certainly the Marlborough of this war.' It was Alexander who reported to Churchill the defeat of all German forces in North Africa, and it was Alexander who became Eisenhower's deputy in the latter stages of the war.

After the war, he was created Earl Alexander and from 1946 to 1952 served as Governor General of Canada. There he was made honorary Chief Eagle, the head of the Blackfoot tribe, the only MCC President with that on his CV. In 1952 he returned from Canada to serve as Minister of Defence in Churchill's cabinet, a post he held until 1954. The Presidency of MCC was just one of many retirement jobs. He was a charismatic and popular man who had the knack of making people seem important, even if they were not. To him, they always were.

Harold Alexander nominated as his successor a Harrow team-mate from Fowler's Match all those years ago. **WALTER TURNER MONCKTON, VISCOUNT MONCKTON OF BRENCHLEY**, was eleven months older than Lord Alexander and their paths were to cross many times, even after they both left Harrow to pursue very different careers. Not that Alexander was Monckton's only close connection with the MCC Presidency. His second wife Bridget, whom he married in 1947, was a Hore-Ruthven, the niece of Lord Gowrie (1948).

After Harrow, Monckton, a brilliant scholar, went on to Balliol College, Oxford, where he did not win a Blue, but did play one first-class game for a combined Oxford and Cambridge side against a combined Army and Navy side, at Portsmouth in 1911. He kept wicket and scored 43 and 29 not out batting at number eleven, leaving him with a lifetime batting average of 72, probably the highest lifetime average for a man who never rose higher in the batting order than number eleven.

After Oxford, he went into the law and quickly made an impact. He was recorder of Hythe, in Kent, from 1930 to 1937, at the same time that another cricketer, Percy Chapman, was working for the Mackeson brewery there, and captaining Kent. From 1919 to 1946, he kept wicket regularly for the Bar, retiring when well into his fifties and less flexible than he was as a young undergraduate. More importantly, he was a close advisor of King Edward VIII, as Attorney-General during the abdication crisis of 1936, which brought him into conflict with Stanley Baldwin (1938). One of MCC's oldest and most distinguished members, Alan King-Hamilton, remembers the day that the ex-King sailed from Southampton to begin his long exile. Monckton went to see the Duke of Windsor off from Southampton, and was thus late for a meeting in his chambers, where King-Hamilton and others were already waiting as Monckton returned. 'He paced up and down, and walked round and round the room for about twenty minutes, slowly releasing the tension he was feeling. Then he sat down, looked at us and said, "Gentlemen, let us begin".' Monckton had the ability to care deeply about things, but also to focus entirely on the matter at hand, a skill that served him well, not least as MCC President.

During the war, he worked behind the scenes in what was 'Information' if our side was giving it out, and 'Propaganda' if the other side was. He joined Churchill's 1945 caretaker government, along with Lord Rosebery, and became an MP for Bristol West from 1951 to 1957. He then retired and was ennobled, which happened during his Presidential year. During his time in Parliament, he was successively Minister of Labour, Minister of Defence (as Lord Alexander had been) and Paymaster-General. Rab Butler, a cabinet colleague, summed Monckton up as:

> a diplomat by nature, a friend of princes, admired by women, of acute intelligence and perception, fearless in defence of his friends, high or low. But he did not like taking executive decisions; his strength lay in an ability to inject his own sweetness and light into the atmosphere.

A good character reference for any MCC President, one might have thought.

Lord Monckton handed the Presidency on to perhaps the last great cricket loving nobleman of our times, **BERNARD MARMADUKE FITZALAN-HOWARD, SIXTEENTH DUKE OF NORFOLK**. The Dukes of Norfolk, the heads of the greatest Catholic family of Britain, have their seat at Arundel Castle and it is there that the Sixteenth Duke developed one of the most beautiful cricket grounds in the world. His father, the Fifteenth Duke, began building the ground in 1895, with the intention of making one with a larger playing area than the Oval. The first game was played there in 1897. Like his father, the Sixteenth Duke was no cricketer himself but loved the game with a passion, and he was determined that the ground at Arundel should be a busy and beautiful ground, staging top class matches as well as club friendlies. In this he succeeded, but his cricketing skills never really improved. The tale of his butler umpiring while his master was batting is often told. The bowler appeals for LBW, and the butler, realising that the Duke was plumb in front and he had no option but to raise his finger, simply said, 'His Grace is not in.' No one ever begrudged the Duke any of the few hard-earned runs he made, and he undoubtedly made more friends than runs over his lifetime.

As Earl Marshal of England, the Duke first came into the public spotlight as the master of ceremonies for the coronation of King George VI in 1937, the year in which he married Lavinia Strutt, grand-daughter of Lord Belper, the 1882 President. In 1953 he was in charge of the coronation of Queen Elizabeth and in that year, as well as organ-ising everything for the Coronation perfectly (except for the weather), he also organised a match at Arundel between the Duke of Norfolk's XI and the Duke of Edinburgh's XI, with both Dukes playing. The scorecard read, 'Duke of Norfolk, b. Duke of Edinburgh, 4'. But 4 was not bad.

Born on 30 May 1908, he inherited the Dukedom, and the title of Earl Marshal, from his father when he was only eight years old. He was educated at The Oratory, but did not excel at cricket. That did not stop him playing, watching and organising cricket all his life. Apart from his year as President of MCC, he was President of Sussex C.C.C. for many years, and manager of several tours abroad, most notably MCC's tour to Australia in 1962/63, under the captaincy of his county captain Ted Dexter (2001). He was ably assisted by Alec Bedser, and when the Duke had to return to England in the middle of the tour for reasons of state (he flew back, even though they had all sailed out together in SS *Canberra*), Billy Griffith (1979) also helped. The Duke and his captain both emphasised their desire to play attacking cricket, but in the event the series was a dour affair, with one game won by each side, and three drawn. By the end of the Fifth Test, the players on both sides were being barracked for their defensive tactics. But it would be unfair to remember His Grace for the management of a not particularly successful MCC tour. It is better to remember him for the great gift to cricket in England that he was responsible for – the cricket ground at Arundel.

The Duke nominated another war leader, Lord Portal, to take on the Presidency for 1958/59. **CHARLES FREDERICK ALGERNON PORTAL, FIRST VISCOUNT PORTAL OF HUNGERFORD**, was born on 21 May 1893, and was educated at Winchester, where he played for the first XI in 1912, and Christ Church, Oxford, where he did not. He was a left-arm opening bowler and not much of a batsman, but did not play at any decent level after his school days. This was partly because he was of the generation that had to face the First World War. If he had any leisure time after that, it was spent fishing. He was an avid and expert angler and never missed an opportunity to go fishing. Churchill tells in his memoirs of a conference in Canada during the war, when the Prime Minister was accompanied by Portal and Sir Alan Brooke, another keen angler. The two caught about one hundred fish a day each, and if the conference had gone on much longer, Churchill reckoned the level of the lake would have gone down considerably.

In 1914, Portal joined the Royal Engineers and worked as a motor cycle despatch rider on the Western front. In 1915 he was transferred to the Royal Flying Corps, and his career in air defence had begun. By the end of the war, he had been promoted to Lieutenant Colonel and had won the M.C. and the D.F.C., and when the R.A.F. was formed in 1918, he was a senior officer from the outset.

Between the wars, he was particularly involved in bombing technology and strategy, and by the start of the Second World War, he was an Air Vice-Marshal. In 1940 he was given responsibility for Bomber Command, and one of his first decisions was to launch a bomb attack on Berlin in August 1940. This so infuriated Hitler that he instructed Goering to bomb London rather than the British airfields which had been the target until then. It may have been the start of the Blitz, but it was also one of the underlying reasons why the Battle of Britain was won.

By the end of that year, Air Chief Marshal Portal was Chief of Air Staff, and throughout the war he was in overall charge of Britain's air defence strategy. Whatever the retrospective views of his strategic bombing policies, such as the raids carried out under 'Bomber' Harris that destroyed Dresden, at the time there was little doubt that the work of Bomber Command, and the whole of the Royal Air Force, had played a huge part in the eventual victory. In 1945, when he was 52 years old, Portal retired from the R.A.F. and was created Viscount Portal of Hungerford, the Berkshire town where he was born. In his retirement, he became a major figure in the city, chairing British Aluminium and eventually losing out in a hostile takeover bid by Tube Investments in 1959. The struggle for power in his company took up a good deal of his time in his MCC Presidential year, which cannot have made his year quite the pleasant relaxation it was meant to be. However, after being replaced at British Aluminium, he was appointed chairman of the British Aircraft Corporation – from one aluminium tube to another.

Portal handed over in 1959 to a true man of cricket, almost as steeped in the lore of MCC and its history as Sir Pelham Warner himself. HARRY SURTEES ALTHAM, born on 30 November 1888, was educated at Repton, where he was in the XI for three summers. *Wisden* noted that 'Altham played some extremely useful cricket for his side,' but he was described as 'more the made than the natural cricketer'. At Oxford, he earned his Blue as a lower order batsman in 1911 and 1912. In 1911 he was the first victim in a hat-trick by the Cambridge captain J. F. Ireland, although he redeemed himself with 47 in the second innings, and Oxford won. In 1912 his captain was Dick Twining (1964), and Oxford lost. In the First World War, he won a D.S.O. and an M.C., and on his return from the front he took up schoolmastering. He seems to be the first MCC President whose principal career was teaching, although Hubert Doggart and Dennis Silk have since followed in his footsteps. Altham taught at Winchester, and coached cricket there, for thirty years, and played irregularly for Hampshire when the school holidays came around. In all, he played 55 first-class matches, and scored 1,537 runs at an average just below 20.

He is also known as a cricket writer. His *History of Cricket*, first published in 1926, was a work of originality and brilliance and still holds its own despite the many revisionist books that have been subsequently published. In 1952, he wrote the *MCC Cricket Coaching Book*: still a very useful guide to the basic skills of cricket. As a player who *Wisden* rightly supposed was more made than natural, he was a brilliant coach. Players who find the game very easy often do not make good coaches, because they find it hard to understand how someone cannot do something they do entirely naturally. Altham could sympathise with the less talented players, and had a knack of bringing out the very best in them. 'He was a terrific enthusiast,' is how John Woodcock puts it, 'a tremendous encourager, a truly great man'. He was also one of the greatest experts on Winchester Cathedral.

The list of Altham's achievements in cricket is long. He was chairman of the Test selection Committee in 1954, the man who selected the almost untried Tyson and the very young Colin Cowdrey to tour Australia in 1954/55, a decision that pretty well ensured that England retained the Ashes. He was President of Hampshire from 1941 to 1965 and at various times also chairman of the MCC Youth Cricket association, President of the English Schools' Cricket Association, MCC committee man and MCC Treasurer from 1949 to 1963. He thus was President and Treasurer in the same year, a unique double. Other men have been President and Treasurer in different years; in fact all the treasurers since Sir Spencer Ponsonby-Fane, who died in 1915, have also been President, up to and including Hubert Doggart in the 1990s, but none of the others have done both jobs at once. Altham also was President of Hampshire that year, never a man to take life easy. It is worth noting that the accounts for 1959 showed an excess of expenditure over income of

£1,892 14s 9d, despite the membership now standing at 7,562 full members and 3,003 associate members. Altham died in 1965, aged 76.

Altham's successor was a Wykehamist and a member of the only brotherhood apart from the Studds who captained their university in three successive years. **Sir Hubert Ashton**, along with his brothers Claude and Gilbert, captained Cambridge from 1921 to 1923. In 1921, the Cambridge side, captained by Gilbert and including all three Ashtons alongside such fine players as Charles Marriott, Percy Chapman and J. L. Bryan, were far too strong for Oxford, even though Douglas Jardine, Greville Stevens and 'Crusoe' Robertson-Glasgow were all playing for Oxford. Hubert hit a brilliant 118 in that game, and was selected as one of *Wisden*'s Five Cricketers of the Year. He played for Archie MacLaren's XI against the Australians at the end of that summer, and helped inflict the only defeat of the summer on the tourists. R. L. Arrowsmith wrote, 'Why he was not picked for England it is impossible to imagine.'

The next year, Hubert's captaincy year, the Varsity match was even more one-sided. Cambridge, now with Gubby Allen in their side, won by an innings and 100 runs over an Oxford side weakened by the absence of Jardine through illness. Ashton made 90 not out, and with Chapman (102 not out) added 172 for the fifth wicket in 135 minutes. But he was never destined to play cricket seriously after graduating. Born in Calcutta on 13 February 1898, he had to go to war after his schooldays, and won an M.C. on the Western Front, as Harry Altham had done. After university, he went to Burma and India for a number of years on business, but used to come home on leave and get in a few matches for Essex most summers. He even played one game for Bristol Rovers in the 1924/25 season, having won a Blue for football (and also for hockey) a few years earlier. Once he returned to Britain on a permanent basis, he took up office as President of Essex from 1948 to 1970, and was elected Conservative MP for Chelmsford in 1950. He had married in 1927 Dorothy Gaitskell, the sister of the future leader of the Labour Party, but that did not appear to affect his political beliefs.

His Presidential year at Lord's was not the easiest. He was still an MP and had to tread warily into the minefield created by South Africa's withdrawal from the Commonwealth and thus their automatic expulsion from the I.C.C., which was linked at that time to Commonwealth membership. The President of M.C.C was also at this time chairman of the I.C.C., so Sir Hubert could not sit back from the debate. In the end, as we were to discover, the problem escalated so that within a decade South Africa was cut off from all official cricketing contact and a generation of great South African cricketers had to ply their trade elsewhere, but it took the D'Oliveira affair to trigger that crisis.

Hubert Ashton nominated **Sir William Worsley** to succeed him for 1961/62. Col. Sir William Arthington Worsley, Fourth Bt., was born on 5 April 1890 and educated at Eton, where he was in the first XI in 1908 and 1909. He went straight into the Army after Eton, and was in many ways lucky to be wounded and captured during the First World War, given the high death rate of those young officers who remained fighting at the front. He was an avid cricketer who turned his home, Hovingham Hall in Yorkshire, into the social centre of cricket in that part of the county. Cricket is still played there, at a social and village level, and the ground competed with Escrick, Lord Wenlock's estate, as one of the prettiest in that part of the country. Sir William spent much of his time in the years immediately after the war playing Army and club cricket, with great success, and in 1928 the Yorkshire Committee turned to him to lead the county side. It would be wrong to say that Sir William, then aged 38, was up to the job as a cricketer, but he was a successful county captain. He did not bring the title back to Yorkshire, but they finished fourth and second, and were a very hard side to beat. It was probably the arrival of Hedley Verity in 1930 that turned them into the very best in England. Sir William played 60 matches in those two seasons, but only scored two fifties and averaged under 16 overall. He did not bowl and was not the most mobile in the field. Still, his contribution to Yorkshire cricket was considerable.

There was more to come, of course. He became President of the County Club in 1960 and remained in position until his death in 1973, so he was yet another MCC President who doubled as a county President at the same time. In 1961, his daughter Katharine married the Queen's cousin, the Duke of Kent, and a few months later he took over as MCC President. He took the opportunity, very rare for an MCC President at the time, of visiting India at the same time as Ted Dexter's side was touring there in the winter of 1961/62, but his presence did not help much. India won the series 2-0.

Worsley's choice was Lt. Col Baron Nugent of West Harling. TERENCE EDMUND GASCOIGNE NUGENT, known universally as Tim, was born in 1895 and educated at Eton, where he played for two years in their XI, in 1913 and 1914, as a batsman who ended up opening the innings. He went into the Irish Guards and won the obligatory M.C. in the First War. He was also wounded and mentioned in despatches. While it would be quite wrong to undervalue the part played by these brave men in the terrible conditions of the Western Front, it does seem that those officers who emerged with their lives also emerged with an M.C. at the very least. Nugent remained a professional soldier for some time after the war, but in 1936 became Comptroller of the Lord Chamberlain's office, a post that Sir Spencer Ponsonby-Fane had held from 1857 until 1901. The Lord Chamberlain is in effect the President of his office, and the Comptroller acts as chief executive. Tim Nugent acted as Comptroller for three different Lords Chamberlain – Lord Cromer (1934), the Sixth Earl Clarendon (son of 1871), and the Eleventh Lord Scarborough. In 1960 he retired and was ennobled. From 1965 until 1969, he was President of Surrey C.C.C. where his good humour, his contacts and his shrewd advice helped the Club enormously during a period of mixed fortunes on the field. He was a man who enjoyed exerting his influence behind the scenes, never pushing himself forward but always managing to know the right person to help out at the appropriate time. He was also, by his marriage, exceedingly well connected with MCC history. His wife Rosalie was the granddaughter of the First Earl of Ancaster, who as Lord Willoughby de Eresby had been President in 1890. She was also the great-granddaughter of Lord Strathavon, the first known President (1821). Her first cousin, the Third Lord Ancaster, was married to the sister of J. J. Astor (1937).

During Nugent's year, Sir Pelham Warner died and it fell to Lord Nugent to give the address at the memorial service. Everybody who was there agrees that the address was worthy of the man. Lord Nugent died in 1973, and the title died with him.

Nugent's successor at Lord's was the man who most closely replaced Pelham Warner as the *éminence grise* of MCC, Gubby Allen. GEORGE OSWALD BROWNING ALLEN was born in Australia on 31 July 1902, and is still, as far as records show, the only Australian-born President to date. At least two other Australians have been offered the Presidency, but both turned it down. Allen's uncle, Reginald, played one Test for Australia in 1886/87, but his nephew was loyal to England. 'Gubby' Allen, so called because of his initials, came to England as a young boy and was educated at Eton and Cambridge, where his cricketing skills earned him a place in the XIs. In 1921 at Eton, he played in the same XI as two other future Presidents, Ronnie Aird (1968) and Sir Alec Douglas-Home (1966). In 1922 at Cambridge his captain was Hubert Ashton (1960). After Cambridge, Allen's life was entirely taken up with cricket. He played regularly for Middlesex, as an amateur, from 1921, and played his final game for them in 1950. He played 25 tests for England between 1930 and 1947/48, and was a part of the MCC Committee, selection committees, treasury and other parts of the hierarchy for most of his adult life. His influence was everywhere from the mid-1930s onwards, and although he always had his view of the good of the Club and the ground at the forefront of any decision he made, there were those who thought of him as a despot, albeit a benevolent one most of the time. He was always utterly opposed to increases in the annual membership, which in the immediate post-war years represented the sporting bargain of the era, provided you could get elected in the first place. But in order to make ends meet without increasing the subs, the Committee decided to sell off many of the properties that they owned around Lord's, a decision that in the new millennium they have come to regret. Allen's edict that the view to the trees at the Nursery End from the Committee Room should never be blocked stymied a few proposals for development in that part of the ground, but some of them were ideas that should have been blocked anyway. It is uncertain what he would have thought of the Media Centre that now dominates his favourite aspect – even though trees are still visible beyond it.

Allen was always a man of principle. Selected as a fast bowling all-rounder for the 1932/33 tour of Australia, he steadfastly refused to bowl what Jardine called leg theory at the Australians, but still played all five Tests and took 21 wickets in the series, a tally second only to Larwood. He captained and managed England on the tour to West Indies in 1947/48, when he was already 45 years old, but it was not a success. It was the first time that any MCC team had returned home from an overseas tour without a single victory to their credit. It would be wrong to blame Allen: several of England's top players declined to tour, including Denis Compton and Bill Edrich who had just scored 7,365 runs between them during the 1947 summer, and Allen, too old to bowl fast, relied on an attack that lacked both Alec Bedser and Doug Wright. Still, it was a sign of his loyalty to the Club and his fierce pride in its history and reputation that he agreed to tour at all, and on balance no one would doubt that Sir Gubby, as he later became, was a massive influence on both MCC and world cricket from about 1930 until he died in November 1989.

Gubby Allen handed over to another MCC insider, Dick Twin-ing. **RICHARD HAYNES TWINING**, born on 3 November 1889, was educated at Eton and Oxford. At Eton, he played in the XI for three years as opening batsman and wicketkeeper (and captain in his final year), without ever recording any remarkable figures. Going up to Oxford, he won his Blue three years in a row, from 1910 to 1912, and was on the winning side twice, losing only in 1912, the year he was captain. He played a few times for Middlesex before the First World War, but during the war he was very badly wounded. He was on crutches for much of the war, a fact that probably saved his life, and it was assumed that any chance of playing serious cricket must be over. However, he fought his way back to a reasonable state of fitness, despite being permanently slightly lame, and went on to play a handful of games most years up to 1928. In 1921, in Pelham Warner's final match, Twining made his highest first-class score of 135 as he and Jack Hearne put on 277 for the second wicket as Middlesex chased 322 to win both the match and the championship. No wonder he and Warner were firm friends for life.

Twining became a financier, and first joined the MCC Committee in 1933. He was involved with the administration of MCC from then until his death, as committee man, as trustee from 1952 until 1969, and as President in 1964. His was the year in which the South Africans toured England for the last time before their twenty-plus years of international seclusion, and his was also the year in which two touring teams were invited to England, splitting the summer between them. New Zealand were the other tourists, and the experiment was deemed to be successful enough to be worth trying again. Almost half a century later, every summer features at least two touring teams, until we have more Test matches and one-day internationals than we can possibly fully appreciate. After Dick Twining gave up his trusteeship, in 1969, he was made a life Vice-President of MCC in honour of all he had done, only the second man to be so honoured. The first was, of course, his old colleague-in-arms Sir Pelham Warner. He had also been, like Plum, President of Middlesex, though only for seven years, not nine like Plum. Despite his war wounds, Twining lived on until 1979, dying a couple of months after his 89th birthday.

Dick Twining nominated another Etonian, **SIR OLIVER LEESE**, to succeed him. Lt. Gen. Sir Oliver William Hargreaves Leese KCB CBE DSO was born on 27 October 1895, and played fitfully in the Eton XI of 1914, but with not enough success to be picked for the Lord's game against Harrow, unlike his exact contemporary, the 1962 President Lord Nugent. The First World War broke out as he left school, and he enlisted at once in the Coldstream Guards. He was wounded, but after the war he stayed on in the Army. By the outbreak of the Second World War, Leese was already a senior officer, but it was the fighting in North Africa that brought him to public prominence. He was promoted to Lieutenant-General during the North Africa campaign, and was knighted in the field by King George VI. He succeeded Montgomery as head of the Eighth Army in 1943, leading them through the invasion of Italy. Harold Macmillan noted the differences between Leese, whom he described as 'a very popular figure' and the generals of the First War. Macmillan wrote, 'It is a remarkable contrast with the last war. Then a general was a remote Blimpish figure in white moustache, faultlessly tailored tunic, polished boots and spurs, emerging occasionally from a luxurious chateau and riding in his huge limousine Rolls.' He might have been describing Lord Plumer, the man who noted that 'if Findlay had been a soldier, I should like to have had him on my staff.' Leese, on the other hand, 'is a youngish man, in shorts and open shirt, driving his own jeep, and waving and shouting his greetings to the troops as he edges his way past guns, tanks, trucks, tank-carriers etc., in the crowded and muddy roads, which the enemy may actually be shelling as he drives along.'

In 1944 Leese went to Burma as British commander of allied forces in south-east Asia, where he was less successful, and after the war, he retired from the Army, devoting much of his time thereafter to his garden and wider issues of horticulture. He was also still a keen follower of cricket, and was President of both Shropshire and Warwickshire during his year at Lord's, making him almost certainly the first man to be President of three major cricket clubs in the same year. He was also President of the Cricket Society from 1968 to 1973, and a keen member of I Zingari and the Eton Ramblers.

His year at Lord's was not the happiest, as there were a number of difficult meetings as the Committee tried to persuade the membership of the wisdom of their plans to redevelop the Tavern stand and the south-west corner of the ground. As Diana Rait-Kerr wrote in *Pavilions of Splendour*, despite a 'lucid explanation of the plans from the President, Sir Oliver Leese', there was much opposition to the plans. 'The feeling of the meeting was that, regardless of the merits of the two resolutions, they should be referred back on the grounds that members had received insufficient information.' The turbulent revolutionary spirit of the 1960s had arrived at St John's Wood. However, Sir Oliver was up to the task. He began the next meeting, held at the Seymour Hall because the Long Room would not have been big enough, by getting the hall on his side:

> The reputation and standing of Lord's is second to none in the cricketing circles of the world. It is the Mecca of cricketers of all nations and the headquarters of cricket from which come forth the Laws of Cricket, the spirit in which it should be played, and the encouragement to men of all ages and all nations to play what we believe to be the finest game of all.

It was stirring stuff, and while he did not entirely quell the riot, his subsequent plea for MCC members to enable the Club to move with the times and provide buildings and playing areas second to none, and to show they had faith in Lord's and its future, was instrumental in helping the Committee largely win the day. The plans for the Tavern Stand were scaled down a little, but the proposals for increased subscriptions and increased membership to help pay for the development went into the rulebook. On 31 December 1965, MCC had 9,486 members and

2,694 associate members. Subscriptions were put up by 50 per cent, and a new upper limit of 10,000 full members and 4,000 Associates was put into place.

Perhaps Sir Oliver knew that the chalice he was handing on might be a poisoned one, and that MCC needed political skills more than ever. Sir Oliver therefore chose **SIR ALEC DOUGLAS-HOME** to be the new President for 1966. Sir Alexander Frederick Douglas-Home was the second former Prime Minister to become President of MCC, and the only President to have renounced a peerage. It is a sign of the rapidly changing times in British society in the 1960s that the last man to hold a hereditary title and be President of MCC was a man who had given up the title. The Duke of Edinburgh was to come back again as President in 1974, but Sir Alec is the last in a very long list of blue-blooded peers to have held the Presidency, nine years after the last man still to be using his hereditary title, the Duke of Norfolk. In the 1800s, there were only fifteen Presidents who did not hold some kind of hereditary title. Since 1900, there have only been 25 Presidents, including Sir Alec, who inherited a title, and since 1975 none at all.

Sir Alec, born on 2 July 1903, is also the only Prime Minister to have played first-class cricket, which he did as Lord Dunglass, playing a handful of games for Oxford University (without gaining a Blue) and several other teams. He played only ten first-class matches in all, but represented six different sides in the process: Oxford University, Middlesex (two matches, both against Oxford University), MCC (in South America), Free Foresters, H. D. G. Leveson-Gower's XI and Harlequins. He was a useful fast-medium bowler from his days in the Eton XI alongside Gubby Allen and Ronnie Aird, and a stubborn batsman described in the 1923 *Wisden* as being better on wet pitches. He was probably never good enough to make a name as a county cricketer, but he never put it to the test, because a political career beckoned.

In 1931, he was elected to Parliament for the first time, as Scottish

Unionist MP for Lanark. In 1938 he accompanied Chamberlain to Munich as his PPS, but shortly thereafter developed spinal tuberculosis, which kept him bedridden and immobile for two years, and inevitably meant that he did not take any active part in the war. In 1945, in the Labour landslide, he lost his seat, but won it back again in 1950. However, the next year his father died and he became the Fourteenth Earl of Home, and was elevated to the House of Lords. From the Lords, he continued his political career, being appointed to the Eden and Macmillan cabinets as Commonwealth Secretary and then as Foreign Secretary. In 1963, when Harold Macmillan resigned through ill-health as his government rumbled towards disintegration, Lord Home was the surprise choice to succeed him as Prime Minister. He renounced his title so that he could take on the job in the Commons, but only lasted a year before he was bound to call a general election. The Conservatives lost, but the margin of defeat was closer than many expected. Sir Alec, as he now was, was hardly charismatic, but even his political opponents liked and respected him. Jo Grimond, a fellow Scot and then leader of the Liberal party, thought of him as a thoroughly professional politician. 'He liked and was well liked by the ordinary Tory. He seems to have run the party well. In addition he was trusted. He made no effort to be other than he was.' All in all, promising qualifications for the job Sir Oliver handed on to him. Sir Alec was still a sitting Member of Parliament when he was President, and a member of Edward Heath's shadow cabinet, but he made time for his cricket responsibilities.

After retiring from politics in 1974, Sir Alec was once again elevated to the House of Lords, as Lord Home of the Hirsel. He had now been an Hon, a Rt. Hon, a knight, a hereditary peer and a life peer, as well as an MP, and had used four different names during his life. He continued to take a keen interest in cricket, as Governor of I Zingari from 1977 to 1989, and was a regular visitor to Lord's at Test match time. He died in 1995, aged 92.

From the end of the war until the mid-sixties, MCC had not appeared to take much notice of the winds of change that were sweeping through all parts of British life, but with the minor membership revolts in 1966, followed by the Presidency of a man who had been seen in politics as the last of a dying breed, there was an underlying mood within MCC which was prepared to welcome the future rather than ignore or defy it. The values that Sir Oliver Leese talked about would not change, but MCC's idea of its role in the game would do so over the next forty years.

CHAPTER EIGHT

1967–1986

EMBRACING MODERNITY, CAREFULLY

In 1967, Sir Alec Douglas-Home handed the Presidency to a great man of cricket, and a member of a distinguished Sussex brotherhood, ARTHUR GILLIGAN. Arthur Edward Robert Gilligan, born on 23 December 1894, was hardly a symbol of a new generation of MCC Presidents, being a decade older than his predecessor. However, he was a former captain of England, and from this time there is a clear change in the perceived qualities required of a President. From 1967 onwards, there have been only eight Presidents who have not played first-class cricket, and of the ones who did, eight were England Test captains. Practical experience of first-class cricket now seems more important than business or political skills.

Gilligan was educated, uniquely for a President to that time, at Dulwich College, where he was captain of the XI in 1913 and 1914, being the most successful bowler for the school in both those years. He was the middle of three brothers, F. W. (Frank) being the eldest and a wicket-keeper, and A.H.H. (Harold) being the youngest, a batsman and like Arthur a Test captain of England. In 1913 all three brothers played for Dulwich College, and in 1919 and 1920, after the war had ended, Frank and Arthur played against each other in the University matches. In 1919, A. E. R. Gilligan, batting at number eleven for Cambridge, was stumped by his elder brother in the first innings, and although Arthur took six for 52 in Oxford's second innings, he could not prevent Oxford winning by 45 runs. Curiously, there was another pair of brothers, the Naumanns, playing against each other in the same game, and J. H. Naumann of Cambridge was bowled by F. C. G. Naumann of Oxford in the second innings. The Oxford brothers had the better of that match in every way. The 1920 match was a rain-affected draw, despite the strength of the teams. Seven future Test players were on show that year, along with two Ashtons and the father of Tim Brooke-Taylor, the cricket-loving comedian.

For a few seasons in the 1920s, before injury put an end to his cricket, he was a very fine fast bowler, a superlative outfielder and an aggressive batsman who often made good scores. In all first-class cricket he took 868 wickets at 23.20 each, and scored 9,140 runs at a shade over 20, with twelve centuries, including one for Cambridge against Sussex in 1919. He was appointed captain of Sussex in 1922, and was so successful that he earned a place on the 1922/23 tour to South Africa. In those days, teams to South Africa were not always the strongest available, but still Gilligan played in two of the Tests, and, as *Wisden* rather archly commented when selecting him as one of their Five Cricketers Of The Year in their 1924 edition, 'with his varied gifts as a cricketer he seems to have every chance of playing in Test cricket at home.' This he did in 1924, when he was picked to captain England against South Africa. His debut as captain was startling: South Africa were bowled out in their first innings for 30, the captain's share being six wickets for 7 runs.

When he decided to retire when injury reduced his effectiveness, he turned to that infant art, cricket broadcasting, as well as to the administration of his beloved Sussex C.C.C. He was succeeded as captain there by his brother Harold, whose daughter would much later marry Peter May (1980).

Gilligan turned to **RONNIE AIRD** to replace him as President. Ronald Aird was born on 4 May 1902 and went to Eton and Cambridge. E. W. Swanton recounts a story of his time at Eton, which neatly sums up the different attitudes of Aird and Gubby Allen. They were both picked to play for the college against the Eton Ramblers, and while batting together, Aird hit the ball straight to cover point, and called for a single. Allen was run out by half the length of the pitch. Afterwards, Aird said, 'You must admit, that was bad luck.' 'I don't know about bad luck', replied Allen through gritted teeth. 'Oh, you must run to a chap in brown suede shoes' was Aird's logic.

He gained his Blue in 1923, alongside Allen, and went on to play for Hampshire, with only slight success. His four centuries and seven first-class wickets will never be his memorial in cricket, because he is best remembered as a great administrator. He was an outstanding all-round sportsman, gaining his Blue for rackets, and reportedly would have won his Blue for football if he could be persuaded to head the ball. He found that heading the heavy, wet ball gave him headaches, so the selectors overlooked him. He was also a fine real tennis player, and a National Hunt steward.

In 1926, aged only 24, he was appointed assistant secretary at Lord's to William Findlay and thus began a career which took him the Secretaryship in 1952 and, after his retirement, to the Presidency in 1968. It was a thankless year. The South African issue, brought on by the non-selection and then the selection of Basil D'Oliveira for the proposed 1968/69 tour by MCC, created a furore the likes of which MCC had not experienced before. The main cast of players were all past or future Presidents – Lord Cobham, who had been told by the South African Prime Minister, John Vorster, early in 1968 that D'Oliveira would never be acceptable as a tourist; Sir Alec Douglas-Home, then shadow Foreign Secretary, who had advised the exact opposite; the selectors, who included Doug Insole (chairman), Peter May and Colin Cowdrey; and the MCC President, Treasurer and Secretary, Arthur Gilligan, Gubby Allen and Billy Griffith. Between these eight past, present and future Presidents, they managed to incense so many people on both sides of the political debate that the new President, Ronnie Aird, found himself chairing a Special General Meeting almost before he had got his feet under the Presidential desk, so to speak. His chairmanship was much praised, MCC did not go to South Africa that winter, nor for another two decades and more, but the crisis was not yet over. When the news of Lord Cobham's discussion with Vorster leaked out, there were further demands from some quarters for change within MCC. Billy Griffith, the Secretary, considered resigning, but Aird and his Committee gave him a unanimous vote of confidence, and he carried on. Having to give votes of confidence to your chief executive is not a sign of a happy administration, and Aird's year was a very difficult one. Just to add a little to the air of change that year, Diana Rait Kerr, daughter of Aird's predecessor as Secretary, retired from the post of Curator and Stephen Green was appointed. That at least proved to be a comparatively smooth transfer of responsibility, as Green stayed for 35 years. Despite all the ups and downs of the year, the self-effacing Aird, who had won an M.C. as a tank officer in the Second World War and who was almost more of a Lord's insider than Gubby Allen, made the best possible job of it.

In 1969, the Presidency passed to **MAURICE ALLOM**. The D'Oliveira affair and its fallout had by no means run their course, and Allom had to play the diplomat as well as the cricket supremo. Maurice James Carrick Allom was born on 23 March 1906 and was educated at Wellington and Trinity College, Cambridge. Although successful as a schoolboy cricketer, he did not win his Blue until his third summer at Cambridge, 1927, the same year that he began his career with Surrey. A fast bowler in the same mould, but not as good, as Maurice Tate, he will always be remembered for the explosive start he gave to England v. New Zealand Tests. In the first ever match, at Lancaster Park, Christchurch in January 1930, Allom, who was playing in his first Test, took four wickets in five balls in his eighth over, including a hat-trick, to reduce New Zealand to 21 for seven. Since then only two men, Peter Petherick and Damien Fleming, have taken hat-tricks on their Test debuts, and only two other men, Chris Old and Wasim Akram, have taken four wickets in five balls in a Test. It remains the only Test hat-trick taken in New Zealand. Allom only played in five Tests in all, and never bettered his analysis in that first New Zealand innings, five for 38.

Before becoming President of MCC, Allom spent many years on the Committee at the Oval, being Chairman of the General Committee during the years of his county's domination of the County Championship under Stuart Surridge and Peter May. For much of this time he was also a member of MCC's Committee. In 1970, his Presidential summer, South Africa were due to tour, but after the debacle eighteen months earlier, public opinion was swinging firmly against the South Africans. It has to be admitted that opinion within cricket was far more divided, but among the general public, ably stirred up by the press and the 'Stop The Tour' campaign led by Peter Hain and others, there was little room for doubt. The South Africans were not welcome. When James Callaghan, the hapless Prime Minister, made it clear the government would or could do little to stop the protests, the tour was called off, and a series against the Rest of the World was played in its place. The cricket was wonderful, and several of the banned South Africans played for the Rest of the World.

Allom was a tall (6ft 3in), energetic, happy man, who in his youth had played the saxophone professionally in a jazz band. He died in 1995, at the age of 89, seventy years after his election to MCC.

Allom's successor was **SIR CYRIL HAWKER**, a banker rather than a cricket administrator. Frank Cyril Hawker was born on 21 July 1900 and after three seasons in the City of London School XI, where he scored many runs as a forcing right-hand batsman, he went into the City. He played a great deal of club cricket when work allowed, mainly for the Free Foresters and the Gentlemen of Essex, and in 1937 made his one first-class appearance, for Essex against Lancashire at Old Trafford. One of the very few other Essex cricketers to have received a knighthood, Sir Geoff Hurst, also played this fixture, twenty-five years later, but with less success. Hawker made 16 and 10 and fielded for a long time while Eddie Paynter made 266 for the hosts. He had a strong family connection with Essex too: his brother-in-law was T. N. Pearce, the Essex captain in 1937. The brothers-in-law were the only two members of the Essex side to reach double figures in both innings in the game, but their efforts were not enough to prevent Lancashire from winning by an innings and 212 runs, nor to prevent Hawker being put on the county scrapheap for ever.

A year after his county career ended, Hawker was elected to MCC. He was also a keen footballer, and later in his career became a Vice-President of the Football Association and President of the Amateur Football Alliance, following there in the footsteps of Lord Alverstone (1903). He was also a vice-president of the National Playing Fields Association, and in that capacity worked in close conjunction with the Lord's Taverners, who gave (and still give) appreciable sums to the NPFA each year. 'The most ill-dressed man I've ever seen', was the opinion of the then secretary of the Lord's Taverners, 'but a lovely man'.

Ill-dressed or not, Hawker's career in banking began in 1920 when he joined the Bank of England. In 1954 he joined the board of the Bank, and in 1962, he became chairman of what was then the Standard Bank, but which in 1970 merged with the Chartered Bank. Sir Cyril remained chairman of the Standard Chartered Bank until 1974. His MCC career began with his election to the Committee in 1964, and he served on the Finance Committee from 1966 until 1983. He was also chairman of the Arts and Library Sub-Committee for much of this time, from 1973 to 1982, and of the Development Committee, from 1971 to 1981. It seems he was hardly ever away from Lord's in the 1970s. He was a man whom Doug Insole remembers as having a great sense of humour, and who was always helpful to younger members of the committees he sat on. He died in February 1991, aged 90.

Sir Cyril passed the Presidency to one of the most charismatic of England's captains, **FREDDIE BROWN**. Frederick Richard Brown was born, uniquely among MCC Presidents, in South America – in Lima, the capital of Peru, on 16 December 1910. Naturally left-handed, his father made him play right-handed, but the end result was an all-round cricketer of great note. He came back to England for his schooling, at The Leys in Cambridge, and then at Cambridge University, where he won a Blue in 1930 and 1931. He joined Surrey and played for them with such success throughout the 1930s that he was nominated one of *Wisden's* Five Cricketers of the Year in their 1933 edition and was selected to go on the tour to Australia in 1932/33. He did not play in any of the Tests in Australia, but he had already made his debut at home against New Zealand in 1931, and also played two matches against New Zealand after the Ashes had been regained by Jardine, Larwood and Voce. His cricket career appeared to have ended with the war, but in 1949 he was offered the captaincy of Northamptonshire. He was such a success in this job that he was asked to lead MCC to Australia in 1950/51, eighteen years after his previous trip. England did not get anywhere near regaining the Ashes, losing by four matches to one in the first post-Bradman series, but Brown was a huge success. He was wholehearted in everything he did, as he was throughout life, and never gave up. The Australians love a loser, unless he is Australian, and soon the market traders of Sydney were offering lettuces with 'hearts as big as Freddie Brown's'. On that tour, he gave J.J. Warr (1987) his only Test caps.

In 1953, he was chairman of selectors, and recalled himself for the Lord's Test, but that was his last experience of play at the highest level. He went on to manage MCC sides in both South Africa (1956/57) and Australia (1958/59), and by this time was a member of the MCC Committee. His year as President was far less fraught than that of his immediate predecessors, but 1972 was no less busy. Times were moving on, and the anomalous position of MCC as a private club governing a public game needed to be looked at in the wake of the D'Oliveira affair. After much discussion and debate, the Cricket Council was formed, as a governing body for the sport 'on the lines generally accepted by other sports in the United Kingdom'. Little did John Arlott realise what changes he was putting in place when he helped D'Oliveira to find a club in England, and move to Britain on a permanent basis, although if he had done, he still would have acted in the same way. The Cricket Council was, needless to say, chaired by the President of MCC, so Freddie Brown was the first of the line. The Cricket Council was still to be based at Lord's, along with the International Cricket Conference. It would be another three decades before the geography changed. The first Cricket Council included no fewer than thirteen past, present and future Presidents in its 29 members, so it was obvious that the power had not moved any real distance from the Committee Room in the Pavilion at Lord's.

Freddie Brown nominated one of his fellow Cricket Council members, a Conservative Member of Parliament and distinguished cricketer and golfer in his younger days, AIDAN CRAWLEY. Aidan Merivale Crawley was born on 10 April 1908 and was educated at Harrow, the first Harrovian for quite some time to be nominated President. He was in the XI at Harrow, and *Wisden* said of him in 1926, 'he was far ahead of the other Harrow boys.' This was proved right the next year, when his innings of 87 against Eton at Lord's was thought to be the best batting seen in these matches for a very long time. His two elder brothers, L.G. (Leonard, the Walker Cup golfer and golf writer) and C.S., were also in the XI before him, as was his younger brother K.E. after him, but Aidan was the man who was destined for greater things. He duly won his Blue at Oxford from 1927 to 1930, being the dominant player at either university in 1928, when he scored over 1,100 runs, hit five centuries and averaged over 54. He hit another century for Kent that summer, too.

However, his first-class cricket career was really over by the end of 1932, although he played occasional further matches. He was elected Labour Member of Parliament for Buckingham, rose almost to cabinet level, but then lost his seat in 1951 and had to find another seat to fight. He tried to be nominated for South East Leeds, but was beaten for the place by a young Denis Healey, who noted in his memoirs that Crawley 'was unwise enough to boast to a Yorkshire audience that he had played cricket for Kent'. However, Crawley was soon back at Westminster, as Conservative MP for West Derbyshire. During the war, he was a fighter pilot who was captured and escaped, and then rather quickly recaptured. After the war, he moved into television and was one of the main powers behind the launch of independent television. He was the first head of ITN, and later the first chairman of London Weekend Television. He still found time for his cricket interests, not only in Kent but also as chairman of the National Cricket Association. In that role he was closely involved with the creation and launch of the National Village Championship, which was first competed for in 1972, the final taking place at Lord's a few weeks before Aidan Crawley took over as President of MCC. Crawley died in 1993, having in his final years lost his wife in a car accident and his two sons in an air crash.

Crawley's successor was a man he got to know well in the corridors of power at Westminster, because **LORD CACCIA**, as Sir Harold Caccia, had been Permanent under-Secretary of State at the Foreign Office since 1962. In fact, their paths first crossed in 1924, when Caccia was at Eton and Crawley was at Harrow. In their match at Lord's that summer, which ended in a draw, Caccia took two wickets as Harrow attempted to chase 183 to win in an hour and three-quarters, and he effectively ended any thoughts of an unlikely Harrow victory. However, as Crawley subsequently recalled, 'He gave me my first boundary at Lord's with a high full pitch outside the off stump.' On such things are lifelong friendships built. Caccia, born in 1906, was a descendant of a Tuscan family, but he was born in England, and after his time at Eton moved on to Trinity College, Oxford. After university, where he did not win his Blue, he joined the Foreign Office and from the early 1930s spent his time in postings at the heart of some of the more fraught regions of the world. He was in Beijing when Chaing Kai-shek was gradually losing control of China to the various warlords and ultimately to the Communists, and when the Japanese were beginning their offensive from the north-east; he was posted to Athens in 1940, which proved to be a brief posting because he was soon expelled by the Germans – nevertheless, there was still time to help rescue the King of Greece from Crete. He was political counsellor to Harold Macmillan, then Resident Minister in North Africa, from 1943, and he went back to Athens in 1944 to watch the Greek civil war from a front-row seat. After a few years as British High Commissioner in Austria during the Harry Lime years of espionage and black marketeering, he took up the top diplomatic post, Ambassador to Washington, just as the Suez crisis began. Whatever his time at Lord's would offer, he had seen it all before.

At the time when Crawley was thinking of his successor, there were still rumblings in the wake of the D'Oliveira affair, to the extent that the subcontinental cricket authorities were highly suspicious of what they considered racial prejudice at Lord's, and there was some serious talk of a breakaway cricket authority being formed. Crawley followed England on their tour of India, Pakistan and Sri Lanka in 1972/73, and despite being able to reassure his hosts that MCC would never tolerate racial discrimination in any form, he was still well aware that there were diplomatic bridges to be built. So Lord Caccia seemed the perfect choice. He proved to be the right man for the job. Not physically particularly imposing but shrewd and with strikingly blue eyes, he commanded attention easily. He wore his authority easily, as a diplomat, as President of MCC and later as Provost of Eton College. He died in October 1990, aged 84.

L ord Caccia's choice as successor was a remarkable one. Maybe because he had saved his successor's cousin, the King of the Hellenes, in the war, Caccia went for the only member of the Royal Family to be

President, and the third man to be invited to do the job for a second time, **H.R.H. PRINCE PHILIP, DUKE OF EDINBURGH**. Prince Philip has no real idea why he was asked a second time: the invitation was just as much a surprise as it had been 25 years earlier. 'I was no longer a naval officer. Perhaps I thought I would be able to do more this time.' He also noticed one item on the agenda for the Annual General Meeting that he was to chair – an increase in membership in fees. 'Perhaps that's why I was invited, to keep the membership in check.' In fact, Prince Philip soon summed up the situation and saw how much the Club and its ways had changed since his previous year as President. The Club was bigger, the ground was being redeveloped rapidly, and there was much more practical work to be done. Also during his year, there was a new Secretary, Jack Bailey, to work with, following the retirement of Billy Griffith in 1974. The President was no longer merely head of the Club: he was also Chairman of the Cricket Council and the I.C.C., so perhaps it was apt that the consort of the Head of the Commonwealth should be the head of world cricket, at a time when Test matches were only being played between members of the Commonwealth.

1975 was an Australian touring year, but more importantly it was also the year of the inaugural cricket World Cup, played almost entirely in glorious sunshine, and culminating in a final at Lord's between West Indies and Australia, which was won by Clive Lloyd's West Indian side by 17 runs, at 8.43 p.m. on a balmy June evening. The competition, which was played over 60 overs, was seen as a huge success, and even though England had lost heavily in the semi-final to Australia, the whole country, indeed the entire cricketing world, took the competition to its heart. The Test series was exciting, if still unsatisfactory for England, as the series was lost 1-0. Tony Greig was the new England captain, David Steele was the hero of the summer, and the general public played a big role in the matches too. At Lord's, the first streaker appeared, as John Edrich ground out a big hundred to make the Second Test safe, and the Third Test, at Leeds, had to be abandoned, with Australia roughly half-way to their target of 445 to win, when vandals dug up and poured oil on the wicket to protest against the jailing of a man for armed robbery. The ringleader of the gang that dug up the pitch was jailed; the armed robber, George Davis, was released on appeal; he was jailed again when caught red-handed undertaking another armed raid. All in all, it was an eventful year.

Prince Philip nominated **Cecil Paris** to be the next President. Cecil Gerard Alexander Paris was born on 20 August 1911 in Kirkee, near Pune in the Indian state of Maharashtra, where his father was serving with the Royal Engineers. He was the first President to be born in India, but not the last, as Colin Cowdrey (1985) was also born there. Coincidentally, both Paris and Cowdrey came back to England to be educated at the same school, Tonbridge in Kent. He was captain of the first XI at Tonbridge for two years, opening the batting and taking plenty of wickets, and he also played for the school rugby XV. His home base in England, once his father came out of the Army, was Hampshire, where in due course he joined the family firm of solicitors, Paris Smith and Randall, in Southampton, where his grandfather and his uncle had worked before him. In many ways his heart was not in the law, and cricket always managed to take up a large part of his time. He first played for Hampshire in 1933, and over the next six seasons he played almost one hundred games for the county, including several in the same side as Ronnie Aird. In 1936 he was appointed vice-captain to the dashing batsman Dick Moore, and in 1938 he took over the captaincy. That year he scored 1,000 runs for the county, but his one season in charge did not revolutionise the Club's fortunes. They finished fourteenth and Paris, whose law work was beginning to take precedence over his cricket, handed over the captaincy to another local solicitor, G. R. Taylor.

The onset of war meant that both cricket and law were set aside, and Paris acted as a Liaison Officer in Eastern Europe, working with Montgomery's 21st Army Group and a Czechoslovakian brigade under General Liske. His was a distinguished record, with medals from the

Czech government if not from the British. In fact, he went through his entire life without any official recognition of his efforts from Britain, despite his years in the law (he retired aged 71 in 1982), his chairmanship of the new Test and County Cricket Board from 1968, his Presidency of Hampshire C.C.C. from 1984 to 1989, and his Presidency of MCC in 1975/76. His time at the T.C.C.B was far from easy. With the new body trying to find its feet in changing times, it needed a quiet diplomatic approach from its leader, and with Paris at its head, that is what it got. He had to oversee the expansion of the one-day game, the rapid expansion of sponsorship in all forms and the entry of overseas players into county cricket, among other things, and Paris and the T.C.C.B proved to be up to the challenges. Almost four decades later, the T.C.C.B has metamorphosed yet again, but that is merely a sign of the changing pace of sports governance rather than a sign that the T.C.C.B failed to work for its times. When Paris died in 1998, aged 86, the Cecil Paris Memorial Trust was set up under the direction of Hampshire C.C.C. to help fund the county's community and ethnic minority coaching programmes. He led a full and happy life and, although he was never a man to push himself forward, is remembered as one of the great men of Hampshire cricket.

Paris went for **TADGE WEBSTER** as his successor. Little did he realise quite what he was letting his friend in for. In 1977, Kerry Packer's plan to win the television rights for cricket in Australia went into action, and the implications threatened to blow international cricket apart. William Hugh Webster was the man in the President's chair when the trouble began. Webster, who for some reason was always known as 'Tadge', was born on 22 February 1910. He went to Highgate School, and then on to Pembroke College, Cambridge, where he won his cricket Blue in 1932. In a high-scoring draw, he opened the batting and was out for 12 in each innings, both times bowled by the South African Tuppy Owen-Smith. At university his left-arm gentle medium-pace bowling was used occasionally, but as a county cricketer he tended only to bat. After graduating he became a stockbroker but spent a great deal of his spare time playing sport. He was a good cricketer, playing around 40 matches for Middlesex in the 1930s, and a handful more in the immediate post-war years, but football was his better sport. He won his Blue at Cambridge and played seven amateur internationals for England in the early 1930s, and retained a strong interest in the game all his life. From 1950 until 1986 he was a member of management committees of the Football Association (where both the Duke of Norfolk and Sir Cyril Hawker were honorary vice-presidents), and he chaired their Finance Committee from 1974, a position he still held during his Presidential year at Lord's.

In April 1977, the first rumours of Kerry Packer's plans to stage his own series of cricket matches emerged in the South African *Sunday Times*, with reports that several leading South Africans had signed to play for Packer's World Series Cricket. The full details of what happened next have been widely reported and discussed in the years that followed, and in England the crucial event was the court case in which Packer, and three of the players he had signed up (Tony Greig, Mike Procter and John Snow) sued the I.C.C. and the T.C.C.B. for what amounted to unreasonable restraint of trade. The case began on 26 September 1977, a few days before Webster was due to hand over his Presidency, and lasted 31 days. Tadge Webster attended every day of the hearing, and was on hand to hear Mr Justice Slade announce the total victory of the Packer side, and the awarding of costs, amounting to about £200,000, against the T.C.C.B. and the I.C.C. It was a bad moment for the cricketing establishment, although clearly not in the longer run a bad thing for cricket and the cricketers.

Webster, who died in June 1986, handed over to **DAVID CLARK**, a Kentish farmer. David Graham Clark, born on 27 January 1919, was a right-hand batsman and very occasional slow bowler who played for the county in the years immediately following the Second World War. Having played four matches in 1946, he played no cricket in 1947 and only three games in 1948. On this basis, he was appointed to succeed Bryan Valentine as captain for 1949. His was, as *Wisden* pointed out, a thankless task, given the county's lack of resources at the time. In his second season as captain, Kent gave nine players their county debuts, but one stood out – the seventeen-year-old Colin Cowdrey, who by the time his first county captain was MCC President 27 years later, had only just finished a long and extraordinary cricket career. Clark captained the side for three years, retiring from cricket at the end of 1951, the season in which he took his only first-class wicket, that of the Nottinghamshire wicketkeeper Meads. In that innings, Kent's wicket-keeper Godfrey Evans took off his pads and captured two wickets, which puts Clark's achievement into context. The match ended in a very dull draw.

In 1951, Kent had three future Presidents playing for them – Clark, Cowdrey and Jack Davies (1985) but although two of the three were often in the same county XI, rather surprisingly all three never played together.

Clark's career in cricket is by no means defined by his time on the field. Having managed the MCC team to India in 1963/64, he was invited by MCC in 1965 to chair a committee that would look into the structure of the County Championship, to examine its future from all angles and with a wide remit to recommend any alterations they thought fit. His committee included four men who had been, or would be, MCC Presidents (Clark himself, Gubby Allen, Ted Dexter and Doug Insole) as well four very distinguished county captains in Stuart Surridge, Brian Sellers, Fred Titmus and Ossie Wheatley, three county secretaries, a county chairman and a journalist. The Clark Committee worked hard between September 1965 and January 1967 in canvassing opinion and putting together its proposals, which were almost immediately rejected by the counties. The reaction of the wider public was much more favourable, and the counties were cast as the reactionary villains of the piece, a role they have found it hard to shake off in the forty years of change that have followed. Many of the Clark

Committee's recommendations have come into effect in the longer term, and there is no doubt that David Clark's efforts have had an influence on the birth of Twenty20 cricket.

Clark was also asked, in 1982, to chair a Lord's working party to scrutinise the role of MCC, to 'look at Lord's' and to review the rules of the Club, especially with reference to the election and formation of Committees and sub-committees. The impetus for this working party was a Special General Meeting held in Hubert Doggart's year, and it put in its first interim report in 1983. It made its final report in September 1984, and among the recommendations it made and which were accepted were plans to reduce the size and number of committees, to increase the proportion of elected rather than nominated members of committees and to make the rule that in future no one over the age of 70 will be elected or nominated an officer of the Club. The very next President nominated, Jack Davies in 1985, was already 74 years old.

Next man in after David Clark was **CHARLES PALMER**, who took office on 1 October 1978. Charles Henry Palmer, born on 15 September 1919, was probably the first President to have been educated at a grammar school, and certainly the first to admit to having then gone up not to Oxbridge, but to the eminently sound redbrick, Birmingham University. He began his first-class career while still an undergraduate, playing for Worcestershire in 1938. *Wisden* wrote that 'Palmer gave indication of real skill' and the next year they were able to record that 'the twenty-year-old amateur from Old Hill ... altogether confirmed the high opinion of him formed of him the previous summer.' He missed scoring his 1,000 runs that war-curtailed summer by just 7 runs, and had to wait until 1946 before having the chance to build on his growing reputation. After the war, he became a teacher at Bromsgrove School, which meant that his appearances for Worcestershire were occasional rather than regular. However, he still managed to find time to tour South Africa with MCC in 1948/49, although he did not play in any of the Tests. He did, however, form a friendship with MCC's reserve wicketkeeper on the tour, Billy Griffith, which was to make his choice of successor as President a little easier.

Palmer was then appointed captain and secretary of Leicestershire, a clever move by the Leicester club, which allowed Palmer to retain his amateur status on the pitch while earning a living as their secretary for the rest of the time. Palmer's time at Leicester was immediately successful. Although he was only a small man, prematurely bald and described by Trevor Bailey as 'a hen-pecked bank clerk in a Whitehall farce', he had the knack of leadership, and Leicestershire began their transformation from perennial back runners to potential champions. Palmer was duly rewarded with the position of player-manager of MCC's 1953/54 tour to West Indies where he played his only Test. It was hardly a reward, proving to be one of the most contentious tours of the post-war era, with trouble both on and off the field. At Kingston during the First Test, an umpire's family was attacked after he had given an unpopular LBW decision, and in Georgetown, during the Third Test, play had to be suspended after the crowd disagreed with a run out decision and threw bottles on to the outfield. The result of the series, two matches all with one drawn, was in retrospect a very fine result, but Palmer's quiet attitude to all the problems that arose was not appreciated everywhere. E. W. Swanton castigated him as being in charge of a tour that was 'a diplomatic and sporting disaster of the first magnitude' and even the sympathetic commentators felt that the experiment of appointing a player-manager should never be repeated. Freddie Trueman missed out on several MCC tours because of his alleged behaviour off the field. If Trueman had been picked for the next winter's tour to Australia, instead of Frank Tyson, would cricket history have been changed for ever?

Palmer's playing career did not continue much longer, although he did manage to baffle the mighty Surrey in 1955 with his occasional bowling. He bowled eleven consecutive maiden overs at them, taking eight wickets in the process, and might have recorded the best eight-wicket analysis of all time, had it not been for the fact that he still had to get rid of the man who did hold the record for the best eight-wicket analysis of all time, Jim Laker. Laker made contact with a couple of swipes, and Palmer had to be content with eight for 7, not quite as good as Laker's eight for 2 five years earlier.

From 1964 Charles Palmer was chairman of Leicestershire and over the following 25 years he and his secretary Mike Turner (who was also a member of the Clark Committee) turned the club into one of the most successful of the era, despite its small size. Inspired signings such as Tony Lock and Ray Illingworth gave the team the leadership they needed on the field, while behind the scenes the Palmer/Turner double-act pushed the county ahead. Palmer's Presidency of MCC, while he was still chairman of Leicester, was followed by a period as chairman of the Test and County Cricket Board from 1983 to 1985. When he died aged 85 on 31 March 2005, he was remembered as 'an all-round good egg', which may of course have had something to do with the shape of his head.

It is remarkable how many MCC Presidents have been wicketkeepers. Even in recent years, Sir Oliver Popplewell, Michael Melluish and Charles Fry have been added to the list that goes back beyond Alfred Lyttelton to John Barnard and the early days of the MCC Presidency. But there is only one man who was not only a wicketkeeper but also scored his maiden first-class century on his England debut, and that is **BILLY GRIFFITH**. Stewart Cathie Griffith was born on 16 June 1914 and was educated at Dulwich College, where he was in the first XI for four years. He went up to Pembroke College, Cambridge, but it was not until his second summer there, in 1935, that he won his Blue, and he lost his place in his final year to another future England wicketkeeper, Paul Gibb. After graduating, he went briefly into teaching at his old school, combining that job with playing cricket for Sussex. When the war came, he joined the Army and became a glider pilot, and finished in 1945 with a D.F.C., won at Arnhem, and the rank of Lieutenant Colonel. When peacetime cricket resumed, he became captain and secretary of Sussex, although he soon gave up the captaincy in favour of his school, university and Army friend and contemporary, Hugh Bartlett. Griffith carried on wicketkeeping, and was selected as Godfrey Evans's deputy for the 1947/48 tour of West Indies, where he made his startling Test debut. Forced into opening the batting because of injuries to all other candidates, he made 140 in six hours, the first century of his career. He was chosen for the tour the next winter, too, to South Africa, and even kept Evans out of the side for two Tests, but he then retired from playing. Within a couple of years he had been appointed assistant secretary at Lord's to Ronnie Aird, and from 1962 to 1974 was Secretary of the Club. These were, as we have seen, momentous years, with the transfer of powers to the T.C.C.B., and the ramifications of the D'Oliveira affair, but Griffith handled every crisis with calm and charm. It sometimes seems that every man in a position of power at MCC was or is a man of calm and charm, but there must have been someone who played the bad cop to everyone else's good cop. The bad cops were men like Frederick Beauclerk, Robert Grimston and, in more recent times, Gubby Allen.

Billy Griffith turned to one of the very greatest cricketers to have been chosen as President of MCC, PETER MAY. In fact, it is easy enough to argue that, in the absence of Sir Donald Bradman who turned the honour down, he is the best cricketer ever to be President. His only challengers would be his near contemporaries Colin Cowdrey and Ted Dexter, but in their playing days May was generally considered the best post-war English batsman, and forty years on there is little reason to change that opinion. Peter Barker Howard May was born on 31 December 1929, and educated at Charterhouse and at Cambridge University. There is no real need to rehearse his playing career: his achievements speak for themselves. By the time he retired from playing, in his early thirties, he had captained England more times than anybody to that time and had given more pleasure to lovers of great batting than any Englishman of his era. A May on-drive was majestic and unstoppable; his off-side play too was beautiful and technically perfect.

After giving up playing, just as the distinction between amateur and professional was abolished, he became something in insurance in the City and went into cricket administration with a will. He was a member of Surrey's committee and the MCC Committee almost from the day he retired (he never formally announced his retirement from playing, he just didn't do it any more: the long awaited comeback never materialised), and, as he relates in his autobiography, 'In early 1980 Billy Griffith rang me up and to my astonishment asked if he might nominate me as his successor as President of MCC. I was staggered.' He was 50 years old – younger than any President since Lord Cobham in 1954, and younger than any of his successors to date – and he enjoyed the experience. He did not have to handle a Packer Crisis or a D'Oliveira Affair, and although he would face many challenges as chairman of selectors, his year as President was a wonderful one. The summer was the summer of Ian Botham's Ashes, and there was goodwill and sunshine all around. May himself thought that he was helped by the fact that he had been a well-known cricketer. Such a President, he wrote, 'is regarded as a cricketer first and foremost with no political axe to grind and with no reputation as a shrewd businessman to uphold'. He himself chose Hubert Doggart, a schoolmaster cricketer, to succeed him, and later Presidents seem to have favoured the well-known cricketer option. Since May there have been 22 Presidents, eight of whom have been Test cricketers (including six England captains) and another eight have played regular first-class cricket. A couple of bankers, a couple of lawyers, a field marshal and a lyricist round out the numbers.

May died young, on 27 December 1994, just four days before his 65th birthday. His last season as a Test selector, 1988, had ended in chaos, with West Indies winning four of the five Tests, and England picking four different captains, including Peter May's godson, Chris Cowdrey, for the Fourth Test. It was a sad exit from cricket for the greatest English batting talent since the war.

GEORGE HUBERT GRAHAM DOGGART, known as Hubert and named for his godfather Sir Hubert Ashton (1960), was born on 18 July 1925. He was educated at Winchester, where Harry Altham (1959) taught him classics. When he was only sixteen, *Wisden* wrote of Doggart, 'if this boy is not a cricketer I shall be prepared to eat his eponymous Coat and Badge.' Even then he was described as 'rich in promise'. He was May's contemporary at Cambridge, having been the captain who, in 1950, awarded May his first Blue as a freshman. The 1950 Cambridge side, full of young men who had already done military service and who were older and stronger than their counterparts today, is generally regarded as one of the strongest university sides of all: Dewes, Sheppard, Doggart and May, the top four batsmen, all went on to play Test cricket, and there was Oliver Popplewell (1994) keeping wicket, and J. J. Warr (1987) to open the bowling, so there were four future Presidents of MCC in the side. When they played the touring West Indies side at Fenner's, Cambridge made 594 for four declared (Dewes 183, Sheppard 227, Doggart 71; Ramadhin 0 for 86, Valentine 0 for 97), but West Indies replied with 730 for three (Weekes 304 not out, Christiani 111, Worrell 160; Warr one for 121, Doggart 0 for 123).

Mind you, Doggart was more than just a cricketer. He won Blues for Association football, rackets, fives and squash, as well as cricket, a collection that beat the three awarded to his godfather Hubert Ashton. Doggart's subsequent career was spent as a schoolmaster, but he played for Sussex as an amateur whenever he could, and in all scored over 10,000 runs and hit 20 centuries. He was also very much involved in schools and youth cricket, and served as President of the English Schools Cricket Association and on many NCA committees. May particularly wanted someone with a direct link to youth cricket to be President, so Doggart was a happy choice. His year was not entirely an easy one: there was a Special General Meeting called to debate the issue of whether MCC should send a side to South Africa, which he had to chair. He also had to referee the tension that was building between MCC and the T.C.C.B.

'The question of power and influence was never far below the surface,' he says. 'For example, MCC originally had five votes on the Cricket Council, the same as the T.C.C.B. and the N.C.A. This pattern of voting was changed to ensure the T.C.C.B. had the whip hand. Gubby Allen, at the centre of Lord's politics, resigned on principle because he thought that the Cricket Council should be representative of all levels of cricket.' In retrospect, we can see this as one of the early steps towards the 'professionalisation' of cricket administration, with the emphasis on the top level of the game rather than on recreational cricket. MCC has nobly battled against this tide, and in recent years has had some small success in seeing the emphasis changed, if only a little.

A sign of modern times was the go-ahead given by members to Sunday cricket, and a sign of MCC's devotion to its history was the 80th birthday dinner given for Gubby Allen in the Long Room. Just as MCC had done for Plum Warner over a quarter of a century earlier, Gubby's age was put up on the scoreboard. It was a happy evening, chaired by one of MCC's most popular Presidents of recent years.

Hubert Doggart went outside the normal avenues to choose TONY TUKE as his successor. Sir Anthony Favill Tuke was born on 22 August 1920 and was educated at Winchester, but did not quite overlap with Doggart there. He also, like so many MCC Presidents, failed to make the first XI there, and at Magdalene College, Cambridge he once again failed to impress the selectors. Both his father and his grandfather having been chairmen of Barclays Bank, it was clear where his future would lie. Before he could go into the family business, the war came and he joined the Scots Guards, but from 1946 his career was bound up with Barclays. He joined the board in 1965 and from 1973 was chairman of the board for eight years. He was knighted in 1979. This was a time when Barclays came under heavy fire for continuing to deal with South Africa, so it was a brave decision of MCC to bring a man so closely associated with continuing links with the apartheid regime to the top position. During his Presidential year, he was also chairman of RTZ, another company not shy of controversy; Sir Anthony was a man of principle who did not shirk confrontation, and whose experience was put to excellent use during his year.

Tuke joined MCC in 1945 and served on the finance sub-committee for sixteen years, including a run of seven years after completing his Presidential year, as chairman of finance. He was, in the words of Doug Insole, 'sports mad, but not much of a player'. Signs of his sports madness were his devotion to Arsenal F.C. and to Hampshire County Cricket Club, as well as his chairmanship of the British Olympic Appeal Committee for the 1980 Olympics. He also got Colin Cowdrey on to the Barclays payroll, and started the process of Barclays becoming a major player in sports sponsorship in the last decades of the century. He loved gardening and in *Who's Who* listed MCC as his only club. He died in 2001, aged 80.

Tuke passed on the mantle to another banker, **ALEX DIBBS**. Arthur Henry Alexander Dibbs was born in 1919, and was educated at Whitgift Middle School, where in 1935 he was captain of the first XI. He joined the Westminster Bank straight from school, and among other achievements played for the Westminster Bank XI for over twenty seasons, apart from the war years. He was not elected to MCC until 1970, having been originally proposed by Doug Insole, so it was by recent standards a very quick progression from new member to President. Of course, by nineteenth century standards, it was positively laggardly. His progress within the bank was also pretty rapid. From being manager of the Croydon branch in 1960, he rose to become Deputy Chairman of what by 1977 was the National Westminster Bank. By the beginning of his Presidential year he was Deputy Chairman of British Airways.

At the time that he was appointed President, there was a significant amount of disagreement between MCC and the T.C.C.B., and Alex Dibbs, who had been active on the finance sub-committee, seemed to be a suitably strong man to try to sort the situation out. However Dibbs, a big man physically and with a big reputation, did not really achieve a great deal. Perhaps the odds were always against him. He had little or no experience of the world of cricket, apart from a few years on MCC's Finance Sub-Committee, and although he proved to be able to grasp the essence of any issue quickly, his lack of contacts and long-lasting friendships within cricket counted against him. He did not have favours to call in. He, as ex officio chairman of I.C.C., made a strong impression on the delegates from outside the U.K., and found himself undertaking work for I.C.C. after his Presidential year, but sadly he did not live for long. Having handed over at Lord's to George Mann in October 1984, he suffered a massive stroke within a year, and died, aged only 66, on 28 November 1985.

FRANCIS GEORGE MANN, born on 6 September 1917, is one of only two pairs of fathers and sons both to have captained England at cricket. George's father, Frank, led England against South Africa in 1922/23, and George captained England in South Africa in 1948/49 and also for the first two Tests against New Zealand in 1949. Only the Cowdreys, Colin and Chris, can match the Manns. George was an unexceptional batsman but a wonderful captain, the Mike Brearley of his day, who turned the comparatively weak 48/49 squad into a very strong team, welded together by his captaincy and brilliant fielding. His highest score in first-class cricket, 136 not out, was made at a time of crisis in the deciding Test at Port Elizabeth.

Mann was educated at Eton, where he captained the XI in 1936, and Pembroke College, Cambridge, where he won his Blue in 1938 and 1939. In the war, he joined the Scots Guards and rose to the rank of Major, winning a D.S.O. and an M.C. along the way. He was, however, always likely to go into the family brewing business, and after the war he had to make the choice between beer and cricket. He had a most enjoyable summer in 1947, as part of the Middlesex side that won the Championship on the back of Compton and Edrich's tidal wave of runs, and again in 1949 when he led the team to a joint title with Yorkshire, but after a couple of seasons playing top class cricket, beer was the winner. Mann did not give up playing altogether: he was a stalwart of the Free Foresters and I Zingari for many more seasons, and played a number of minor games for MCC, but his interest in cricket turned increasingly to the administration of the game. He was honorary secretary of Middlesex, for whom he had first played in 1937, from 1951 to 1965, chairman of the county from 1980 to 1983, and President from 1983 to 1990, thus making him yet another MCC President who doubled up as a county President.

In 1965 Mann was asked to chair a committee that looked into the throwing controversy of the time (there's always a throwing controversy, from the days of David Harris and John Willes, past Arthur Mold to Tony Lock, Geoff Griffin, Ian Meckiff and on to James Kirtley and Muttiah Muralitharan). He was also chairman of the T.C.C.B. when the control of cricket was passing from MCC to the new body, and just a year after giving up that job, he took on the MCC Presidency. As John Warr remarked of his influence behind the scenes, 'a traditionalist by instinct, he recognised the need for change in some areas and was tenacious in the pursuit of his opinions.' He was one of the last true amateurs of the game, the type of man that MCC relied on so heavily over the years, and of which there had always seemed to be an inexhaustible supply. He was appointed C.B.E. in 1983 and died, aged 83, on 8 August 2001. His son, Simon, did not follow the family line of Eton, Cambridge, Middlesex and England. At the time of writing, he is languishing in a Zimbabwean prison, having been found guilty of mercenary activities in relation to a coup attempt in West Africa. George Mann, a very brave man, would never have been so foolhardy.

In 1985, George Mann nominated **JACK DAVIES** to succeed him. Jack Gale Wilmot Davies was born on 10 September 1911, in Devon. He was, however, a Man of Kent (or a Kentish Man) from an early age, and

was educated at Tonbridge, the school that later would help Colin
Cowdrey on his way to greatness. After four years in the Tonbridge
XI, it seemed inevitable that he would gain his Blue when he won a
Classical Scholarship to St John's College, Cambridge. Davies was
as spectacular an all-rounder, intellectually and athletically, as Lord
Desborough or C. B. Fry, but his academic brilliance never seemed to
get in the way of his sporting success. In 1931, however, he sprained
an ankle just before the Varsity match, in which his replacement, A. T.
Ratcliffe, scored a double-century. The next year he hardly played any
cricket, (though Ratcliffe scored another century at Lord's) so it was not
until 1933 that he won his Blue. In 1934 he caused a sensation by bowling Don Bradman for a duck when the university played the Australians
at Fenner's; it was the first duck Bradman had ever made in England.
He also, for good measure, ran out Len Hutton for a duck on his debut
in the same week.

Davies played for Kent in the summer holidays, and for Blackheath
R.F.C. in the winter. He also won the Rugby fives national singles title
three times, and took a second degree in psychology, so that by the
onset of war, he joined the War Office as chief psychologist in the Direc-
torate of Personnel Selection, picking the right person for the right
– and often very strange and dangerous – job. In the early 1950s, he
returned to Cambridge University as Secretary of the University
Appointments Board, and became mentor to generations of university
cricketers. He even played against them in a first-class fixture in 1961,
for MCC, but made a duck. He did however take one final first-class
wicket with his off-breaks, and is one of the very few men who have
played first-class cricket with both Kenneth Farnes and Garry Sobers,
and against both Don Bradman and Mike Brearley.

At MCC, Davies was Treasurer from 1976 to 1980, and a Committee stalwart for many years. Outside cricket and the university, he was
also an executive director of the Bank of England (where he would
have come across Sir Anthony Tuke and Alex Dibbs), and a sporadic
reporter of cricket matches for the *Daily Telegraph*. He was far too
clever for most of his friends and colleagues, but he was never superior

or dull. His laugh is what most people remember of him. He died, aged 81, on 5 November 1992.

J ack Davies nominated as President the man who, at the time, had won more Test caps (114) for England than anyone else. He also chose a second consecutive Tonbridge boy. MICHAEL COLIN COWDREY, C.B.E., was born in Ootacamund, near Bangalore in India, on 24 December 1932, and came to England as a small boy. His career at Tonbridge, where he was initially known as a leg-spinner, and at Oxford, where he stood out as one of the best and most stylish batsmen for years, are too well known to be documented again here. His years as captain of Kent were on the whole very successful. He led Kent to a variety of titles in the early 1970s, and was central to perhaps the longest period of sustained success in the county's history. He went on playing for longer than most, racking up tours to Australia in 1954/55, 1958/59, 1962/63, 1965/66, 1970/71 and 1974/75. Although he captained England 27 times (winning nine successive tosses in the process), he was not captain on any of his tours to Australia. In 1974/75 he was flown out a few days before his 42nd birthday as a replacement for the injury-riddled England side, and four days after landing was drafted into the team for the Second Test. He made 22 and 41 against the might of Lillee and Thomson at their peak, after introducing himself to Jeff Thomson at the start of his innings. 'How do you do, Mr Thomson. My name's Cowdrey.' Thomson's response was not suitable for a family audience.

Cowdrey, who became first Sir Colin and then Lord Cowdrey of Tonbridge, was a delightful, unassuming man, who had the knack of making the person he was talking to seem like the most important person in the world. Some critics believe his apparent lack of ruthlessness was what made him finish his career one rung below the very great batsmen of his era, but cricket for him was always meant to be fun, not a matter of victory or nothing. Those who saw him play when he was in form will say that there was never a man who timed the ball so sweetly, or who could make it fly away to the extra-cover boundary with such delicate grace. At his best, he was impossible to bowl to.

As an administrator, Cowdrey was indefatigable. He worked tirelessly within the rapidly changing framework of world and domestic cricket administration, facing up to the challenges, and managing most of the time to reach compromise where none seemed possible. When it looked as though there was a real possibility of a breakaway from the I.C.C. by the sub-continental cricketing nations, it was Cowdrey's diplomacy as much as anything that pulled them back from the brink. His year at Lord's ended unhappily, with Cowdrey needing a heart bypass operation and a fractious Annual General Meeting. The issue causing the friction at the 200th A.G.M. was the relationship between MCC and the T.C.C.B., alongside the resignations of David Clark as Treasurer and Jack Bailey as Secretary, which MCC were keen to point out to members were purely coincidental. In the words of his successor, John Warr, 'Colin didn't handle it all that well.' So his time as one of the Lord's heavyweights finished on a downbeat note.

But most of all, he was a man who enjoyed the company of other people, and when he could not be with them, he wrote them notes. Every Kent batsman got a note from Cowdrey when he scored his first championship century for the county, and they all treasure their letters. He was elected President of Kent in 2000, and it was after hosting a day in the President's Tent during Canterbury Cricket week in August 2000 that he suffered the stroke that ultimately killed him. He did peacefully in his sleep in December 2000, just three weeks before his 68th birthday, mourned by everyone in cricket.

CHAPTER NINE

1987–2007

MODERN TIMES

The past twenty years have seen more changes in the role of President of MCC than any period before. The Presidency evolved originally from a playing role, with William Ward for one absolutely adamant that the President should play in games organised by his Club. By the 1850s, the view was gaining strength that the President should be a powerful member of Victorian society, as well as a keen cricketer, but if only one qualification was on offer, the keen cricketer bit could go by the board. But still the role of the President off the field was to chair Committee meetings if he could arrange to be there, and to chair the Anniversary Dinner at which a successor would be announced. By the end of the nineteenth century, distinguished men were beginning to make way for distinguished cricketers, but they were men in upper middle age or older. The average age of Presidents has increased steadily decade by decade throughout the past two hundred years, and it is still increasing. The three most recent Presidents, Messrs. Graveney, Marlar and Insole, are all men who were over 75 on taking office, and Doug Insole, the President for 2006/07 is the oldest man ever to take on the job.

The early years of the twentieth century saw a mixture of war heroes, cricketers and peers of the realm (sometimes all three in one man) take on the Presidency, but from the Second World War the key qualification seems to have been administrative skill. Several former secretaries of the Club, civil servants, bankers and schoolteachers have become President; they are men who combine a devotion to cricket with a vast experience of running big organisations, which is what MCC was now becoming. From the late 1980s it changed again. We should also note that, as at the time of writing, whereas only three men who were President before 1987 are still alive, of the sixteen men who have been President since then, only two men, Colin Ingleby-Mackenzie and Lord Alexander, have died. So these men are still influential at Lord's and their stories are unfinished.

J. J. WARR, who was Colin Cowdrey's choice to succeed as President, played for Cambridge University, Middlesex and England from 1949 onwards. Born on 16 July 1927, John James Warr was educated, remarkably for a future MCC President, not at Eton, Harrow or Winchester, but at Ealing County Grammar School, and from there he went to Cambridge, where he was given his Blue in his first season, 1949. He was part of a very strong Cambridge XI who included four future MCC Presidents – Warr, Doggart, Insole and Popplewell – and who would get even stronger the next year when a fifth future President, Peter May, arrived at Cambridge. Warr's presence in the Cambridge side shocked even *Wisden*, who described him as 'a comparatively unknown newcomer from Ealing County Grammar School', but he won his Blue three years in a row and proved his worth. He was given his Middlesex cap by George Mann at the end of the 1949 season and was picked to tour Australia on Freddie Brown's tour of 1950/51. Trevor Bailey broke a finger fielding and Doug Wright pulled a hamstring, so J.J. played in two Tests, at Sydney and Adelaide, taking just one wicket for 281 runs. His one victim was not a particularly spectacular one – Ian Johnson, the off-spinner, caught Evans bowled Warr for 3 in the second innings at Adelaide, where England lost by 274 runs and J.J. finished his Test career with a pair. In 1956, playing for Middlesex against Kent at Lord's, he very nearly became the first man since Gubby Allen in 1929 to take all ten wickets in an innings at Lord's. He took the first nine wickets, but then, with Kent still needing 77 more runs to avoid the innings defeat, their Australian number eight, Jack Pettiford, charged down the wicket to Fred Titmus and John Murray could do nothing else but stump him. Warr was not amused, and no one has taken all ten at Lord's since.

Warr moved seamlessly into cricket's corridors of power, first by being invited to join the Middlesex committee and then coming on to the MCC Committee, where he served for upwards of ten years. As soon as he reached his seventieth birthday, he had to step down from the Committee, but was rewarded with the Presidency, which he thoroughly enjoyed. He was also Australia's representative on the I.C.C., a job he got when Ben Barnett decided for family reasons to return to Australia. The Australian Board wrote to Warr, 'In view of your services to Australian cricket while playing for England, we would like you to be our representative on the I.C.C.' The one wicket for 281 runs proved valuable in the end.

Warr's year at Lord's was, in his words, 'as quiet as can be'. When his year was over, he was appointed Chairman of the Racecourse Association, based on his membership of the Jockey Club since 1977, and his lifelong love of racing. He also became a trustee of Lord's, and as such was very much involved in the rebuilding of both the Mound Stand and the Grand Stand. Sir Paul Getty, who had been so extraordinarily generous in helping to fund the Mound Stand redevelopment, refused to put a penny into the Grand Stand. In his view, the old Grand Stand was a historic monument and he did not want it taken down, and Lord's turned into a stadium. 'If you want to knock it down, do it without me', was what he said to J. J. Warr, and in Warr's view, he was right. 'The architect had no idea about cricket'.

J. J. Warr is one of the most distinguished and funniest speakers ever to have been President of MCC. Any dinner where he was one of the speakers was worth attending, any memorial service where he delivered the eulogy was sure to be an inspiring occasion. 'If only I hadn't done all this speaking for free', he says.

J. J. Warr nominated **DWIN BRAMALL** as the President for the 1989 season. Field Marshal Edwin Noel Westby Bramall, Lord Bramall of Bushfield since 1987, was born on 18 December 1983 and educated at Eton, where he captained the XI in 1942. *Wisden* said of him that 'Bramall handled his attack adroitly and, as a batsman, was in a class by himself.' He scored plenty of runs, and would clearly have been able to enjoy a solid first-class career had there not been a war waging. He joined the Army, being commissioned into the King's Royal Rifle Corps in 1943, and served out the war in northern Europe. Even though the Army was able, in 1945, to field four future Presidents of MCC (Brown, Davies, Griffith, Palmer) in a match at Lord's against the Royal Navy, there was no place yet for Bramall, who was away winning his M.C. He did, however, open the batting regularly for the Army a couple of summers later, after his return from duty in occupied Japan. But most of Bramall's cricket from now on would be for Free Foresters and I Zingari, whenever he had the chance.

Bramall went to the Far East again in 1973, as commander of British forces in Hong Kong, which is where he met the man he chose to be his successor as President, Sir Denys Roberts. He was knighted while in that post, and on his return to Britain in 1976 was promoted to full General and made Commander in Chief of British Land Forces. He was Chief of the General Staff from 1979 and promoted Field Marshal in 1982. On his retirement from the Army in 1983, he became firstly a trustee and then chairman of the Imperial War Museum, a J.P. in London and, from 1986, Lord Lieutenant of Greater London, a post he still held during his Presidential year.

He had always tried to take an active role in the affairs of MCC, and at a time when some clear leadership was needed at Lord's, Dwin Bramall was the right choice. During his year, a draft of new Club rules were laid before the membership, and Lord Bramall made a strong statement at the AGM in May 1989 that if MCC was to retain its role as 'a sort of guardian and conscience of the game', then it had to be an active member of the T.C.C.B. and the Cricket Council, and not merely snipe at these bodies' efforts from the sidelines. Membership of MCC was now officially put at 19,528, with another 8,600 on the waiting list. Given that only 418 vacancies had occurred during the year, and that the Club was aiming to reduce by 2,000 its total membership, the waiting list was then at least 25 years long.

By the time that **SIR DENYS ROBERTS** took over the chair at Lord's, the only thing that was unchanging at Lord's was that things were always changing. Denys Tudor Emil Roberts was born on 19 January 1923 and was educated at Aldenham School in Hertfordshire. He played in the first XI there, topping the batting averages in 1940, when *Wisden* said that the school's batting 'was not sound – only D. T. E. Roberts being anything like reliable'. That was the year before John Dewes first played for Aldenham: Dewes transformed Aldenham's fortunes and went on to play for Cambridge and England alongside Peter May, Hubert Doggart and David Sheppard. Denys Roberts, on the other hand, did not get a Blue when he belatedly went up to Wadham College, Oxford, after three years in the Royal Artillery. But if he did not get a Blue, he got a good law degree in 1948 and began a dual career as a lawyer and a novelist.

The law career was more profitable in the long run, but to begin with it looked as though writing would claim him. His first novel, *Smuggler's Circuit*, was filmed in the late 1950s as *Law And Disorder*, directed by Michael Crichton (who also directed *The Lavender Hill Mob* and *A Fish Called Wanda* among many others) and starred Michael Redgrave as a career criminal who uses his loot to educate his son as a gentleman. By this time, Roberts was already working as a lawyer in Nyasaland (now Malawi) and in 1960 he was appointed Attorney-General in Gibraltar. He wrote more novels, including *Beds and Roses* and *The Bones of the Wajingas*, but he was by now too busy with the law to pursue his writing career more enthusiastically. In 1962 he moved to Hong Kong, first as Solicitor-General, and apart from a 1964 book, *How To Dispense With Lawyers*, remained largely unpublished during these years. When he retired aged 65, it was as Chief Justice of the colony for the past nine years, the last non-Chinese to hold the post. He was simultaneously Chief Justice of Brunei, and later President of the Bermuda Court of Appeal. Once safely retired, he was able to write again. Three volumes of autobiography have followed, with the most recent, *Another Disaster: Hong Kong Sketches*, being published in 2006.

Throughout his time in Hong Kong his interest in cricket remained. In 1964, he toured Thailand with E. W. Swanton's XI, a side captained by another future President, Colin Ingleby-Mackenzie. He was also Hong Kong's representative to the I.C.C. from 1983 to 1987. It was an inspired choice by Lord Bramall to pick a comparative outsider to come into Lord's and take on the Presidency, but when Sir Denys finished his year, he handed over to a man with a more local connection to cricket, although he stayed within the legal profession to make his choice.

Lord Griffiths, who took over in 1990, was born **WILLIAM HUGH GRIFFITHS** on 26 September 1923, and was educated, like Lord Somers and Peter May, at Charterhouse in Surrey, where he topped the school bowling averages in 1940. He was a fast bowler by school standards, although only rated fast-medium when he made the step up to first-class cricket. Before he could make that step up, he went to war, serving in the Welsh Guards from 1942 to 1946, winning an M.C. along the way. He went up to St John's College, Cambridge and won his Blue in 1947 and 1948, and played for Glamorgan in the vacations. Like many a President before and since, he shared in a Championship triumph, when Glamorgan won the title for the first time in their history in 1948. He only played four games, all away from Wales, and took eight wickets at 40 apiece, but he was part of a championship-winning team.

However Hugh Griffiths' first-class career was short-lived as his legal obligations took over. He finished in 1949, with a first-class batting average of 3.91 (still almost three times as good as his fellow Welshman J. H. Scourfield over a century earlier) and 102 wickets at 31.47. He was called to the Bar in 1949, and was appointed a High Court judge in 1971, when he was knighted. By this time, golf had taken over from cricket as his main active pastime, although even at Cambridge he won a Blue for golf as well as cricket. Sir Hugh Griffiths was created Baron Griffiths of Govilon in the County of Gwent in 1985 when he was appointed Lord of Appeal in Ordinary, and in 1993 he became only the second man, after Lord Forster, to have held the offices of President of MCC and Captain of the Royal and Ancient Golf Club. As a golfer, he won the Bing Crosby trophy at St Andrews in the autumn of 1988, and must be, alongside Ted Dexter, one of the best golfers to have held the office of MCC President. He is certainly the only one to have won a golf trophy donated by Bing Crosby, although Sir Tim Rice did write the final track on side two of the Old Groaner's final album.

L ord Griffiths went for another Cambridge man, who had sat on various Lord's committees for three decades. MICHAEL EDWARD LOVELACE MELLUISH, born on 13 June 1932, was educated at Rossall School, where he was a good enough wicketkeeper to play in the Public Schools side at Lord's, captained by Colin Ingleby-Mackenzie. He went up to Cambridge after National Service in 1953, and won his cricket Blue for three years in a row, from 1954 to 1956, captaining the Light Blues in his last year. Among his team-mates were Dennis Silk and Ted Dexter, as well as players of the quality of Bob Barber (a man Melluish remembers as a great leg-spinner in the nets, but not so much in the middle) and Gamini Goonesena. He played for the Gentlemen against the Players in 1956, in a side that included six future MCC Presidents – in batting order Cowdrey, Insole, Palmer, Warr, Melluish and Marlar. Playing for the professionals was a seventh – Tom Graveney. The old family connections of Victorian times that created so many Presidents may be a thing of the past, but the cricketing connections of today are just as strong. It is impossible to be absolutely sure, but a first-class XI that includes six future MCC Presidents must surely be a record.

His business career as a merchant banker left him little time for top class cricket, and in truth he knew he was never quite good enough. But he had some wonderful times, notably keeping wicket against Hampshire at Southsea with his two boyhood heroes Bill Edrich and Denis Compton at first and second slips. It was Billy Griffith who put him up for the MCC Committee as the beginning of a thirty-year involvement with the running of the Club. When he was nominated as President, he claims that Hugh Griffiths handed him a hospital pass by saying that there would be logos on the grass at Lord's 'over my dead body'. But they happened and happily Lord Griffiths is still alive.

Melluish's Presidency was notable for many reasons. Firstly, MCC handed over the chairmanship of the I.C.C. in his year: he was quite happy about this as I.C.C. had to be in charge of its own destiny. Secondly, South Africa came back into the international fold, something that Melluish says was 'a wonderful experience'. However, MCC were now realising that the Presidency was a big job – 'mentally you are there all the time' is how Melluish described it – and the club decided to make changes in the way they administered themselves. Melluish was thus the last man for a while to be President for just one year. This was something for which Lord Bramall had been pressing for some time, and in 1992 it was agreed that Michael Melluish's successor and future Presidents should hold the job for two years. The thinking was that it took the best part of a year to get into the job, and by the time a man was just getting good at it, he had to make way for his successor. When Melluish stepped down, he became Treasurer, a post he held for seven years, and a trustee, a position he held for three years, so there was a logic in extending the term of the Presidency. But in his view, MCC did not quite get it right. 'He should be a figurehead who serves for two years.' What MCC created was a post that lasted two years, but was far from a figurehead.

The first man nominated President under the new system, appointed to serve for two years from October 1992, was **DENNIS SILK**.

Dennis Raoul Whitehall Silk was born in Eureka, California, where his father was a medical missionary on an Indian reservation, on 8 October 1931. His mother died of pneumonia when Dennis was only four years old, and the family returned to Primrose Hill where his grandmother raised the young Silks. He was at school at the beautiful Christ's Hospital in Sussex, and at Cambridge he earned cricket and rugby Blues. Robin Marlar, his captain at Cambridge, 'thought I was a pretty useless player' but when Silk scored 116 not out in the Varsity match of 1953 to win the match for Cambridge by two wickets, he no doubt changed his mind. *Wisden* reports that 'Cambridge supporters and MCC members gave Silk an ovation as he took out his bat after an innings lasting three and a quarter hours'. Silk thought Marlar was a pretty good bowler then. 'It's the only time I've heard the ball hum in the air. We thought he was better than Laker.' Silk's cricket thereafter was limited by his teaching career, in which he spent the final years as Warden of Radley College (where Melluish was a governor).

His two years as President he remembers as being free of really contentious happenings. 'There was a fraught meeting about the fact that Jack Russell and David Gower were excluded from the England touring party to India in 1992/93, but it is not MCC's job to pick the touring team.' It was actually the job of a future President, then chairman of selectors, Ted Dexter. Silk also attended an I.C.C. meeting chaired by Colin Cowdrey, who was very ill at the time, which got out of hand as the subcontinental countries argued the case for a World Cup in India, Pakistan and Sri Lanka. It lasted seventeen hours and 'was the most unpleasant I've ever been at'. He was also involved in the selection of a successor to Colonel John Stephenson, who retired as Club Secretary in 1993. Stephenson, like his predecessor as Secretary Jack Bailey, and the President himself, were all old boys of Christ's Hospital, and he had described the job as 'tougher than commanding a battalion'. MCC, however, decided against the military option and went for another cricketing schoolmaster, Roger Knight, who took over in 1993 and retired at the end of 2006.

In his time Silk has seen many changes. He remembers Lord Cobham 'fulminating with rage' to Colonel Rait Kerr, the Secretary, when the Oxford team arrived for their game in tweed coats and flannels rather than proper suits. 'Rat catchers' outfits' is how Lord Cobham described them. Nowadays dress codes are far more relaxed. But in his view, the Presidency demands most of all a 'capacity for friendship' and stamina, things that Silk has always had in abundance.

The second man to take on the two-year stint was a man who had already turned down the job twice before. **Sir Oliver Bury Popplewell**, Mr Justice Popplewell to a generation of criminals, was born on 15 August 1927, and was educated at Charterhouse, where he was in the same school XI as Peter May. Like Michael Melluish, Popplewell was a wicketkeeper, and when he moved on to Cambridge he won his Blue in 1950 and 1951, having been overlooked in favour of Doug Insole, a part-time wicketkeeper at best, in 1949. After he graduated, the law took up all of his time, and his playing days at first-class level were over. He played for Free Foresters and other club sides when he could, and came back into the MCC's reckoning in 1969 when the trouble over the proposed 1970 tour by South Africa was brewing. From then on, he was on the Committee as often as not and by the time Dennis Silk was ready to step down, Sir Oliver could no longer refuse.

In his time, the main issues were the rebuilding of the Grand Stand, which in turn unleashed a horde of other, very sticky, issues. The old Grand Stand, designed by Sir Herbert Baker, was 'a nightmare' with about one third of the seats having a restricted view, but that did not stop many members, notably Sir Paul Getty, from being very attached to it. To build a new one would cost a great deal of money, and the Committee therefore had to find ways of funding it that would be acceptable to a membership that was not desperately keen on the idea in the first place. Then there was the new Media Centre, to be built at the Nursery End in such a way that Gubby Allen's view of the trees would not be disturbed. The design finally chosen, by no means the

1974, HRH Prince
Philip, Duke of
Edinburgh

1975,
Cecil G. A. Paris

1976, William H. Webster

1977, David G. Clark

Two of England's finest post-war batsmen: Colin Cowdrey (1986) and Peter May (1980).

1978, Charles H. Palmer

1979, S. C. 'Billy' Griffith

1980, Peter B. H. May

1981, G. Hubert G. Doggart

1982, Sir Anthony Tuke

1983, Alexander
H. A. Dibbs

1986, M. Colin Cowdrey

1989, Sir Denys Roberts

1990, Hugh, Baron Griffiths of Govilon

1991, Michael E. L. Melluish

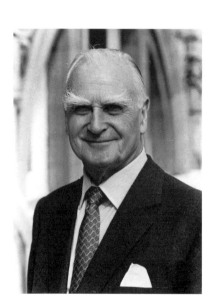

1992, Dennis R. W. Silk

1994, Sir Oliver Popplewell

1996, A. Colin D. Ingleby-Mackenzie

1998, Anthony R. Lewis

2000, Robert, Lord
Alexander of Weedon

2002, Sir Timothy Rice

2003, Charles A. Fry

cheapest option on show, was supposed to cost £1.5 million, but in
the end costs spiralled to around £5 million, and had it not been for the
sponsorship of the NatWest Bank, it may never have been completed.

The rebuilding of the Grand Stand left a legacy that Sir Oliver's
successor, COLIN INGLEBY-MACKENZIE, would have to tackle:
the issue of women members of MCC. Alexander Colin David Ingleby-
Mackenzie, born on 15 September 1933, was educated at Eton, where he
played some of his very best cricket and first came up against Robin
Marlar in the Eton v. Harrow match at Lord's in 1949, and in the Navy,
before emerging to captain Hampshire to their first ever Championship
title in 1961. A free hitting and free thinking left-handed batsman and
captain, the dapper Ingleby-Mackenzie was one of the happiest and
most loved men in the cricket world. He also had possibly the smallest
feet of any MCC President – size 5. After he died on 9 March 2006, his
memorial service had to be held at St Paul's Cathedral because there was
not another venue big enough to hold all the people who wanted to
attend. He was a man who lived his life to the full, memorably stating
in Hampshire's championship year that his team trained on wine,
women and song, and that yes, there was a curfew. They had to be in
bed in time for breakfast. As an obituarist noted, 'Wherever Colin
Ingleby-Mackenzie went, he brought a lightness and laughter, not only
among his uncommonly wide circle of friends. He radiated goodwill.'

After giving up playing for Hampshire in the early sixties, he joined
the insurance brokers Holmwood, and became the backbone of their
schools insurance business. His life was not that of an ordinary insurance salesman, however. He was an inveterate risk-taker, after carefully
assessing the odds as any good insurance man should do, and loved
horse racing and gambling of most types. He built a lifelong friendship
with Keith Miller, perhaps his nearest Australian counterpart, and with
Denis Compton, who shared completely the view that cricket should
always be fun. He was also the last man to see Lord Lucan, a close friend

from the gaming clubs, before his disappearance. Ingleby-Mackenzie lived right next door to Lord's, and so was in and out of his favourite ground all the time.

The biggest thing he did for MCC, indeed the biggest thing that any President has seen through since the first MCC touring teams went overseas to play Tests, was to bring women into the Club. If the Club were to be granted Lottery funding to help meet the cost of the Grand Stand, then the Club had to be open to everybody, regardless of all the usual caveats of gender, race, class, disability or love of cricket. Until women were allowed in, MCC could never hope for government funding, indirectly or indirectly, and Lord's would never be able to be considered for national events which might involve such funding. This was the trigger for the debate, although many members had taken up positions on the matter far earlier. What Ingleby-Mackenzie did that was so brave and so enlightened was to refuse to accept a vote by membership against women members in February 1998, which really only failed on a technicality, and to go back to the membership the same November for another vote. This time it passed, with the required two-thirds majority (69.8 per cent) voting for women members. Within a few months the first women had been elected, among them Rachael Heyhoe-Flint, whose original application for membership a couple of years earlier, proposed and seconded by Sir Tim Rice and Brian Johnston, had been another spark to ignite the flame. The irony of it all was that despite the vote, MCC did not get Lottery funding to rebuild the Grand Stand, and had to finance it by other means, including the sale of debenture seats and offering life memberships for £10,000. The Grand Stand got built, and is an improvement on its predecessor.

Colin Ingleby-Mackenzie thus carved his name indelibly onto the walls of Lord's and left his successor, **TONY LEWIS**, with plenty more still to do. Anthony Robert Lewis was born on 6 July 1938 and was educated, like J. J. Warr, at, of all places, a grammar school: Neath

Grammar School to be exact. There he excelled at cricket and rugby, and at music, to such an extent that he played violin in the Welsh National Youth Orchestra. He went up to Christ's College, Cambridge in October 1959, where he gained Blues at both cricket and rugby (in his first term). He captained the cricket side in 1962. Almost inevitably, something had to give, and the violin was the first to go. The rugby went soon after, but it left him with a bad knee, which would eventually hasten his retirement from cricket. He was seen from his earliest days in the Glamorgan side as a future England captain, a curse that has hindered many a career, and his Test debut was a long time coming. In 1966 he scored more runs than anybody else in Britain – 2,198 at 41.47 – and he was made twelfth man for the Fifth Test against West Indies, but there was no tour that winter. When he did make his Test debut it was as captain on the tour to India and Pakistan in 1972/73. Not many men have made their debut as captain, and Lewis joins a list that includes the Hollywood film star Sir Aubrey Smith and another MCC President, George Mann.

He qualified for MCC as a playing member on their tour to Argentina in 1964/65, and as captain of Glamorgan soon found himself on several MCC sub-committees. As a junior member of the registration sub-committee, one of the first cases he had to deliberate on concerned Barry Knight, an England all-rounder who wanted to move from Essex to Leicestershire. 'That was the first time I realised the Committee Room was a room in which you dare not speak unless you know what you are going to say.' By 1973 he was, in his own words, 'joined at the hip to MCC'.

He became President when Colin Ingleby-Mackenzie cornered him and asked him some questions about how much time he had, and what his attitude to women members was. He must have answered correctly, because he was duly nominated. But Lewis was the last of the two-year Presidents, an experiment that did not last for long. 'There was an urgent need for a reform of the structure of MCC. It was becoming a very big business.' Together with Sir Michael Jenkins, then Treasurer (and incidentally one of the very few Treasurers not to have become

President – yet), Lewis agreed to recommend to the Committee that the position of chairman be created, a facilitative rather than executive position to last for three years, and that the Presidency revert to one year, and be restricted to a more ceremonial role. The Jenkins Report, as it was known, was accepted.

Lewis, who was the BBC television cricket man for many years, as well as a distinguished cricket journalist for even longer, also found time to chair the Welsh Tourist Board and get involved with many music organisations in Wales, and continues to involve himself in cricket at many levels. During his time as President, the Media Centre was the big issue, women having been duly elected as members and their existence generally tolerated within the Long Room. The original vote was 13 to 2 against the design, but Lewis describes it with affection as 'a thumping piece of architecture'. His one complaint is that, at the end of their year, each President 'falls off stage left and is never seen again'. To fight against this, Lewis has devised the new International Committee of MCC, which had its first meeting in the spring of 2006 and which is planned to act as a kind of House of Lords, to question and support I.C.C. on difficult issues. The Committee has established links with Imperial College, London, to study such matters as the mechanics of throwing, rather than leaving it all to I.C.C. MCC, after all, remains the ultimate custodian of cricket's Laws.

Tony Lewis had originally planned to hand over to another England captain, Ted Dexter, but such were the requirements of the moment that he turned instead to a lawyer, Lord Alexander of Weedon. ROBERT SCOTT ALEXANDER was born on 5 September 1936, and was educated at Brighton College and King's College, Cambridge. He did not make the XI at either establishment, and throughout his life his passion for cricket was more as a spectator than as a participant. At 6ft 6in, he might have been an imposing fast bowler, but his unplayable balls were delivered in the law courts rather than on the green swards of England.

Lord Alexander first came to the notice of Lord's when he acted, successfully, for Kerry Packer in the fight against the Test and County Cricket Board. He was also engaged by Ian Botham when Somerset suspended him for bringing the game into disrepute, but perhaps his highest profile case was not one that had much, if anything, to do with cricket. He acted for Lord Archer in his libel trial against the Daily Star, which he won with some devastating advocacy. It was only a pity that it turned out much later that Archer had lied throughout the trial. Bob Alexander, a most unstuffy man, subsequently became chairman of the takeover panel, and then chairman of NatWest, a bank that had plenty of troubles of its own at the time, but was a firm supporter of cricket. Lord Alexander, who was created a life peer in 1988, was a member of various MCC committees for a number of years, and became a natural choice as the first of the reinstated one-year Presidents, with the expectation (duly realised) that he would go on to become chairman when he stepped down from the Presidency. He was a great partygoer, and his time as President was filled with good parties celebrating a number of different happenings that he deemed worthy of celebration. He brought a remarkable degree of informality to Lord's. Sadly, he was not long to outlast his time as chairman, which ran from 2001 to 2004. In 2005, he was struck down by a massive stroke, and he died, aged 69, on 5 November 2005.

If Lord Alexander was one of the less able cricketers to have become President, he made up for it by handing over to one of the greatest – TED DEXTER. Edward Ralph Dexter, born in Milan on 15 May 1935, was educated at Radley and Jesus College, Cambridge. From his earliest days, he was obviously going to be an outstanding sportsman, and after three years in the Radley XI, he clinched his Blue at Cambridge in his first year, and went on to captain the side in his final year. He played for Sussex on the basis – as his captain Robin Marlar put it – that Sussex is close to Milan, and was very soon in the England side. He played 62

Tests for England, and finished with an average of 47.89. He would have played more Tests, but the combination of a broken leg in 1965, caused by running himself over in his own car (a tricky but obviously achievable feat) and a restlessness to do other things limited his playing career. His 70 in 73 balls at Lord's in 1963 against Wes Hall and Charlie Griffith at their fastest will remain in the memory of everybody who saw it as one of the great attacking innings ever seen there: when his batting worked, there was an imperiousness that perhaps only Viv Richards has matched in the past fifty years.

He was also a wonderful golfer, probably good enough to have become a successful professional, and has won the President's Putter competition, for Oxford and Cambridge golf Blues, at Rye three times. Even in his seventies, one would not put it past him to win it a fourth time. He also stood for Parliament in 1965, in the Conservative cause in James Callaghan's Cardiff constituency. Not surprisingly, he was defeated, but in most other endeavours he has been successful. He was the driving force behind the ratings system for cricket which has now become a standard measure of an international cricketer's standing, and he even co-wrote two novels, murder-mysteries with a sporting theme, called *Test Kill* and *Deadly Putter*. His co-author was Clifford Makins, one-time editor of the boy's comic *Eagle*, and there is something about Ted Dexter's entire life that is best presented in comic strip form. He was also for several years chairman of selectors, but eventually he stepped down when England's lack of success over too long a period proved too much. 'Lord Ted', as he was always known to his admirers, has yet to earn the title for real, but he was created C.B.E. for his services to cricket in the New Year's Honours list of 2001.

If Ted Dexter wanted his Presidential year to be sandwiched between two lesser cricketers, he could not have done better than to choose **SIR TIM RICE** as his nominee as next man in. Timothy Miles Bindon Rice, born in Amersham on 10 November 1944, is no cricketer, but his love for the game is unrivalled. Famous for his lyrics, he is almost as well known to the public for his enthusiasm for cricket, and his willingness to talk about the game and write about the game, as well as playing it and watching it at every opportunity. His writing partnership with Lord Lloyd-Webber first foundered because Sir Tim went to the Test Match at Lord's rather than attend the final dress rehearsal for *Evita*. In fact, Sir Tim probably fulfilled the wishes of William Ward 180 years earlier better than all the post-war generation of Presidents. He still played cricket during his Presidential year, even if it was not necessarily of the highest class. His team, Heartaches C.C.(founded in 1973 because no one else would pick him), has progressed well into its fourth decade of activity, and Sir Tim is still the captain, leader and perennial personality. He has never, however, been President of the club: that privilege is reserved for captains of England such as Bob Wyatt, Tony Lewis and David Gower (or England A in the case of Mark Nicholas). In 2003, his year as President of MCC, Sir Tim played eleven matches, one of which was his four hundredth for his club, but only batted four times. He remained undefeated twice, and despite this, his average was only 6.00, but the heartening thing is that there were nine men in the season's averages with a worse average than that. He bowled, too, taking seven more wickets to add to his ever-lengthening list of batsmen who just can't believe bowling can be that easy.

Sir Tim had paid his dues, as a long-serving member of the MCC Committee and of the Arts and Library sub-committee, and was a role model for the more ceremonial style of President that the new constitution of the Club required. That is not to say there is anything ceremonial about Rice, especially his dress sense, but his abilities as a public speaker and his links with other fields of endeavour meant that he was instrumental in raising the profile of MCC, and persuading a few people, at least, that the Club is not still stuck firmly in the nineteenth century.

When Sir Tim thought of a successor, one of the first names
that came to his mind was that of Tom Graveney, but he was
worried that his health might not be good enough, and did not ask him.
Instead, he turned to **CHARLES FRY**, grandson of the great C. B. Fry,
who was an England Test captain who was offered the throne of
Albania but not, as far as we can discover, the Presidency of MCC. Fry
was first elected to the Committee of MCC in the 1970s, in the after-
math of the D'Oliveira affair, and was the first man to be elected
unstarred. In those days, the preferred candidates of the Committee
were given a star next to their names, to advise members how to vote.
Fry, an iconoclast, was not a preferred candidate, but he was elected all
the same. 'I suppose the Fry name helped a great deal. At the time, the
Committee was about thirty strong, and eight of them were over eighty
years old. Gubby Allen had been on the Committee for fifty years!
Michael Sissons and I were the rebels.'

Charles Anthony Fry, born on 14 January 1940, was never as
good a cricketer as his grandfather (very few men were), but he was
good enough to win his Blue at Oxford University and play for
both Hampshire and Northamptonshire, as a wicketkeeper-batsman,
in the 1960s. His father Stephen captained Hampshire occasionally in
the early 1930s, also as a wicketkeeper, but his career was curtailed by
his mother, who had had enough of cricket in the family and used to
hide her son's car keys so that he could not get to the ground to play for
the county. Charles remembers most fondly opening the innings
for Northamptonshire second XI with the young Colin Milburn, and
putting on 138 together. Fry's share of the stand was 12: 'Milburn was
a wonderful player.'

Fry's year as President was unremarkable enough, but on stepping
down, he was elected chairman in succession to Lord Alexander. When
it came to thinking about a successor, he did what most Presidents
have done in recent years – he consulted a few other people, past Presidents like Colin Ingleby-Mackenzie and Tony Lewis, and the chairman
Bob Alexander. But, as with every nomination, when the announce-
ment is made at the Annual General Meeting, there are usually no more

than half-a-dozen people in the room who know what name is about to be spoken. In Fry's case, the name he gave was that of Tom Graveney.

The nomination of **TOM GRAVENEY** as President was unique in that he was the first, and quite likely only, President to have played first-class cricket as an old-style professional. It is now over forty years since the distinction between amateur and professional was made, and although men like Dexter, Cowdrey and Lewis have all been paid for playing cricket since then, Graveney is the only man to have made it to President who came through the professionals' gate on to the pitch at Lord's. Thomas William Graveney, born on 16 June 1927, may have been a pro, but he played cricket like a Golden Age amateur. His cover drive was a thing of beauty and timing, but the ease of his stroke-play gave some the impression of a looseness that could be interpreted as unreliability in a crisis. Nothing could have been farther from the truth, but it may explain why a man who scored almost 48,000 runs in a 23-year career, and who scored 122 centuries and averaged over 44 in Tests, only played 79 times for England.

Graveney, like Fry, was a bit of an outsider in his younger days, and spent years in the wilderness for one reason or another. He had no reason to love the powers that be at Lord's, as they prevented him from moving from Gloucestershire to Worcestershire in the 1960s when he was over-looked as captain in favour of the Old Etonian amateur Tom Pugh. Graveney lost two seasons of his career while qualifying for Worcester-shire, but he repaid them with a glorious Indian summer of his career, helping them to their first ever Championships in 1964 and 1965. His Test career ended abruptly when he opted to play a benefit game on the Sunday of the Old Trafford Test in 1969 (which was a rest day, of course) against the wishes of the selectors. He was never chosen again.

Although he became a successful journalist, television and radio commentator, pub landlord and purveyor of artificial pitches, not to mention President of Worcestershire, he was not a Lord's insider in the

way that most of his predecessors have been. His nephew David is at
the heart of English cricket as chairman of selectors and for many years
head of the Professional Cricketers' Association, but Tom was never a
committee man.

We can begin to see in Graveney's appointment the way that the Presidency is becoming an honour rather than a job, and it seems likely that
in the future the Presidency will go to famous names within the world
of cricket, whether or not they have taken active roles off the field at
Lord's. This is not a problem or an issue, because the chairman is there
to run meetings and act as the Club spokesman, and it allows MCC
to pick men who will add to the lustre of the Club as viewed from the
outside. 'Any Club with Tom Graveney as President must be a good
one' would be the message conveyed.

G raveney took many people by surprise when he announced the
President for 2005/06. **ROBIN GEOFFREY MARLAR**, born on 2
January 1931, is a different type of man altogether. A very fine off-spin
bowler and intuitive captain of Sussex from 1955 to 1959, he was never
known for doing things the regulation way. He was educated at Harrow,
where he played in the first XI, and at Magdalene College, Cambridge,
where he won his cricket Blue from 1951 to 1953, captaining the side in
his final year. After a year teaching at Eton, he took up a position as
librarian at Arundel Castle, which allowed him to play cricket pretty
well full time, under the benign eye of the Duke of Norfolk.

Once he finished his playing days, he became an opinionated but
highly regarded cricket correspondent for the *Sunday Times*, and also
set up his own consultancy firm that specialised in personnel and head-
hunting. Like Ted Dexter, he was an unsuccessful candidate in the
Conservative cause, but he topped Dexter by losing twice – at Bolsover
in 1959 and at Leicester North-East at a by-election in 1962. A long-
serving member of MCC committees, it was not that Marlar was not
thoroughly qualified for the position, it was the anti-establishment

position he had always taken up that might have worked against his chances of ever taking the top job. However, as President, he managed to outrage women by being misrepresented in his comments on women cricketers, but he also took the first steps towards bringing Afghan cricket to public attention, by organising a game between MCC and Afghanistan in India early in 2006. He has also been an assiduous attendee of all MCC Committee meetings, not afraid to ask the awkward question people had hoped might remain unasked.

Robin Marlar never quite made the England side, having to compete with such spinners as Jim Laker, Tony Lock, Bob Appleyard and Johnny Wardle, but he did manage one piece of representative cricket that has almost gained the status of urban myth. Playing for The Rest against the Champion County, Surrey, at the Oval in September 1955, he was asked to go in as night-watchman by his captain, Doug Insole. Marlar was not pleased by this decision, as he had already changed into his dinner jacket for a night out, but he bowed to Insole's demands and went out to face Tony Lock. Two balls later he was back in the pavilion, stumped McIntyre bowled Lock for 6. 'As I was saying', he said to his captain on his return, 'I am not a night-watchman.'

His captain that day, Doug Insole, has obviously forgiven his headstrong off-spinner, because he accepted Marlar's invitation to succeed him as President for 2006/07. DOUGLAS JOHN INSOLE C.B.E. was born in Clapton in the east end of London on 18 April 1926, and so the very last President in this book becomes the oldest man ever to take on the office, and the only man over eighty years old when his term began. But he holds this record only because he turned down the honour several times (estimates vary from five to eight) earlier in his life. Insole was educated at Sir George Monoux Grammar School (the third grammar school boy after J. J. Warr and Tony Lewis to become President) and at St Catherine's College, Cambridge, where he won his Blue from 1947 to 1949, captaining the side in his final year. He was also a very fine footballer, not only winning three Blues on the soccer field, but also playing regularly for the top amateur sides Corinthian Casuals and Pegasus, winning an Amateur Cup Final runners-up medal in 1956, when Bishop Auckland beat Corinthian Casuals 4-1 at Ayresome Park after a 1-1 draw at Wembley. Insole is by no means the only man to have played at both Lord's and Wembley (my younger brother did so in the space of three days), but he is the only one also to have become President of MCC.

Insole captained Essex for much of his playing career, from 1950 to 1960, and after his playing days were finished in 1963, he became deeply involved behind the scenes at both Lord's and Chelmsford. He served on the MCC Committee for twenty years, and was a Test selector for nineteen. Ronnie Aird told him when he was elected to the Committee in 1955 at the age of 29 that he was the youngest ever committee man, but actually that is not nearly the case. There have been at least two dozen Presidents younger than 29 years old, but still Insole's total span of service to MCC, at just over the fifty years Gubby Allen served on the Committee, is remarkable. He was Chairman of the T.C.C.B. at the time of the Packer rumpus, and later became Chairman of the European Cricket Council. President of MCC was about the only job he hadn't done.

Why did he take on the job now? 'Well, I suppose there's no fool like an old fool.' When he was asked to take on the job in the past, it was either at a time of personal tragedy (his first wife died of motor neurone disease in 1982) or when things at Essex or the T.C.C.B. were too busy to abandon. 'They always managed to find a President for MCC, but there were not too many candidates for the jobs at Essex.' But in his view the job has now changed immensely, and he is happy to take on the role that many people have been urging him to take for the past quarter of a century. With a new Chief Executive to help into the post, it is a good thing that the new President knows Lord's, the E.C.B. and the I.C.C. extremely well and thus, in Insole's words, 'might be able to help'.

'Might be able to help' is as good a job description as any for the Presidency of the Marylebone Cricket Club. MCC remains a private club with a public function, but is still coming to terms with the huge changes and the huge finances that are now sweeping into cricket, and into all professional sport. When Insole began playing, a professional would be paid a few pounds a week and if he was lucky could expect a benefit that might yield £5,000 after the best part of two decades. Now the likes of Shane Warne and Sachin Tendulkar are millionaires in anybody's currency, and Andrew Flintoff sets a target of £3 million for his 2006 benefit. Yet the financial position of the county clubs is still precarious and MCC is evolving all the time. Like Britain, MCC has lost an empire and is still searching for a role to play. Choosing the right President every year will help define MCC's role, and ensure that the Club does not fade into the background as merely the owner of the greatest cricket ground in the world.

APPENDIX

MCC PRESIDENTS

Test captains

G. O. B. 'Gubby' Allen (1963)

Hon. Ivo Bligh (1900)

Frederick R. Brown (1971)

M. Colin Cowdrey (1986)

Edward R. Dexter (2002)

Arthur E. R. Gilligan (1967)

Thomas W. Graveney (2005)

Lord Harris (1895)

Lord Hawke (1914–1918)

Hon. F. Stanley Jackson (1921)

Anthony R. Lewis (1998)

F. George Mann (1984)

Peter B. H. May (1980)

Allan G. Steel (1902)

Sir Pelham Warner (1950)

Other Test cricketers

Maurice J. C. Allom (1969)
5 Tests

Stanley Christopherson (1939)
1 Test

G. Hubert G. Doggart (1981)
2 Tests

S. C. 'Billy' Griffith (1979)
3 Tests

Douglas J. Insole (2007)
9 Tests

Hon. Alfred Lyttelton (1898)
4 Tests

Charles H. Palmer (1978)
1 Test

John J. Warr (1987)
2 Tests

Other first-class cricketers

Ronald Aird (1968)

Harry S. Altham (1959)

Sir Hubert Ashton (1960)

Lord Bridgeman of Leigh *(as W.C. Bridgeman)* (1931)

Hon. Edward Chandos Leigh (1887)

Viscount Chelmsford *(as F. J. N. Thesiger)* (1922)

David G. Clark (1977)

Ninth Viscount Cobham (1935)

Tenth Viscount Cobham *(as Hon. C. J. Lyttelton)* (1954)

Lord Cornwallis *(as Capt. W. S. Cornwallis)* (1947)

Aidan M. Crawley (1972)

Lord Dartmouth *(as Viscount Lewisham)* (1893)

Jack G. W. Davies (1985)

Rt. Hon. Sir Alec Douglas-Home *(as Lord Dunglass)* (1966)

William Findlay (1951)

Charles A. Fry (2004)

Charles E. Green (1905)

Baron Griffiths of Govilon *(as W. H. Griffiths)* (1990)

Sir Cyril Hawker (1970)

A. Colin D. Ingleby-Mackenzie (1996)

Robin G. Marlar (2006)

Michael E. L. Melluish (1991)

Viscount Monckton of Brenchley *(as Walter Monckton)* (1956)

Sir Oliver Popplewell (1994)

Sixth Earl of Rosebery *(as Lord Dalmeny)* (1953)

Dennis R. W. Silk (1992)

Sir Kynaston Studd, Bt. (1930)

Richard H. Twining (1964)

V. Edward Walker (1891)

William H. Webster (1976)

Prime ministers

Rt. Hon. Lord Baldwin of Bewdley (1938)

Rt. Hon. Sir Alec Douglas-Home (1966)

Cabinet ministers

Lord Bridgeman of Leigh *(as W. C. Bridgeman)* (1931)

Earl Cawdor (1908)

Viscount Chelmsford (1922)

Robert Grosvenor, Baron Ebury (1865)

Viscount Hailsham (1933)

Lord George Hamilton (1881)

Sir William Hart-Dyke, Bt. (1880)

Marquess of Lansdowne (1869)

Walter H. Long (1906)

Lord Loreburn (1907)

Viscount Monckton of Brenchley *(as Sir Walter Monckton)* (1956)

Sixth Earl of Rosebery (1953)

Baron Skelmersdale *(as Earl of Lathom)* (1860)

Earl Spencer (1861)

Viscount Ullswater *(as J. W. Lowther)* (1923)

Members of House of Commons

Viscount Alverstone *(as Richard Webster)* (1903)

Sir Hubert Ashton (1960)

Col. The Hon. John J. Astor (1937)

Lord Belper *(as Hon. Henry Strutt)* (1882)

Duke of Buccleuch *(as Earl of Dalkeith)* (1888)

Viscount Chelsea (1873)

Ninth Viscount Cobham *(as Hon. J. C. Lyttelton)* (1935)

Aidan M. Crawley (1972)

Earl of Dalkeith (1913)

Lord Dartmouth *(as Viscount Lewisham)* (1893)

William E. Denison (1892)

Lord Desborough *(as William Grenfell)* (1911)

Lord Ernle of Chelsea *(as Rowland Prothero)* (1924)

Lord Fitzhardinge of Bristol *(as Col. Francis Berkeley)* (1878)

Lord Garlies (1858)

Lord Guernsey (1850)

Earl Howe *(as Viscount Curzon)* (1901)

Sir Henry James (1889)

Sir Charles Legard, Bt. (1875)

Viscount Lewisham *(as Sir William Legge)* (1932)

Earl of Lucan *(as Hon. George Bingham)* (1928)

Hon. Alfred Lyttelton (1898)

Earl of March (1842)

Viscount Monckton of Brenchley *(as Walter Monckton)* (1956)

William Nicholson (1879)

Earl of Pembroke *(as Sidney Herbert)* (1896)

Lord Charles Russell (1835)

John H. Scourfield (1870)

Lord Strathavon (1821)

Earl Vane (1854)

Lord Willoughby de Eresby *(as Gilbert Heathcote)* (1890)

Marquess of Worcester (1853, 1877)

Colonial administrators and diplomats

Field Marshal Earl Alexander of Tunis (1955) *Canada*

Lord Caccia (1973) *Washington*

Viscount Chelmsford (1922) *India, Queensland, N.S.W.*

Viscount Chelsea (1873) *Ireland*

Tenth Viscount Cobham (1954) *New Zealand*

Duke of Devonshire (1912) *Canada*

Lord Forster of Lepe (1919) *Australia*

Lord Gowrie, V.C. (1948) *Australia*

Lord Harris (1895) *Bombay*

Earl of Jersey (1894) *New South Wales*

Marquess of Lansdowne (1869) *Canada*

Lord Somers (1936) *Victoria, Australia*

Earl Spencer (1861) *Ireland*

Lord Wenlock (1885) *Madras*

Lawyers

Lord Alexander of Weedon (2001)

Viscount Alverstone (1903)

Hon. Edward Chandos Leigh (1887)

Baron Griffiths of Govilon (1990)

Hon. Robert Grimston (1883)

Sir Henry James (1889)

Hon. Alfred Lyttelton (1898)

Viscount Monckton of Brenchley (1956)

Cecil G. A. Paris (1975)

Sir Oliver Popplewell (1994)

Sir Denys Roberts (1989)

Sir Archibald L. Smith (1899)

Allan G. Steel (1902)

Warriors

General Sir Ronald Adam Bt. (1946)

Field Marshal Earl Alexander of Tunis (1955)

Col. The Hon. John J. Astor (1937)

Field Marshal Baron Bramall of Bushfield (1988)

Lord Cornwallis (1947)

Admiral of the Fleet Sir John de Robeck, Bt. (1925)

Viscount Downe (1872)

Duke of Edinburgh (1949, 1974)

Lord Fitzhardinge of Bristol (1878)

Lord Gowrie, V.C. (1948)

Algernon F. Greville (1828)

General Viscount Hampden (1926)

Lt Gen Sir Oliver Leese (1965)

Lord Methuen of Corsham (1868)

Lt Col. Lord Nugent (1962)

Field Marshal Baron Plumer (1929)

Marshal of the RAF Lord Portal of Hungerford (1958)

Earl of Sandwich (1866)

Col Sir William Worsley, Bt. (1961)

Schoolteachers

Harry S. Altham (1959)

G. Hubert G. Doggart (1981)

S. C. 'Billy' Griffith (1979)

Robin G. Marlar (2006)

Charles H. Palmer (1978)

Journalists

Col. The Hon. John J. Astor (1937)

Anthony R. Lewis (1998)

Robin G. Marlar (2006)

Sir Pelham Warner (1950)

Businessmen and financiers

Benjamin Aislabie (1823)

Earl of Cromer (1934)

Alexander H. A. Dibbs (1983)

Earl of Dudley (1864)

Charles A. Fry (2004)

Marquess of Hamilton (1874)

Henry R. Kingscote (1827)

William Nicholson (1879)

Sir Anthony Tuke (1982)

Priests

Lord Frederick Beauclerk (1826)

Oscar winners

Sir Tim Rice (2003)

MCC PRESIDENTS

listed alphabetically

Sir Ronald Adam Bt.	1946	Viscount Chelsea	1873
Ronald Aird	1968	Sixth Earl of Chesterfield	1839
Benjamin Aislabie	1823	Tenth Earl of Chesterfield	1909
Harry S. Altham	1959	Stanley Christopherson	1939–45
Earl Alexander of Tunis	1955	Fifth Earl of Clarendon	1871
Lord Alexander of Weedon	2000	David G. Clark	1977
G. O. B. Allen	1963	Aidan M. Crawley	1972
Maurice J. C. Allom	1969	Ninth Viscount Cobham	1935
Viscount Alverstone	1903	Tenth Viscount Cobham	1954
Hon. Anthony H. Ashley	1834	Second Lord Cornwallis	1947
Sir Hubert Ashton	1960	Ninth Earl of Coventry	1859
Hon. John J. Astor	1937	M. Colin Cowdrey	1986
First Earl Baldwin of Bewdley	1938	Second Earl of Craven	1841
John Barnard	1829	Second Earl of Cromer	1934
Charles J. Barnett	1825	Earl of Dalkeith	1913
Sir John Bayley, Bt.	1844	Sixth Earl of Darnley	1849
Lord Frederick Beauclerk	1826	Sixth Earl of Dartmouth	1893
Eighth Duke of Beaufort	1877	Jack G. W. Davies	1985
Tenth Duke of Beaufort	1952	William Deedes	1831
Second Baron Belper	1882	William E. Denison	1892
Hon. Ivo Bligh	1900	First Baron Desborough	1911
Lord Bramall of Bushfield	1988	Ninth Duke of Devonshire	1912
First Viscount Bridgeman of Leigh	1931	Edward R. Dexter	2001
Frederick R. Brown	1971	Alexander H. A. Dibbs	1983
Sixth Duke of Buccleuch	1888	G. Hubert G. Doggart	1981
Lord Caccia	1973	Sir Alec Douglas-Home	1966
Third Earl Cawdor	1908	Eighth Viscount Downe	1872
Thomas Chamberlayne	1845	Second Earl of Ducie	1843
Hon. Edward Chandos Leigh	1887	First Earl of Dudley	1864
First Viscount Chelmsford	1922	Viscount Dupplin	1852
		First Baron Ebury	1865

HRH Prince Philip,
  Duke of Edinburgh   1949, 1974

Fourth Earl of Ellesmere   1920

First Baron Ernle of Chelsea   1924

Second Marquess of Exeter   1838

William Findlay   1951

Second Baron Fitzhardinge
  of Bristol   1878

First Baron Forster of Lepe   1919

Charles A. Fry   2003

Lord Garlies   1858

A. E. R. Gilligan   1967

First Earl of Gowrie   1948

Marquess of Granby   1904

Thomas W. Graveney   2004

Charles E. Green   1905

Algernon F. Greville   1828

S. C. Griffith   1979

Lord Griffiths of Govilon   1990

Hon. Robert Grimston   1883

Fourth Viscount Grimston   1837

Lord Guernsey   1850

First Viscount Hailsham   1933

Lord George Hamilton   1881

Marquess of Hamilton   1874

Third Viscount Hampden   1926

Fourth Lord Harris   1895

Sir William Hart-Dyke, Bt.   1880

Seventh Baron Hawke   1914–1918

Sir Cyril Hawker   1970

Sir Frederick H.
  Hervey-Bathurst, Bt.   1857

Henry Howard   1832

Fourth Earl Howe   1901

A. Colin D. Ingleby-Mackenzie   1996

Douglas J. Insole   2006

Hon. Sir Stanley Jackson   1921

Sir Henry James   1889

Herbert Jenner   1833

Seventh Earl of Jersey   1894

Henry R. Kingscote   1827

Henry T. Lane   1824

Fifth Marquess of Lansdowne   1869

Third Baron Leconfield   1927

Sir Oliver Leese   1965

Sir Charles Legard, Bt.   1875

Second Earl of Leicester   1848

Anthony R. Lewis   1998

Viscount Lewisham   1932

Third Earl of Lichfield   1897

Henry J. Lloyd   1822

First Lord Londesborough   1876

Second Lord Londesborough   1910

Walter H. Long   1906

First Baron Loreburn   1907

Fifth Earl of Lucan   1928

Hon. Alfred Lyttelton   1898

Fifth Lord Lyttelton   1886

F. George Mann   1984

Earl of March   1842

Robin G. Marlar   2005

Peter B. H. May   1980

Michael E. L. Melluish   1991

Second Baron Methuen
  of Corsham   1868

Viscount Milton   1856

First Viscount Monckton
  of Brenchley   1956

William Nicholson   1879

Sixteenth Duke of Norfolk   1957

Lord Nugent of Harling   1962

Charles H. Palmer   1978

Cecil G. A. Paris	1975	Twelfth Earl of Strathmore & Kinghorne	1847
Fourteenth Earl of Pembroke	1896	Sir Kynaston Studd, Bt.	1930
Lord Plumer	1929	Fourth Lord Suffield	1836
Viscount Portal of Hungerford	1958	Fifth Lord Suffield	1863
Hon. George Ponsonby	1830	Richard H. Twining	1964
Sir Oliver Popplewell	1994	Sir Anthony Tuke	1982
Sir Timothy Rice	2002	First Viscount Ullswater	1923
Sir John de Robeck, Bt.	1925	Earl of Uxbridge	1855
Sir Denys Roberts	1989	Earl Vane	1854
Sixth Earl of Rosebery	1953	First Earl of Verulam	1840
Lord Charles Russell	1835	Second Earl of Verulam	1867
Seventh Earl of Sandwich	1866	V. Edward Walker	1891
John H. Scourfield	1870	Sir Pelham Warner	1950
Fourth Earl of Sefton	1862	John J. Warr	1987
Dennis R. W. Silk	1992	William H. Webster	1976
Second Baron Skelmersdale	1860	Third Baron Wenlock	1885
Sir Archibald L. Smith	1899	Twenty-Second Baron Willoughby de Eresby	1890
Baron Somers	1936		
Fifth Earl Spencer	1861	Fourth Earl of Winterton	1846
Seventh Earl of Stamford	1851	Fifth Earl of Winterton	1884
Allan G. Steel	1902	Marquess of Worcester	1853
Lord Strathavon	1821	Sir William Worsley, Bt.	1961

MCC PRESIDENTS

Year of office

1787 to 1820   No records remain – the fire of 28 July 1825 destroyed them.

1821   Charles Gordon, Lord Strathavon

1822   Henry J. Lloyd

1823   Benjamin Aislabie

1824   Henry T. Lane

1825   Charles J. Barnett

1826   Lord Frederick Beauclerk, D.D.

1827   Henry R. Kingscote

1828   Algernon F. Greville

1829   John Barnard

1830   Hon. George Ponsonby

1831   William Deedes

1832   Henry Howard

1833   Herbert Jenner (afterwards H. Jenner-Fust)

1834   Hon. Anthony H. Ashley (afterwards A. H. Ashley-Cooper)

1835   Lord Charles Russell

1836   Edward Harbord, Fourth Baron Suffield

1837   James, Fourth Viscount Grimston

1838   Brownlow Brownlow-Cecil, Second Marquess of Exeter

1839   George Stanhope, Sixth Earl of Chesterfield

1840   James Grimston, First Earl of Verulam

1841   William, Second Earl of Craven *(last to be elected)*

1842   Charles Lennox, Earl of March *(first to be nominated)*

1843   Henry Moreton, Second Earl of Ducie

1844   Sir John Bayley, Bt.

1845   Thomas Chamberlayne

1846   Edward Turnour, Fourth Earl of Winterton

1847   Thomas Bowes-Lyon, Twelfth Earl of Strathmore & Kinghorne

1848   Thomas Coke, Second Earl of Leicester

1849   John Bligh, Sixth Earl of Darnley

1850   Heneage Finch, Lord Guernsey

1851   George Grey, Seventh Earl of Stamford

1852 George Hay-Drummond, Viscount Dupplin

1853 Henry Somerset, Marquess of Worcester

1854 George Vane-Tempest, Earl Vane

1855 Sir Henry Paget, Earl of Uxbridge

1856 William Spencer Wentworth-Fitzwilliam, Viscount Milton

1857 Sir Frederick H. Hervey-Bathurst, Bt.

1858 Alan Stewart, Lord Garlies

1859 George, Ninth Earl of Coventry

1860 Edward Bootle-Wilbraham, Second Baron Skelmersdale

1861 John, Fifth Earl Spencer

1862 William Molyneux, Fourth Earl of Sefton

1863 Charles Harbord, Fifth Baron Suffield

1864 William Ward, First Earl of Dudley

1865 Rt. Hon. Robert Grosvenor, First Baron Ebury

1866 John Montagu, Seventh Earl of Sandwich

1867 James Grimston, Second Earl of Verulam

1868 Frederick, Second Baron Methuen of Corsham

1869 Henry Fitzmaurice, Fifth Marquess of Lansdowne

1870 John H. Scourfield M.P.

1871 Edward Villiers, Fifth Earl of Clarendon

1872 Hugh Dawnay, Eighth Viscount Downe

1873 George Cadogan, Viscount Chelsea K.G.

1874 James, Marquess of Hamilton

1875 Sir Charles Legard, Bt.

1876 William Denison, First Lord Londesborough

1877 Henry Somerset, Eighth Duke of Beaufort

1878 Francis Berkeley, Second Baron Fitzhardinge of Bristol

1879 William Nicholson

1880 Sir William Hart-Dyke, Bt.

1881 Lord George Hamilton

1882 Henry Strutt, Second Baron Belper

1883 Hon. Robert Grimston

1884 Edward Turnour, Fifth Earl of Winterton

1885 Rt. Hon. Beilby Lawley, Third Baron Wenlock

1886 Charles, Fifth Baron Lyttelton

1887 Hon. Edward Chandos Leigh

1888 William Montagu-Douglas-Scott, Sixth Duke of Buccleuch

1889 Sir Henry James

1890	Sir Gilbert Heathcote-Drummond-Willoughby, Twenty-Second Baron Willoughby de Eresby
1891	V. Edward Walker
1892	William E. Denison
1893	William Legge, Sixth Earl of Dartmouth
1894	Victor Child-Villiers, Seventh Earl of Jersey
1895	George Canning, Fourth Baron Harris
1896	Sidney Herbert, Fourteenth Earl of Pembroke
1897	Thomas Anson, Third Earl of Lichfield
1898	Hon. Alfred Lyttelton
1899	Sir Archibald L. Smith
1900	Hon. Ivo Bligh
1901	Richard Curzon-Howe, Fourth Earl Howe
1902	Allan G. Steel
1903	Richard Webster, Viscount Alverstone
1904	Henry Manners, Marquess of Granby
1905	Charles E. Green
1906	Walter Hume Long
1907	Robert Threshie Reid, First Baron Loreburn
1908	Frederick Campbell, Third Earl Cawdor
1909	Edwyn Scudamore-Stanhope, Tenth Earl of Chesterfield
1910	William Denison, Second Earl of Londesborough KCVO
1911	William Grenfell, First Baron Desborough
1912	Victor Cavendish, Ninth Duke of Devonshire
1913	John Montagu-Douglas-Scott, Earl of Dalkeith
1914–18	Martin, Seventh Baron Hawke
1919	Henry William, First Baron Forster of Lepe
1920	John Egerton, Fourth Earl of Ellesmere
1921	Col. The Hon. Sir Stanley Jackson
1922	Frederick Thesiger, First Viscount Chelmsford
1923	James William Lowther, First Viscount Ullswater
1924	Rowland Prothero, First Baron Ernle of Chelsea
1925	Admiral of the Fleet Sir John de Robeck, Bt.
1926	General Thomas Brand, Third Viscount Hampden
1927	Charles Wyndham, Third Baron Leconfield
1928	George Bingham, Fifth Earl of Lucan
1929	Herbert, Field Marshal Baron Plumer
1930	Sir Kynaston Studd, Bt.

1931	William, First Viscount Bridgeman of Leigh
1932	Rt. Hon. Sir William Legge, Viscount Lewisham
1933	Rt. Hon. Douglas Hogg, First Viscount Hailsham
1934	Sir Rowland Baring, Second Earl of Cromer
1935	John Lyttelton, Ninth Viscount Cobham
1936	Arthur Somers-Cocks, Sixth Baron Somers
1937	Col. The Hon. John J. Astor
1938	Rt. Hon. Stanley, First Earl Baldwin of Bewdley
1939–45	Stanley Christopherson
1946	General Sir Ronald Adam Bt.
1947	Rt. Hon. Wykeham, Second Baron Cornwallis
1948	Alexander Hore-Ruthven, First Earl of Gowrie, V.C.
1949	HRH Prince Philip, Duke of Edinburgh
1950	Sir Pelham Warner
1951	William Findlay *(Term of Office: 1 October – 30 September)*
1952	Henry Somerset, Tenth Duke of Beaufort
1953	Harry Primrose, Sixth Earl of Rosebery
1954	Charles, Tenth Viscount Cobham
1955	Harold, Field Marshal Earl Alexander of Tunis
1956	Walter, First Viscount Monckton of Brenchley
1957	Bernard Fitzalan-Howard, Sixteenth Duke of Norfolk
1958	Charles, Marshal of the RAF Viscount Portal of Hungerford
1959	Harry S. Altham
1960	Sir Hubert Ashton
1961	Col Sir William Worsley, Bt.
1962	Terence, Lt Col. Lord Nugent of Harline
1963	George O. B. 'Gubby' Allen
1964	Richard H. Twining
1965	Lt Gen Sir Oliver Leese
1966	Rt. Hon. Sir Alec Douglas-Home
1967	Arthur E. R. Gilligan
1968	Ronald Aird
1969	Maurice J. C. Allom
1970	Sir Cyril Hawker
1971	Frederick R. Brown
1972	Aidan M. Crawley
1973	Harold, Lord Caccia
1974	HRH Prince Philip, Duke of Edinburgh

1975	Cecil G. A. Paris
1976	William H. Webster
1977	David G. Clark
1978	Charles H. Palmer
1979	SC 'Billy' Griffith
1980	Peter B. H. May
1981	G. Hubert G. Doggart
1982	Sir Anthony Tuke
1983	Alexander H. A. Dibbs
1984	F. George Mann
1985	Jack G. W. Davies
1986	M. Colin Cowdrey
1987	John J. Warr
1988	Field Marshal Baron Bramall of Bushfield
1989	Sir Denys Roberts
1990	Hugh, Baron Griffiths of Govilon
1991	Michael E. L. Melluish
1992	Dennis R. W. Silk *(Term of Office: two years)*
1994	Sir Oliver Popplewell
1996	A. Colin D. Ingleby-Mackenzie
1998	Anthony R. Lewis
2000	Robert, Lord Alexander of Weedon *(Term of Office: one year)*
2001	Edward R. Dexter
2002	Sir Timothy Rice
2003	Charles A. Fry
2004	Thomas W. Graveney
2005	Robin G. Marlar
2006	Douglas J. Insole

Note: Year of Office refers to the year in which the term of office began. Since 1951 this means that the cricket season of the Presidential term is the following year.

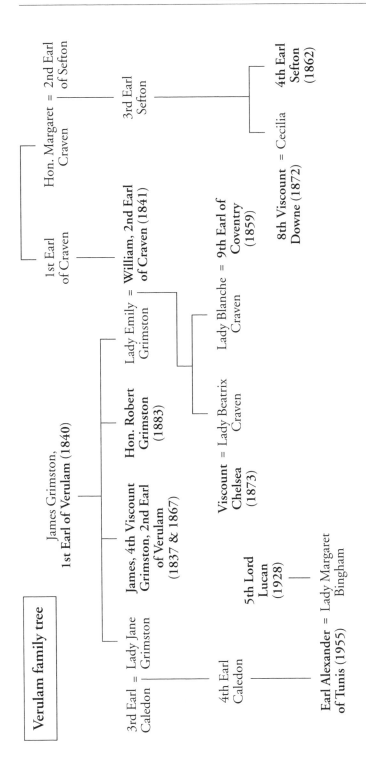

Verulam family tree

James Grimston,
1st Earl of Verulam (1840)

1st Earl of Craven — Hon. Margaret = 2nd Earl of Sefton / Craven

3rd Earl Sefton

3rd Earl Caledon = Lady Jane Grimston

James, 4th Viscount Grimston, 2nd Earl of Verulam (1837 & 1867)

Hon. Robert Grimston (1883)

Lady Emily = **William, 2nd Earl Grimston / of Craven (1841)**

Lady Blanche = **9th Earl of Craven / Coventry (1859)**

Lady Beatrix Craven

Viscount = Lady Beatrix Chelsea Craven (1873)

8th Viscount = Cecilia Downe (1872)

4th Earl Sefton (1862)

5th Lord Lucan (1928)

4th Earl Caledon

Earl Alexander of Tunis (1955) = Lady Margaret Bingham

NOTE: 1. The Earl of Uxbridge's nephew married Victoria, daughter of the 8th Duke of Rutland, who was president (as Marquis of Granby) in 1904.

2. Lady Jane Grimston was half-sister to James and Robert Grimston, by a different mother.

Hamilton family tree

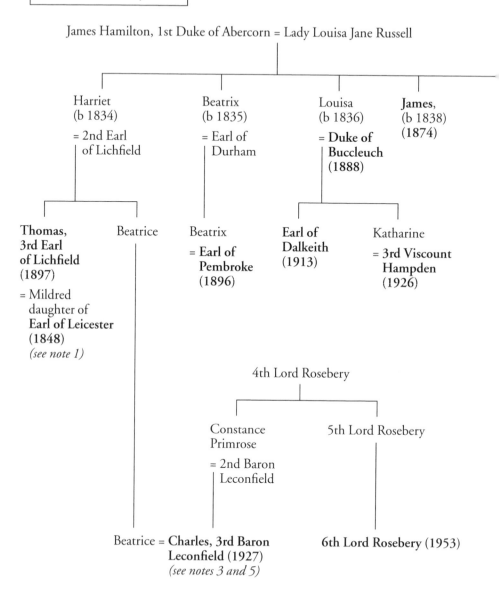

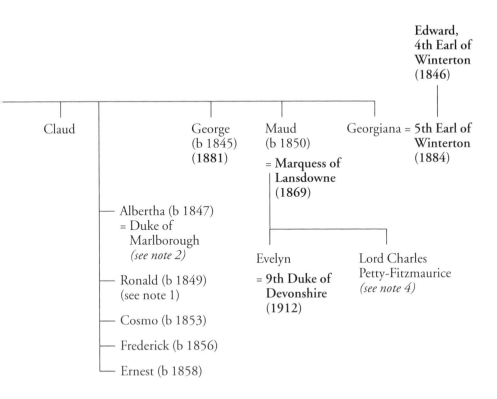

NOTES:

1. When 3rd Earl of Lichfield married Mildred Coke, daughter of the Earl of Leicester, he became the brother in law of the 6th Earl of Dartmouth (1893), who was himself the nephew of Lord Strathavon (1821) and father of Viscount Lewisham (1932), the first of only two men to follow both father and grandfather to the presidency.

2. James, Marquess of Hamilton married Lady Mary Anna Curzon-Howe, the half-aunt of 4th Earl Howe (1901). Earl Howe married Lady Georgiana Spencer-Churchill, daughter of Albertha Hamilton.

3. 4th Earl of Ellesmere (1920) married Lady Violet Lambton, granddaughter of Beatrix Hamilton and the Earl of Durham, making him nephew-in-law to the Earl of Pembroke (1896) and second cousin-in-law to Lord Leconfield (1927). His brother married Lady Bertha Anson, daughter of the 3rd Earl of Lichfield (1897). His wife's sister married the 13th Earl of Home, making him uncle to Sir Alec Douglas-Home (1966).

4. Lord Charles Petty-Fitzmaurice, son of the Marquess of Lansdowne and brother-in-law of Duke of Devonshire, married, firstly, Lady Violet Elliot-Murray-Kynynmound. She subsequently married Col. The Hon. J.J. Astor (1937), while her sister married 2nd Earl of Cromer (1934).

5. 4th Baron Leconfield, younger brother of 3rd Baron Leconfield (1927), married the sister of 9th Viscount Cobham (1935).

INDEX